uide to
ses

Books in the series

Students' Guide to Business Computing
Students' Guide to Data Communications
Students' Guide to Expert Systems
Students' Guide to Information Technology
Students' Guide to Office Automation
Students' Guide to Spreadsheets

Students' Guide to Databases

Malcolm Bull

BUTTERWORTH
HEINEMANN

Newnes
An imprint of Butterworth-Heinemann Ltd
Linacre House, Jordan Hill, Oxford OX2 8DP

PART OF REED INTERNATIONAL BOOKS

OXFORD LONDON BOSTON MUNICH
NEW DELHI SINGAPORE SYDNEY
TOKYO TORONTO WELLINGTON

First published 1990
Reprinted 1991

British Library Cataloguing in Publication Data
Bull, Malcolm
Students' Guide to databases
1. Information systems. Databases. Design and construction
I. Title
005.74

ISBN 0 7506 0285 6

Printed and bound in Great Britain by
Biddles Ltd, Guildford and King's Lynn

Contents

Preface

The Heinemann Informatics series

This new series of books from Heinemann gives up-to-date coverage of significant developments in information technology. It is aimed at college students whose courses include IT components, including BTEC National and Higher Level courses, RSA and City & Guilds courses, as well as courses designed for professional bodies.

The books in this series adopt much more active learning strategies than traditional textbooks. Each chapter begins with a statement of what learning objectives students are expected to achieve. At key points in a chapter students are given the opportunity to achieve these objectives by carrying out short tasks, and by undertaking the assignment at the end of the chapter. Where appropriate, feedback on the tasks is provided at the end of a chapter, so that students can assess their learning, and as a further check a résumé of the chapter's contents is given.

Most chapters include an assignment with a distinctly practical flavour. It may require students to put their learning into practice using a computer or other item of IT equipment, or it may require an in-depth investigation into topics covered in the chapter.

Roger Carter
The Information Technology Unit
The Buckinghamshire College

The Students' Guide to Databases

It is becoming increasingly important for systems analysts and programmers to realize that the systems which they develop are only a small part of the whole data processing activities of the organization. This is particularly true in the computer systems used in business and commerce where a very large number of systems and programs interact with one another, handling the same files, processing the same information.

Preface

The data which an organization processes is one of its most valuable resources. It is important that this data be processed accurately and satisfactorily, otherwise the management may draw the wrong conclusions and may make the wrong decisions causing the entire structure of the organization to collapse.

It is essential that the data resource be viewed as a whole: an invoicing program will use just a part of that data; a payroll program will use another part of the data; a program which produces an internal telephone directory will use an even smaller part of the data. If there is not enough data held, then management decisions may be threatened; if too much unnecessary data is held, then the computer programs will waste time and money handling this data; if the same data is held in many places, then who is to know which version of that data is correct?

Clearly, the data must be organized as a coherent unit – a database. All the computer users must be able to find the data which they need. We cannot simply assemble the data piece by piece as we go along, relocating a field, adding a new field there, deleting an old field here. We must plan, design and control the data.

When the subject of systems development is studied, time constraints only allow a small system (or, less frequently, a small part of a large system) to be investigated in any one project. But the student must be prepared to go into the real world of commercial computing where huge databases are common. The student must be able to develop and maintain a program which interacts with the data possibly used by hundreds of other users. If things go wrong, it may be serious and it is always expensive.

The aim of the present book is to introduce you to databases, to see why they are needed, how they are organized and controlled, and how they are used. We shall look at some of the database management systems which are used to control and monitor the data and we shall see how they fit in with programming languages and other aspects of data processing which you have encountered. Finally, we shall come to appreciate how efficient utilization of the database enables the organization to derive even greater value and benefit from its data resources.

The book is suitable for college students following BTEC and City and Guilds courses in computer studies and IT topics. The book will also be of general interest in the business world – particularly for those commercial users and end-users who are increasingly being confronted with a wide range of jargon and techniques in their daily work, and who feel that they would like to know what database and database management systems are all about.

Because of the advanced nature of the subject, we are assuming a certain preliminary knowledge of the general concepts of data processing and information technology and of the elementary features of the hardware and the software which is used. We also assume that the reader is familiar with the use and meaning of a number of fundamental terms such as *file*, *record*, *field*, *input* and *output*. As important terms are introduced here, they are defined explicitly or explained implicitly by means of examples and illustrations.

Malcolm Bull

Acknowledgements

A number of people have contributed directly or indirectly to the conception and the final presentation of this book: the various students and teachers, be they British, Arabic or Chinese, who over the years, have enabled me to develop the contents of the lecture material upon which the present book is based.

Special thanks are due to a number of people who have read the various drafts and added their comments and suggestions, particularly Roger Carter, Mal Jackson, and Andrew Maszyr.

I should also like to be able to thank the various software suppliers for providing software for use in the book.

If, after all this support, there are any omissions or any errors remaining in the book, then the responsibility and blame for these can only be laid at my own door.

Malcolm Bull

1: Files or database?

Objectives

After reading this chapter, you should be able to:

- explain what the difference is between a collection of files and a database
- describe the problems which can arise as a result of an integrated computer system which has not been carefully planned and designed
- define the term *database*
- recognize and use the term *database management system* and its abbreviation DBMS
- describe the requirements of a database management system
- recognize situations in which these requirements are important
- identify those features of a system which should be handled by a database management system.

The data which is used by an organization—a college, a library, a bank, a manufacturing company—is one of its most valuable resources. It is expensive to gather, to store and to protect the data. This is particularly true when the data is held on a computer system. For these reasons, it is essential that the organization should make the best use of its data. It is important that the data be organized and arranged so that each user gets the maximum benefit from that data.

In many small computer systems, files are frequently established for use by just one program. Even in some large computer systems there may be small components which, for historical reasons, still have their own peculiar files.

Let us imagine that you are writing a program to keep student records. You are doing this because you need to produce a register of the students, showing when they started studying at the college, which course they are following and when they are expected to graduate. In order to be able to do this, you might decide to hold information such as:

- student's name
- address
- telephone number

- course
- date of entrance into the college
- duration of the course.

Your student record system would then consist of a program or possibly several programs organized to input, validate, store, read, write, and print reports about these various data *fields*.

Activity 1

In this and subsequent activities, we shall look at four small programs which will make up a simple data processing system for a local college. As we proceed with our look at databases, your work on these four programs will enable you to practise some of the topics.

At each stage, you should *keep your results* and use these as a basis for later work.

1 Make a list of the data fields shown above. Add any others which you think necessary for a student record system.

2 The secretary of the college Scientific Society owns an Amstrad computer and she has asked you to write a program which she can use to make her work lighter. As secretary, she is concerned with the organization of lectures, meetings and visits to local industries and factories. Therefore she needs to know the members' interests. She also needs to be able to post notices about forthcoming meetings, so she must know where the students are located and which courses they are following.

At the moment, she keeps a card index to hold details of each member, and a cash book to record all the money she handles. Samples of the various documents are shown in Figure 1.1.

Make a list of the data fields which you suggest she should keep on file.

3 A senior lecturer has a home computer and he has asked you to help him to develop a system for allocating tutors to students. He is interested in the students and the lecturers who give tutorials to those students. At the moment, he writes the information in a notebook and produces a notice which gives details of the next tutorial. Samples of the various documents are shown in Figure 1.2.

Make a list of the data fields which you suggest he should keep on file.

4 The secretary of the Sports and Social Club is responsible for organizing sports fixtures—such as football and rugby matches and the college half-marathon—and social functions such as car rallies, barbecues and jumble sales. He needs to know the members' sporting interests, and he also needs to keep records about the members and whether or not they have paid their subscriptions—and information about the functions being

```
Name: Arthur Rimbaud

Course: HND Maths and computer science

Location: Woolf Building

Interests: Visit to a bank; Manufacturing Plant
```

(a) Card index

```
Date: Monday 23rd August

Description: Westland Bank computer centre

Attending:    Secretary
              A. Rimbaud
              L. Housman
              J. Singh
              R. Tannahill
              T. Livy
```

(b) Notice

```
Visit: Westland Bank / 23 August

Coach: Booked with P.R.C Coaches 6th June

Bookings                                   Cash
7 June        A. Rimbaud                   1.50
7 June        L. Housman
8 June        J. Singh                     1.50
8 June        R. Tannahill                 1.50
9 June        T. Livy

Expenses:

6 June        Telephone call               0.50
6 June        Coach deposit               10.00
```

(c) Cash Book

Figure 1.1 Scientific Society records and documents

Tutor: Mrs Drabble

Subject: A level maths

Student	Telephone
R.Manning	836754
R.Paltock	836445
A.Huxley	836998
K.Digby	875544
R.Tagore	836754

(a) Notebook

** TUTORIAL **

Mrs Drabble

A level maths

10:30 Monday 19th November

Woolf Building: Room A755

(b) Tutorial announcement

Figure 1.2 Tutor allocation records and documents

organized. The secretary has a BBC computer at home and would like to use this to help him in his work for the Sports and Social Club.

At the moment, the secretary records the details in a notebook and produces notices which gives details of forthcoming events. Samples of the various documents are shown in Figure 1.3.

Make a list of the data fields which you suggest he should keep on file.

Keep these four lists. We shall use them later.

As you can see, we have got four separate computer applications. At the moment each of these is just a program (or there may be a number of programs) running on a separate computer. Each has its own file or files.

```
Name: Arthur Rimbaud

Address: 43 St Margaret's Avenue

Sports: Hockey, Tennis, Squash, Football

Subscription: Paid 10 October
```

(a) Card index

```
                 ** FOOTBALL MATCH

Date: Saturday 21st August

Against: Heath Old Boys

Venue: Widdicombe Playing Fields

                  A. Rimbaud - Captain
                  C. Nairne
                  C. Perrault
                  E. Drood
                  J. Powys
                  J. Singh
                  L. Housman
                  O. Glendower
                  R. Edwards
                  R. Tannahill
                  T. Livy
                  W. Byrd
```

(b) Sports fixture

Figure 1.3 Sports and Social Club records and documents

- For the Scientific Society, there may be: name; course code; interests. Your experience may also suggest that the secretary holds details about visits: date; description of visit; names of people attending; details of the coach booking; cash received for tickets; any expenses to be paid.
- For the Tutor Allocation system, you may have suggested: student name; tutor name; course code; student telephone number.

- For the Sports and Social Club, there may be more than one file. For example:
  A member details: name; subscription paid; address.
  B function details: date; description of event; expenses paid out; money received from ticket sales.
  C Team details: title of team; members; fixtures; dates; results.

Each file (or group of files) represents the data which is needed by just one user (or by just one program).

An integrated system

Here we have four separate computer systems. Notice that here and elsewhere in this book we use the term *computer system* informally to mean any collection of computer hardware, software and data which is used to do a particular job. We shall be mainly concerned with the software and the data aspects of such computer systems.

Let us imagine that these four systems have been working nicely for some time, each on a different computer. Then the college authorities decide that these separate activities should be allowed to make use of the large computer at the college. A systems analyst is called in to control the transfer of the systems to the college computer. The decision is taken to have an *integrated system*, an all-embracing environment in which each program will become a small part of the total data processing requirements within the college. One of the first things that the systems analyst notices is that some of these small programs use data which is very similar to that used by the others.

Activity 2

1 Using the suggestions made above, together with any other piece of data which you wish to add, draw up a table like the section in Figure 1.4 showing the data used by the various programs.
2 Indicate those areas where one program uses the same data as one or more of the others.
3 Highlight any data which is particular to each program and which is not used by any of the other programs.

Programs =======> Data (v)	ST. RECORDS	SCI.SOCIETY	TUTOR ALLOC	SPORT+SOCL.
Student's name	*	*	*	
Student's address	*			
Student's telephone number	*			
Course code	*	*	*	
Location of student		*		
Tutor name			*	

Figure 1.4 Data and programs

You will have noticed that data such as:

- the student's name
- his address
- his telephone number
- the course which he is following

are used in several of the programs, whereas data such as:

- tutor's name
- scientific interests
- coach bookings
- sports fixtures

are only used in one program.

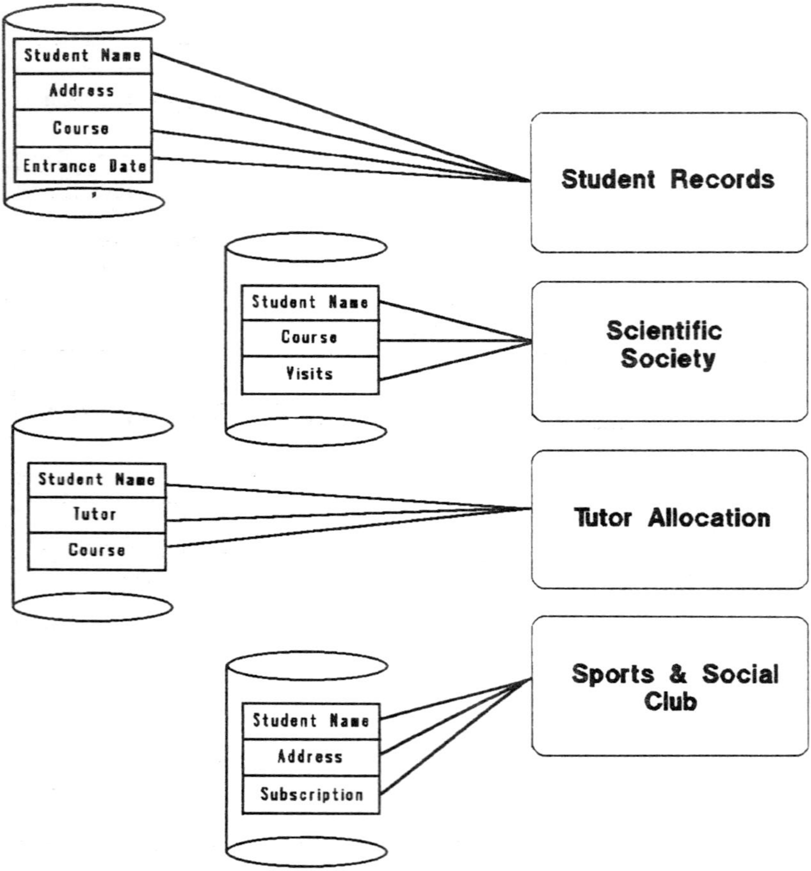

Figure 1.5 Files versus integrated database. (a) Holding the data on separate files.

When the programs are moved to run on the same computer, we could continue to allow each program to handle its own data on its own files as shown in Figure 1.5(a). This means that some data such as the student's name and his address which are used by several programs would be held on several different files.

Another possibility is to reorganize the data holding *all* the data in one place so that each program can use just that part which it needs as shown in Figure 1.5(b). Any data which is only used by a particular

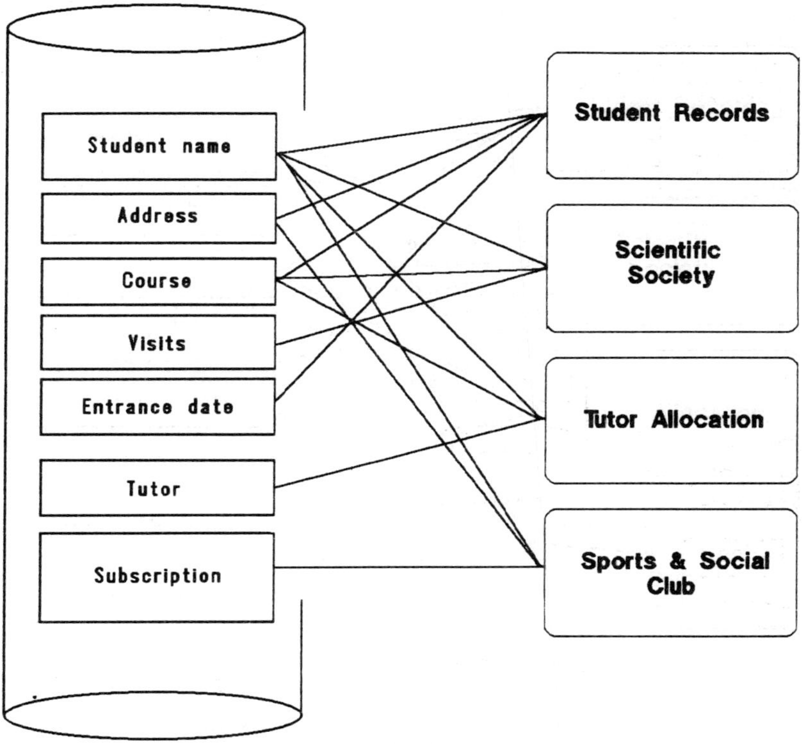

(b) Holding the data on an integrated database.

program could be made available to that program but the other users can ignore it.

In contrast with the previous situation where each file (or group of files) represented the data needed by just one user (or by just one program), the integrated database represents the data which is needed by all users (and by all programs).

Activity 3

1 List some of the disadvantages of holding the same—duplicated—information on several separate files.
2 Make a list of some of the effects which you think these disadvantages might have.

The least important consequence of holding the same data in several places is that it takes up more room than it would if it were only held in one place—disk space is becoming cheaper and storage space is not as important as it once was. More important is the fact that ...

> if data is held in several places there may be inconsistencies in the data.

If Mary Shelley moves house and only tells the College Secretary, then her address on the student record files will be changed but her address on the Sports and Social Club files will be left as it was.

I am sure that you or your friends have been in the situation where you have written to your bank or the library or some other large organization to tell them that you have changed your address. Many months later, they are still sending you mail to the old address. In many cases, this is a consequence of the organization holding your address in more than one place: your address is updated on one file, but not on another.

A database

The systems analyst, therefore decides to use a *database* to hold the data for the various programs. This database will hold each piece of data so that it is accessible to all the programs in the system. We shall use this as our definition:

> A *database* is a collection of data which is organized in such a way that each piece of data is available to those who need it and such that there is minimal duplication of data.

Note that, in certain circumstances this definition does allow duplicated data. This is called *controlled redundancy* and is permitted because there may be situations when we need to hold the same information in several places in order to have cross-references between files. We shall meet some examples later, but in general each piece of data will be held in one place only.

Activity 4

1 Make a list of any disadvantages in holding all the data in a manner such that any part of it can be accessed by anyone using the computer.
2 For each disadvantage, give some examples of situations where it would be particularly serious.

If we make *all* the data universally accessible there will be problems of *security*, *privacy* and *confidentiality*. Would you want everyone to know what your last exam results were? Would it be safe to hold the staff salary details on an open file? What would you do if you discovered that you were able to update your own salary record? Would it be a good idea to hold details of the design of a new sports car on the computer where anybody could look at them, even spies working for your competitors? And if the data is only held in one place, what happens if it gets lost or damaged?

So a computer system must be able to combine the requirements of our definition of a database with these other operational requirements. A computer system which controls the use of the data in this way is known as a *database management system*, or DBMS for short.

What a database should do

We can summarize our requirements by listing the things which we would like the DBMS to do for us:

- It must ensure that each piece of data is available to all those users who need it: each piece of data must be accessible, in other words, the DBMS must provide *data accessibility*. This was our original and most important requirement.
- It must protect the data and ensure that it is not lost or damaged: it must offer *data security*.
- It must protect the data from access and change by unauthorized users: it must offer *data privacy* or *data confidentiality*.
- It must also guarantee that the data is consistent: it must offer *data integrity*. This means that we must be confident that the data is accurate and reliable and we must be able to insist on certain values for the data.

  For example, every student must have a name; anyone who is a member of the Scientific Society must be a student at the college; a student's date of birth must be acceptable (30th, February 1973 would be invalid). Just as data security and data privacy are concerned with damage caused by unauthorized users, so data integrity is concerned with possible damage and harm caused by authorized users.

  In many cases, data integrity (usually in the form of data validation) will be handled by the programmer within each application program. But it would be valuable if the DBMS could also do a double-check for us.

- On a system where several users may be handling the same data at the same time, the DBMS must also ensure that there is no confusion when two or more users try to update the same record at the same time: it must resolve any problems of *data concurrency*.

And in order to simplify the work of the programmers who are writing programs for use on a DBMS, we could also ask that:

- the individual users and programmers should not have to worry about how the data is held
- nor should they need to know exactly where the data is held
- nor should they be concerned with pieces of data which are not used by their particular program.

When these last three features are available, the DBMS is said to offer *data independence* or *data transparency*.

Another feature which, whilst not essential, is worthy of mention here since it makes the use of a DBMS much easier for large companies and organizations, is the ability to house the equipment—the disk storage devices and possibly even individual computers—at a number of different sites. For example, the accounting information might be held on a computer housed at the Head Office in Inverness, the sales information might be held at the Sales Headquarters in Coventry, and the product information may be held at the Manufacturing Plant in Cardiff. By means of a network linking the database and the users together, such a *distributed DBMS* will allow information to be drawn together from all the various sites just as if it were held on one single computer.

Questions

The local radio station plans to use a computer program to record the money pledged by telephone callers in a charity radio-thon. The system must afford data security (they don't want to lose details of any money donated), and it must resolve data concurrency (they have 150 telephone lines and need to handle more than one donation at a time).

Describe some other data processing systems in which you think that the following features would be particularly important:

1 Data accessibility
2 Data security
3 Data concurrency
4 Data privacy and data confidentiality

5 Data integrity
6 Data transparency and data independence.

Which of the above features are important in the following situations:

7 A car company holds details of its designs for new cars on a computer.
8 Your exam results are held on the college computer.
9 Bank accounts are held on a computer which is linked to terminals via telephone lines and modems.
10 An airline booking system has one seat remaining on the flight from London to Delhi. A booking clerk in Delhi is enquiring about seats on the flight. A travel agent at Bombay airport has been asked to put someone on the same flight.
11 The college used to have a system which allowed students to borrow sheet music. This has been discontinued and the lending system is to be removed from the computer.
12 On a hospital registration system, we need to know the age and sex of the patients.
13 A programmer is writing a program for a new system, but the files have not yet been designed.
14 A company manufactures photocopying equipment and holds its future sales and promotion plans on the computer.
15 The data processing manager has decided to buy more disk storage and he is going to move the payroll file on to the new disks.

The place of a DBMS

We have listed a great many requirements for our database management system and this is obviously a lot to demand of a computer system. A great many man-years of effort would be expended on the design and development of a DBMS. This is why you would never be asked to write a DBMS. A DBMS is normally bought from a software house or a computer manufacturer and lies between your programs and the data, as illustrated by the diagram in Figure 1.6. This diagram shows us that, in order to reach any of the data, a program must go via the DBMS. By doing so, we can leave it to the DBMS to take care of data security, data transparency and all the other requirements which we listed above. As the diagram shows, some DBMSs provide a *query language* or an *enquiry language* which allows you and your users to make enquiries about their data and to handle the data without having to write a program. We shall look at a number of query languages later.

In practice, some DBMSs read and write the data directly whilst others use the computer's own operating system to handle the data on

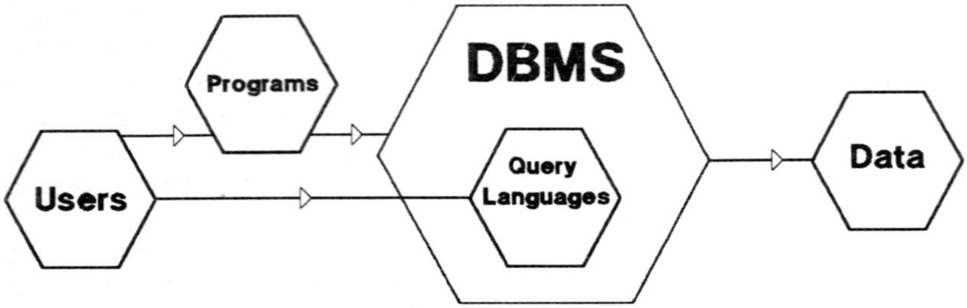

Figure 1.6 The place of a DBMS

their behalf. For this reason, we shall often use the informal expression *file handling system* to refer to that part of the combined software which actually finds, reads and writes data on the disk.

Recap

It is essential that the best possible use is made of the data stored on a computer system. In contrast to the situation where the data needed by each user (and each program) is held on a separate file which is used only by that one user (or by that one program), an integrated database represents the data which is shared by all users (and by all programs).

Most commercial computer systems now use an integrated database where each piece of data is held once. That single occurrence of the data is then accessed and shared by all the programs which need it.

A database management system—DBMS—is a piece of software lying between you and your data which controls data accessibility, data security, data concurrency, data privacy and confidentiality, data integrity, data transparency and independence.

Answers

1 Data accessibility is always important. If the data is not accessible—or if none of the users needs to access it—then there is no point in holding the data on the computer.

2 Data security is important wherever it is needed to protect the data against unauthorized disclosure, alteration or deletion. Some examples might be: payroll information, military secrets, trade secrets, next year's examination questions.

3 Data concurrency is important whenever data is to be (or may be) accessed by several users at the same time. Some examples might be: airline booking details, banking information (you may be drawing money out at the same moment that your cheque is being credited to your account), stock control information (goods may be received and recorded on the stock records at the same time as another clerk is removing goods from stock).

4 Data privacy and data confidentiality is important when you are holding personal details (medical records, police records, data about debts and debtors), protecting commercial information (accounts, sales figures and profits, future plans, formulas) and sensitive information (military and intelligence data, national and government policies).

5 Data integrity is important whenever data is being entered into the system and when data is being changed. Some examples might be: adding new student record details (the course and qualifications must be consistent so that a student cannot start a degree course until he/she has gained the required A level passes); a sales ordering system (users should not be able to delete orders if the customer has not yet paid).

6 Data transparency and data independence are important for programmers so that they can write their programs without too much concern about the way in which the data is held physically. It also means that if the format of any of the data is changed or data is moved to another location then it should not affect the program. Furthermore, if any data is removed completely from the system, then it should not be necessary to change or recompile the programs which do not use that data.

7 Data security, data privacy and data confidentiality would be important and necessary to protect the information.

8 Data privacy and data confidentiality would be important to prevent unauthorized people looking at your results.

9 Data security, data concurrency, data privacy and data confidentiality, and data integrity would be important.

10 Data concurrency would be particularly important.

11 Data transparency and data independence would be important so that other systems on the computer will not be affected when one system is removed.

12 Data privacy and data confidentiality would be important, and data integrity would also be important to ensure that valid sex and ages are specified.

13 Data transparency and data independence would be important.

14 Data security, data privacy and data confidentiality would be important.

15 Data transparency and data independence would be important.

2: Files revisited

Objectives

After reading this chapter, you should be able to:

- explain the meaning of the names *key*, *primary key*, and *secondary key*
- identify suitable *primary keys* for records
- recognize the word *attribute*
- describe the purpose, the nature and the use of *inverted files*
- explain how *indexes* are used
- outline the ways in which records are accessed on disk
- describe the ways in which records are added to a file and deleted from a file
- outline some ways in which file overflow may be handled
- explain the principles of a *binary search*
- describe the structure and use of a *B-tree*
- describe and apply the principles of *Soundex indexing*
- describe the purpose and action of a *hashing algorithm*
- use a simple hashing algorithm.

In your computer studies, you will already have done a large amount of basic work concerning the ways in which records and files are used on computer systems. You will have met a number of I/O devices such as:

- magnetic tapes
- magnetic disks
- optical disks

and you will have seen how application programs use these to hold data organized as:

- sequential files
- direct access files.

Much of this is relevant to a study of databases. But before we go any further we must clarify a number of assumptions which we shall make and we must introduce a few new ideas. The first important point is that:

all the data which we shall hold in our database will be held on magnetic disk.

This makes the data more easily accessible than it would be if we held it on magnetic tape or any of the other devices. It also means that the data can be updated more easily than current techniques for *optical* disks allow.

Indeed, it was the introduction of random access disk files by IBM in 1959, and the ability to access files in a non-sequential manner, that opened up the way taking us from purely sequential magnetic tape files to the database concepts which we shall look at here.

Keys

All the files are written and read using direct access techniques. Each record contains one or more data fields—the word *attribute* is frequently used to refer to a data field and we shall use both words here. The most important of these attributes is that which allows us to identify each record uniquely—this attribute (or it may be a combination of several attributes) is called the *key* of that record. We shall spend a lot of time looking at keys later, and in Chapter 11 we shall be in a position to give a formal definition of what we mean by the key. For the time being however, we shall content ourselves with an intuitive idea of what constitutes a key.

A key may be a meaningful piece of data such as:

a student's name: GEORGE ELIOT

or it may be a fictitious number invented just to make it unique on the file such as:

a student registration number: 89/37461

The student registration number will certainly be unique, but we should find it very difficult to ensure that the student's name was unique.

The important point is that the key must be *unique*. If we use the student's name to identify the record, then there must only be one student with that name; if we use the student's registration number to identify the record, then there must only be one student record with the record key 89/37461. If there were more than one record with the same key, how would the computer know which one we wanted?

What does the computer do if we attempt to create two (or more) records with the same key? On many operating systems, if you try to write a record which has the same key as a record already on the file, then the new record will overwrite and replace the old record. On other operating systems, you can only WRITE (that is, create) a completely new record. You will not be allowed to write a record which exists; you must REWRITE such a record, thereby destroying the earlier record.

Questions

1 Why would it *not* be such a good idea to use the student name as the record key for our student record system?
2 What could we use to identify the lecturers on the files used by our tutor allocation program?
3 I am writing a system to handle reference books in the library. What piece(s) of data do you suggest that I use as the key for the books?
4 A company assembles electronic equipment and holds data about transistors and other components. A systems analyst has been called in to design a stock control system and she has been talking to the people who will use the system. Ivan works in the stores where the goods are delivered and he identifies the components by the suppliers' reference code; Barbara works in the assembly department and identifies the products by the type (transistor or resistor or switch, and so on); Carl works in the sales department and identifies each component and each assembled product by its number in the company's sales catalogue.
Which attribute would you choose as the key for the stock records?

You may wish to check your answers to these questions before you attempt the following activity.

Activity 1

Look at the attributes on the files for the four college programs and choose (or invent) a suitable key for each of the data records which are used.

Accessing the physical files

Let us now look at the way in which the operating system or the DBMS uses the key to find the actual physical record on disk.

We should first understand that different computers handle files and records in different ways. To demonstrate this, let us imagine that I wish to create a new collection of information—a list of the names and addresses of my friends, for example, then:

- some operating systems will consider this to be a new file with individual *lines* for each of my friends, each line having individual *fields* for the name, the address, the telephone list, the postcode and so on. The unit of physical storage in this case is the file, and I read and write the entire file whenever I wish to look at or change a single name and address.

  The information for each of my friends will be identified by its record key or (in this case, more likely) by its position within the name and address file. This allows me to process all my names and addresses at once. This is the way in which data is organized on the DOS operating system.
- other operating systems will consider this to be a new file with individual *records* for each of my friends, each record having individual lines for the name, the address, the telephone list, the postcode and so on. The record for each of my friends will be identified by its record key. The unit of physical storage in this case is the record and I read and write just a single record whenever I wish to look at a single name and address. This allows me to process each name and address individually.

These two methods are illustrated in Figure 2.1. As you can see, they are closely related. One is just a special case of the other.

In our discussion of files and records, we shall use the second model which reads and writes each record individually on the disk and more easily allows us to retrieve a specific record by means of its key. As you or your program creates a new record, then the file handling system simply writes each new record into the next available space on the disk.

The entire disk storage space is divided into units called *pages*. A page is roughly equivalent to a disk sector. Each page is identified by a unique *page number* or *page id*. The size of the pages depends upon which operating system you are using. Some systems use pages of 500 bytes, others use 1000 or 2000 bytes. When your program needs to find a particular record, the system has to read in the page which contains

0551	A MCINTOSH	Bradfax	744352	391, HIGH ST
1002	F CASH	Bradfax	711576	92, BROWN RD
1922	E SMITH	Bradfax	727342	34, HIGH STREET
2298	W GREEN	Bradfax	744329	49, HIGH GROVE
2831	I WALKER	Elmdale	2988	276, BROAD RD
4016	N WILSON	Bradfax	744325	19, DERBY AVE
6069	M BROWN	Elmdale	1934	45, SMITH AVE

(a) The file as a set of lines of data

0551	A MCINTOSH	Bradfax 744352	391, HIGH ST
1002	F CASH	Bradfax 711576	92, BROWN RD
1922	E SMITH	Bradfax 727342	34, HIGH STREET
2298	W GREEN	Bradfax 744329	49, HIGH GROVE
2831	I WALKER	Elmdale 2988	276, BROAD RD
4016	N WILSON	Bradfax 744325	19, DERBY AVE
6069	M BROWN	Elmdale 1934	45, SMITH AVE

(b) The file as a set of records of data

Figure 2.1 Files or records?

that record and then scan through all the data on that page until it finds the record that you need. But, if the file handling system writes each record into the next available space on disk, how does the system know which page your record is held on?

Indexes

Obviously, we cannot hold all the records of a file in a single page. A large file might occupy many hundreds of pages. The system overcomes this by holding some of the records on one page, then some more on the next page, and so on. Rather than read through all the pages on the disk

STOCK	PAGE
1000	1401
1111	1401
1200	1401
1234	1402
1500	1402
2000	1402
2200	1403
2222	1403
2500	1403
3000	1404
3333	1404
3500	1404
4000	1405
4200	1405
4500	1405
4545	1406
5000	1406
5500	1406
5555	1407
6000	1407
6666	1407
7000	1408
8000	1408
8500	1408
9000	1409

(a) Full index

Page	STOCK	DESCRIPTION..............
1401	1000	DESK, GREEN-BLUE, WOODEN
	1111	STOOLS, GREEN, PLASTIC
	1200	DESK, GREY, WOODEN
1402	1234	CHAIR, RED, STEEL
	1500	CHAIR, ORANGE, PLASTIC
	2000	SETTEE, YELLOW, STEEL
1403	2200	SETTEE, BROWN, STEEL
	2222	DESK, BLUE, STEEL
	2500	TABLE, GREEN, LAMINATE
1404	3000	SIDEBOARD, BLUE, WOODEN
	3333	CHAIR, WHITE, LAMINATE
	3500	STOOL, WHITE, PLASTIC
1405	4000	DESK, BLACK, SPECIAL
	4200	SETTEE, GOLD, WOODEN
	4500	CHAIR, RED, LAMINATE
1406	4545	SETTEE, BLUE, SPECIAL
	5000	SETTEE, ORANGE, WOODEN
	5500	TABLE, YELLOW, PLASTIC
1407	5555	TABLE, RED, PLASTIC
	6000	SIDEBOARD, GOLD, STEEL
	6666	SIDEBOARD, ORANGE, STEEL
1408	7000	DESK, WHITE, WOODEN
	8000	SETTEE, RED, SPECIAL
	8500	TABLE, ORANGE, LAMINATE
1409	9000	SIDEBOARD, YELLOW, WOODEN

(b) Data file

STOCK	PAGE
1000	1401
1234	1402
2200	1403
3000	1404
4000	1405
4545	1406
5555	1407
7000	1408
9000	1409

(c) A short index

Figure 2.2 File indexes

to find your record, the file handling system keeps an *index* showing the keys of the records which are held on each page, and uses this index whenever it needs to find a record. This is illustrated in Figure 2.2 which looks at an index of the records on a furniture file. For example, if we wanted to find record 3333, then the file handling system would scan through the index until it found the key 3333. The Page reference would then direct it to page 1404, so it would scan through page 1404 until it found record 3333. If we wanted to find record 7777, then the file handling system would scan through the index, as before, but it would not be able to find an entry for record 7777 and would send a signal that the record could not be found.

An index such as that in Figure 2.2(a) contains an entry for every record on the file. The index itself is usually organized as a file. If there are thousands of records on the file, then the index itself may be large. In such situations, it is not uncommon to have *indexes* to *indexes*. Another possibility is to have an abbreviated index such as that in Figure 2.2(c). This contains an entry for the *first* record on each page. For example, in order to find record 8000, the system would scan the index and find that record 7000 is on page 1408 and record 9000 is on page 1409. So it would scan through page 1408 until it found record 8000—or until it reached the end of the page (this would imply that record 8000 did not exist) in which case the system would send a signal that the record could not be found. Note that, unlike the previous full index, such an abbreviated index does not tell us whether or not a record exists, only where it *might be*. We have to search the appropriate page until we either find the record we want or we reach the end of the page.

The files illustrated here are said to be organized in an *indexed sequential* manner, because the actual records are held in sequence. We could save ourselves (and the file handling system) some time, and we could also avoid the problems of adding a new record when there is no space if the file were to be organized in an *indexed random* manner, with new records being placed on any convenient page and the index directing us to the appropriate place. This is illustrated in Figure 2.3. When the file is organized in this way, only the index needs to be kept in the right sequence. Can you see why it is not possible to use a short index in this situation?

Binary search

Whenever we use an index like this, we must, of course, search through the index to find the entry we need. Elsewhere in your computer

STOCK	PAGE
1000	1406
1111	1403
1200	1406
1234	1402
1500	1403
2000	1401
2200	1401
2222	1405
2500	1404
3000	1403
3333	1408
3500	1404
4000	1404
4200	1408
4500	1401
4545	1409
5000	1407
5500	1405
5555	1407
6000	1402
6666	1407
7000	1408
8000	1406
8500	1402
9000	1405

Page		
1401	2000	SETTEE, YELLOW, STEEL
	2200	SETTEE, BROWN, STEEL
	4500	CHAIR, RED, LAMINATE
Page 1402	6000	SIDEBOARD, GOLD, STEEL
	1234	CHAIR, RED, STEEL
	8500	TABLE, ORANGE, LAMINATE
Page 1403	3000	SIDEBOARD, BLUE, WOODEN
	1111	STOOLS, GREEN, PLASTIC
	1500	CHAIR, ORANGE, PLASTIC
Page 1404	3500	STOOL, WHITE, PLASTIC
	4000	DESK, BLACK, SPECIAL
	2500	TABLE, GREEN, LAMINATE
Page 1405	9000	SIDEBOARD, YELLOW, WOODEN
	5500	TABLE, YELLOW, PLASTIC
	2222	DESK, BLUE, STEEL
Page 1406	8000	SETTEE, RED, SPECIAL
	1000	DESK, GREEN-BLUE, WOODEN
	1200	DESK, GREY, WOODEN
Page 1407	6666	SIDEBOARD, ORANGE, STEEL
	5000	SETTEE, ORANGE, WOODEN
	5555	TABLE, RED, PLASTIC
Page 1408	3333	CHAIR, WHITE, LAMINATE
	4200	SETTEE, GOLD, WOODEN
	7000	DESK, WHITE, WOODEN
Page 1409	4545	SETTEE, BLUE, SPECIAL

Figure 2.3 An index for a random file

studies, you may have come across the concept of a *binary search*. This is a way of finding an entry within a list of sorted information. Using this method, we look first at the centre of the list and then discard the half which does not contain the entry we seek; then we look at the centre of this list, and discard the half which does not contain our entry, and so on until we find our entry or until we find that it is not present in the list. Because we chop the list into successively smaller and smaller sections, this method is also known as the *binary chop*.

To illustrate this, let us look again at some of the keys which we used in Figure 2.2. This is reproduced in Figure 2.4 where we have numbered the entries to help our explanation. In order to find the entry for, say, key 2500, the first step is to look at the entry at the centre of the list: this is key 2200 and we have marked it with an asterisk. Key 2500 is *higher* than 2200 so we discard the first half of the list because all the keys in the first half must be *lower* than 2200. At the second step, we look at the centre of this list: this is key 3333. Key 2500 is *lower* than 3333, so we discard the second half of this list. At step 3, we look at the

1)	1000	1401				
2)	1111	1401				
3)	1200	1401				
4)	1234	1402				
5)	1500	1402				
6)	2000	1402				
7)	2200	1403*				
8)	2222	1403	2222	1403	2222	1403
9)	2500	1403	2500	1403	2500	1403*
10)	3000	1404	3000	1404	3000	1403
11)	3333	1404	3333	1404*		
12)	3500	1404	3500	1404		
13)	4000	1405	4000	1405		
14)	4200	1405	4200	1405		
15)	4500	1405	4500	1405		
	----1-----		----2-----		----3-----	

Figure 2.4 Binary search

centre of this list: this is key 2500, and we have found the key we require and we can therefore find the number of the page we want—1403—and go to Page 1403 to search for our record.

If we had not performed a binary search but instead looked for entry 2500 by scanning through the entire index from the beginning, we should have had to look at 9 entries in all and compare each of these with the one we want. In fact, since there are 15 entries in this list, we should *on average* have to check half the list—making 7.5 comparisons to find any particular entry.

Using the binary search on this particular file, we scan to find any entry in 4 or fewer comparisons. A little thought will convince you that 4 comparisons will enable us to find any entry in a list of 16 (that is 2 to the power 4) entries. Even if we *double* the length of the list, we only need one extra comparison. Ten comparisons will locate an entry in a list of over 1,000 entries (1024 to be exact), and 20 comparisons will locate an entry in a list of over one million entries. Of course, if you happen to hit upon the one you want, as we did with key 2500 at the third comparison, then the process will be even quicker. If we had been looking for key 2222, for example, then we should have needed that fourth comparison.

Activity 2

Draw a diagram similar to that in Figure 2.4, showing the lists which you would scan in looking for each of the following keys in the index shown there:

- 2200
- 4500
- 1234
- 1000

Make a note of the number of comparisons which you make in each case.

B-trees

The principles of the binary search are applied in a data structure known as the *B-tree*. An example of such a structure is shown in Figure 2.5. In a moment we see how such a tree is built. Note that, for simplicity, our illustration shows only the keys (and not the page number where the records are to be found).

The tree is organized into groups of entries, one entry for each key. These groups are called *nodes*. Within each node, the entries are sorted into order. The first node—the top of the tree—is called the *root node*. As the tree grows, new entries are added to the root node until it becomes too large. It is then broken up into sub-trees, as shown in Figure 2.5(e). Entries are added so that they are always in sequence with the lowest entry at the bottom left corner. By looking at all the entries in the leftmost node, and then the element in the root node, then following the pointers to the next leftmost node, then back to the root node, and so on, we can *traverse* the tree, accessing all the entries in sequence.

Some people use the name B-tree to mean a *binary tree*, others use the name to denote a *balanced tree*. The name is also used to denote a *Bayer tree*, which is a variation of the balanced tree and named after the man who introduced the concept.

We shall look at a balanced tree, and this must obey certain rules including:

- There is a limit to the number of entries in each node. Let us call this limit n. The tree is then said to be of order n.
- No node may have more than n entries.
- No node may have fewer than $n/2$ entries (unless it is the root node and there are fewer than $n/2$ entries in the tree).

3000; 2222; 1234; 2500; 1500; 3500; 3333; 4500; 2000; 1200; 4200; 1000; 4000; 2200; 1111.

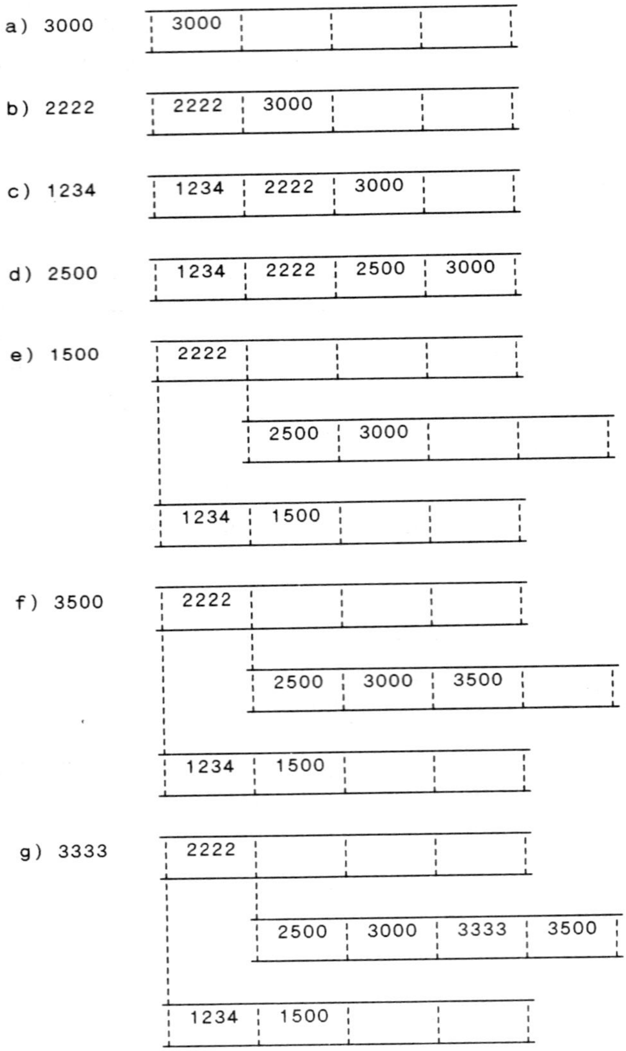

Figure 2.5 Building a B-tree

h) 4500

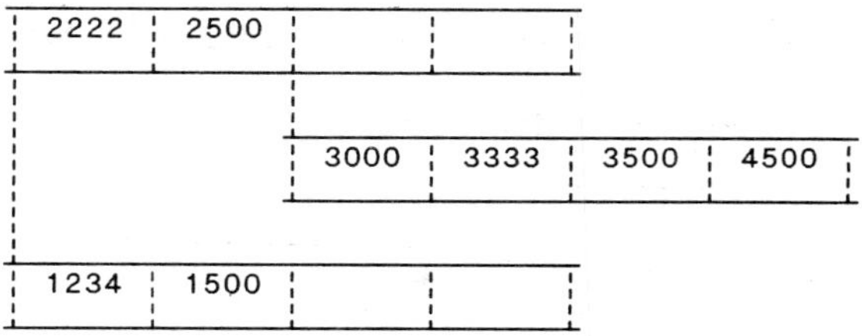

i) 2000

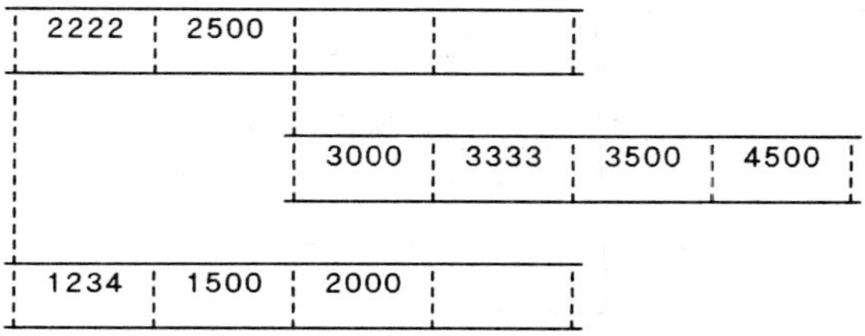

j) 1200

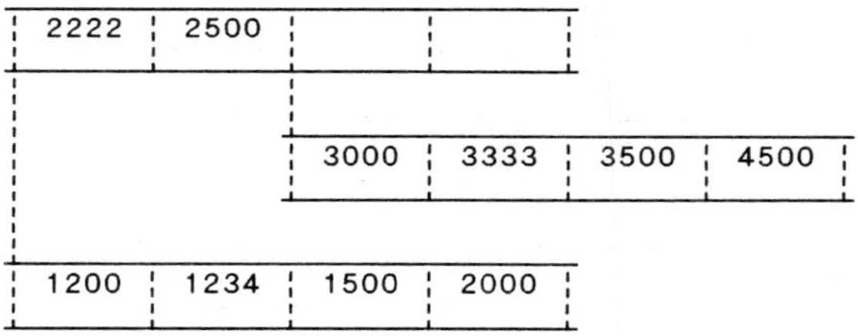

k) 4200

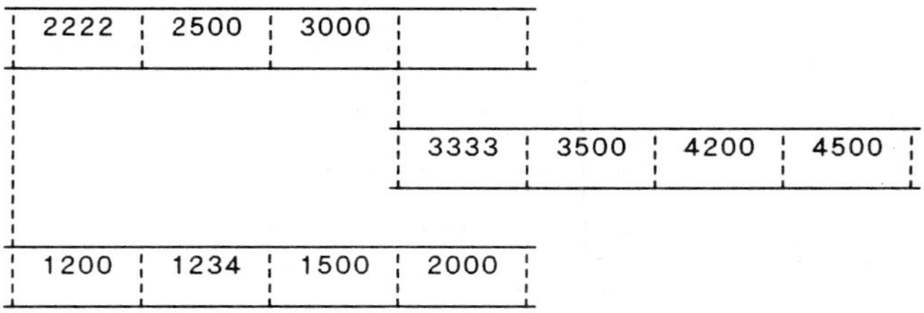

continued

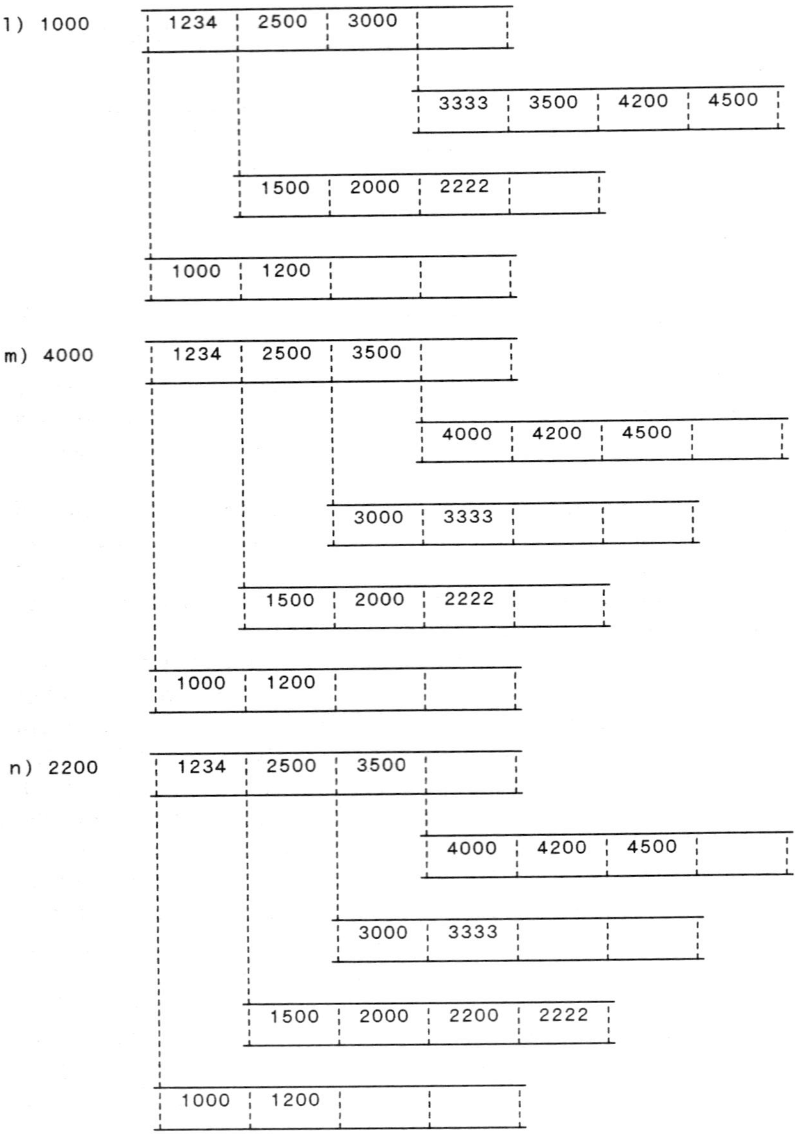

Figure 2.5 – *continued*

o) 1111

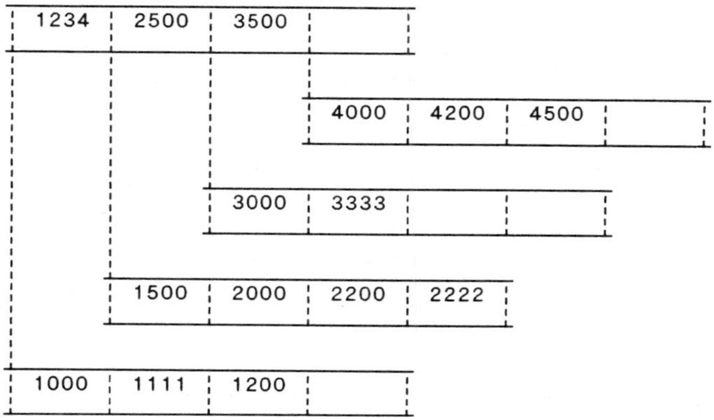

We shall construct a balanced tree of order 4. Therefore, no node may have more than 4 entries and no node (other than the root node) may have fewer than 2 entries. If any node becomes too large, then it will be reorganized into a sub-tree.

The process of adding new entries to the index and deleting old entries is complicated because, at each stage, each node may have no more than 4 entries and no fewer than 2 entries. A set of standard processing routines is normally provided to build, to maintain and to retrieve data from a B-tree.

To illustrate the manner in which a B-tree is handled, let us imagine that we are creating a B-tree by adding the keys shown at the head of Figure 2.5. These are presented to us randomly and we must add them to the tree in accordance with the rules for balanced trees. Each diagram shows the state of the B-tree after each of the keys has been added. We leave the diagrams to explain themselves, but you should note the way in which the nodes are reorganized to obey the rules.

As a new node is established, pointers are set within the root node: the pointer *in front of* an entry there indicates the node containing keys which come *before* that entry; the pointer *following* an entry, indicates the node containing keys which come *after* that entry.

Typically, when B-trees are implemented physically, each node is represented by a record on the index file. A physical representation of the final state of the above index might look like that shown in Figure 2.6. In diagram 2.6(a), we have reproduced the B-tree and numbered the nodes. This identifier is called the *node-id*. Diagram 2.6(b) shows the contents of the node records for the index. Note that we have included the page numbers so that the index may be used to retrieve

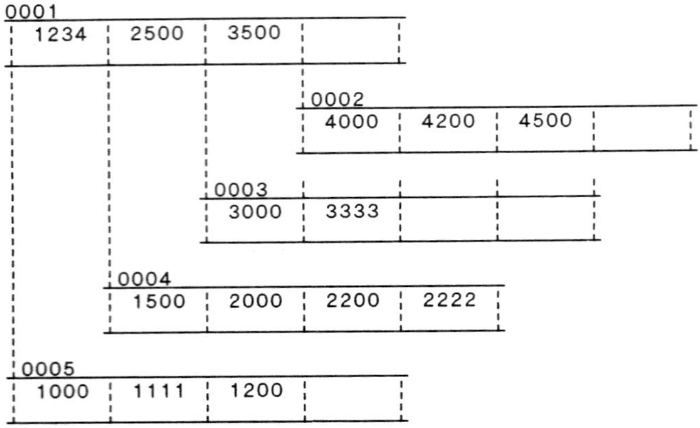

(a) The numbered nodes

```
Node id: 0001
           Key          Page Number
Entries:   1234         1402
           2500         1403
           3500         1404

Links   :  0005
           0004
           0003
           0002

Node id: 0002
           Key          Page Number
Entries:   4000         1405
           4200         1405
           4500         1405

Links:     0
           0
           0
           0

Mode id: 0003
           Key          Page Number
Entries:   3000         1404
           3333         1404

Links:     0
           0
           0

Node id: 0004
           Key          Page Number
Entries:   1500         1402
```

Figure 2.6 Physical implementation of a B-tree

```
            2000           1402
            2200           1403
            2222           1403

Links:      0
            0
            0
            0
            0
-----------------------------------------------------
Node id:    0005
-----------------------------------------------------
            Key            Page Number
Entries:    1000           1401
            1111           1401
            1200           1401

Links:      0
            0
            0
            0
-----------------------------------------------------
```

(b) The node records

records on the main file. The *link* indicates the node-id of the node to which you should go if you cannot find the entry you want in this node. Note that there will be one more link field than there are entries in the node; each links to a node before and/or after each entry.

In the root node, we see three entries:

- 1234
- 2500
- 3500

and four links:

- 0005
- 0004
- 0003
- 0002

This tells us that, if we want a key lower than 1234, we must go to node 0005; if we want a key between 1234 and 2500, we must go to node 0004; if we want a key between 2500 and 3500, we must go to node 0003; if we want a key higher than 3500, we must go to node 0002.

A link field of zero means that this node goes no further. If you encounter a zero link field, then it means that the entry which you are looking for does not exist here, and you must return to the previous (higher level) node. However, if you find an entry which is *after* the one you want, then you know that your entry does not exist.

To illustrate the way in which we use the tree to search for a particular entry, let us imagine that we wish to use the B-tree to find key 2000. We always start at the root node (0001). Scanning the entries, we do not find the one we want here, but we see that it comes *between* keys 1234 and 2500, so we follow the link field to node 0004. Scanning the entries, we find the key we want.

If we are searching for a key which does not exist, then we repeat the above process until we find a key higher than the one we want. For example, if we want key 3100, we start again at the root node. Scanning the entries, we do not find the one we want, but we see that it comes between keys 2500 and 3500, so we follow the link field to node 0003. Scanning the entries, we find key 3000, which comes before the one we want and key 3333, which comes after the one we want, but all the lower links are 0. This means that key 3100 does not exist.

In practice, B-trees are much larger than this, with each node having its own sub-trees. Nevertheless, the general principles on which they are organized are identical to those described here.

Activity 3

1 Describe the actions which would take place whilst you were searching the B-tree in Figure 2.6 for the following entries. Write down the ids of the nodes which are searched and the result of the search in each case.
   a) 2100
   b) 1111
   c) 2200

2 Describe the actions which you would take and draw a diagram showing the final state of the B-tree as each of the following keys is added:
   a) 4555
   b) 1201
   c) 1202

Soundex indexing

In commercial data processing, it is often required to identify data such as names and addresses by the *sound*, rather than by the actual spelling. This is particularly important when data is being captured by telephone operators and by the spoken word. For example, when you telephone the registrar's office, it is more efficient if the telephonist can locate your record on the computer without getting the exact spelling correct. How can the telephonist tell whether you are saying JONSON or JOHNSON? We must have a *precise* means of identifying a name if we are to use it to retrieve a record.

The Soundex technique offers a solution to this and represents a powerful means of indexing in situations where spelling mistakes can cause serious problems. The technique encodes each word according to the approximate sound of the word, returning a unique code for similar-sounding words. So Smythe, Smith and Smithe would all be encoded in the same way. This code could then be used as the key to the index entries to find a list of surnames, and this list would be displayed, together with the date of birth and student number or some other identifying information, to enable the telephonist to retrieve your student record. This is illustrated in Figure 2.7.

The Soundex algorithm returns the first letter of the word followed by a number derived from the next three consonants of the word according to a table such as that shown in Figure 2.8(a). Each letter is

Name	Code
JAMESON	J525
JAMIESON	J525
JENSEN	J525
JENSON	J525
JOHNSON	J525
JONSON	J525

(a) Names and Soundex equivalent

J525	JAMESON	31/05/75	02678
	JAMIESON	04/03/75	01274
	JENSEN	08/08/77	04364
	JENSON	14/12/74	06815
	JOHNSON	19/08/75	05000
	JOHNSON	03/08/75	01303
	JONSON	19/10/74	00706
	JOHNSON	10/12/74	06775

(b) Indexed on the Soundex code

Figure 2.7 Use of Soundex

```
A, E, I, O, U, H, W, Y ...... Ignored
B, F, P, V .................. 1
C, G, J, K, Q, S, X, Z ...... 2
D, T ........................ 3
L ........................... 4
M, N ........................ 5
R ........................... 6
```

(a) Letters encoded by Soundex

```
J O H N S O N
^     ^ ^   ^
|     | |   |
|     | |   |
J     5 2   5       ==> J525

S M Y T H E
^ ^   ^
| |   |
| |   |
S 5   3             ==> S530

S M I T H
^ ^   ^
| |   |
| |   |
S 5   3             ==> S530

W A T K I N S O N
^   ^ ^   ^
|   | |   |
|   | |   |
W   3 2   5         ==> W325

B U L L
^   ^
|   |
|   |
B   4               ==> B400
```

(b) Encoding some surnames with the Soundex algorithm

Figure 2.8 The Soundex algorithm

converted to its coded form. Note that vowels, H, W and Y are ignored. If there are any double letters, only the first is accepted, the second is ignored. The code is padded out to three digits by adding zeroes at the right.

Figure 2.8(b) illustrates how some names would be encoded.

Question

5 Using the algorithm outlined above, derive the Soundex code for the following surnames:

a) HARDING
b) HARDY
c) LEWIS
d) LOUIS
e) ROBINSON
f) SHAKESPEARE
g) STANLEY
h) STONELEIGH
i) LIVINGSTONE
j) WILSON

Some Soundex algorithms are more complicated than this, allowing for TH and WH and SH and NG as single letters. The above algorithm is based upon the frequencies and sounds of the letters in English. Obviously, other foreign languages might devise a similar system more appropriate to their sounds and their surnames.

In our examples, we used the Soundex technique to enable us to find the *student number* by means of the *name*. We would then have to use the *student number* as the key to find the true student record. It is quite feasible to devise a Soundex algorithm which would enable use to find the *page number* directly by means of the *name*.

Hashing algorithms

A more common method of associating a particular record with a particular page is by the technique of *hashing*. When using this method, the disk space which is allocated for the file is divided into separate areas known as *buckets*. Each bucket occupies one or more pages of disk storage and the system uses a *hashing algorithm* to decide which bucket a record is to go into. This algorithm is an arithmetic process which takes the record key and uses it to arrive at a number which indicates the bucket where the record is to be placed.

Here is a simple algorithm:

1 take each character in the record key, find their ASCII equivalent and add them all together. Figure 2.10 shows the ASCII codes for the letters and numbers.
2 divide the result by the number of buckets in the file.
3 add one to the remainder and the result is the bucket where this record should be placed.

Let us imagine that we have established a SUBJECT file with 7 buckets, and that there is one page in each bucket, as illustrated in Figure 2.9. If we have a record with the key BIOLOGY and wish to know the number

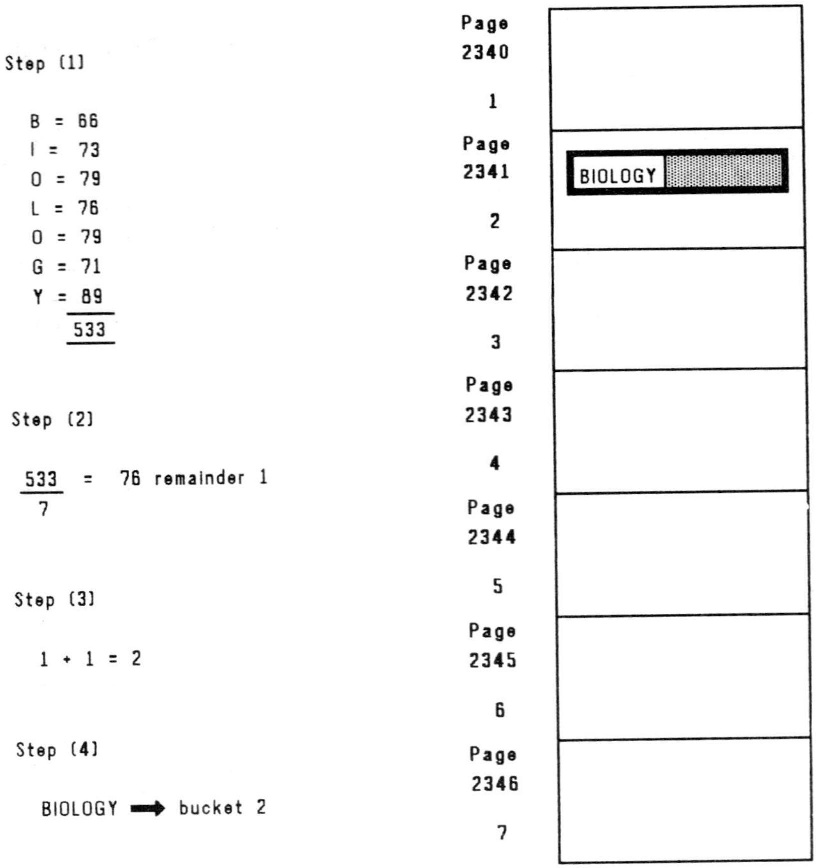

Figure 2.9 A hashing algorithm

of the bucket into which this record will go. We follow the steps of the algorithm and:

1 taking each character of the key in turn, we find its ASCII value (A has the value 65, B is 66, and so on) and add these up for all the characters in the key. The result is 533.
2 we divide the result by 7, the number of buckets in our file, to get 76 remainder 1.
3 add 1 to the remainder to get the final result 2.

So the BIOLOGY record would go into bucket 2 of our file. If we know that the file starts at, say, page 2340 and each bucket is one frame in size, then the BIOLOGY record would be found in page 2341. This is illustrated in Figure 2.9.

To read a record which has been written away to disk, we perform the same algorithm and then, having found the right bucket, scan through the contents of that bucket to find the correct record.

When I say *we perform the algorithm*, I should really say that the file handling system does these calculations on our behalf. As a user—and even as a programmer—it is not necessary to know too much about the physical file organization or how the algorithm works, we simply give the required key to the system and ask it to get the record we require.

Questions

6 Do we need to use the same algorithm to read and to write the records away to disk?
7 A hashing algorithm is based upon certain parameters about the file. What are they?
8 What are the values of these parameters for the COURSE-SUBJECT file we have used?
9 Can you think of an arithmetic formula to derive the page number of the correct bucket from the remainder without having to find out the number of the bucket? Will your formula always work?
10 Using the ASCII table shown in Figure 2.10, calculate the number of the bucket and the number of page where the following records would go on the SUBJECT file. You may assume that the page ids are as shown in Figure 2.9.
   a) ARTS
   b) HUMANITIES
   c) SOCIAL SCIENCES

Space	32	G	71
&	38	H	72
–	45	I	73
.	46	J	74
0	48	K	75
1	49	L	76
2	50	M	77
3	51	N	78
4	52	O	79
5	53	P	80
6	54	Q	81
7	55	R	82
8	56	S	83
9	57	T	84
A	65	U	85
B	66	V	86
C	67	W	87
D	68	X	88
E	69	Y	89
F	70	Z	90

Figure 2.10 Some ASCII characters

d) SOCIO-POLITICAL STUDIES
e) C & G 417
f) C & G 714

11 What do you notice about the solution to parts (e) and (f) of Question 10? Why is this so?

Ours is just a simple hashing algorithm. Typically an algorithm will base its calculations on the character values of the record key, as ours did. It may also *weight* the character values by multiplying the value of the first character by 2, the second character by 3 and so on, or in some similar fashion. By weighting the character positions, you will avoid the situation where *C & G 417* is placed in the same bucket as *C & G 741*: these two records are said to *collide*.

In practice, we really want to avoid such collisions. The more records there are in a bucket, the more you will have to climb over to get to the one you need, and we don't want to waste a lot of time looking at records we don't want.

Unless you have exactly the right number of buckets—one for each record—then you will always have the situation where two or more records collide. In practice, even if you have arranged to have a very large number of buckets, your algorithm may still produce collisions. There are many possible algorithms and much time and effort is expended to produce one which avoids collisions and distributes the records evenly through the file.

Deleting records

When a file is organized in the manner which we have described, an unwanted record can be removed simply by writing another record on top of it, as illustrated in Figure 2.11(b) where we delete record B by overwriting it with record X.

In practice, however, this is not always possible, we may simply want to delete one record without writing another. For this reason, a record is usually deleted by either:

- Setting a flag to show that it has been deleted and is no longer active, as in Figure 2.11(c), or
- Moving the unwanted record to the end of the bucket and setting an end-of-bucket marker, as in Figure 2.11(d). When this marker is encountered by the file-handling system, it is interpreted as the physical end of that bucket.

In either situation, the file handling system will ignore the deleted record.

Coping with overflow

No matter how well designed the algorithm and how many buckets we provide, there may be files in which certain buckets are completely empty, and there will be situations in which a bucket fills up and there is no more room to add further records. So what do we do when a bucket is full? How do we handle data *overflow?*

One solution is to put the record into the next available bucket. When we try to read a record, we must go to the bucket which is indicated by the hashing algorithm then:

- If the bucket is full, go to the next bucket and look there. We repeat this sequence until we find the record, or
- If the bucket is not full and we have not found the record, then we know that it must not exist.

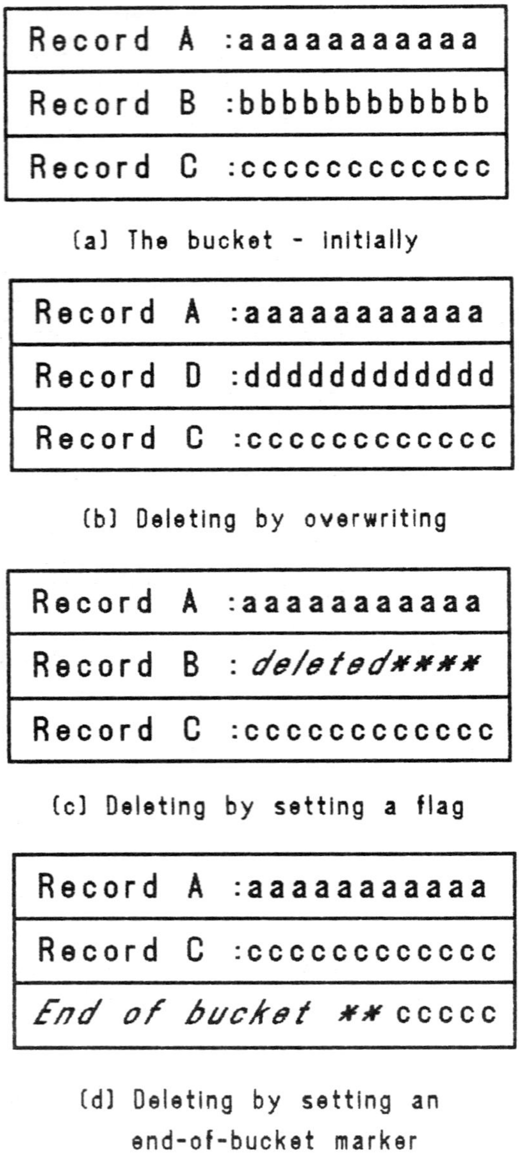

Figure 2.11 Deleting records

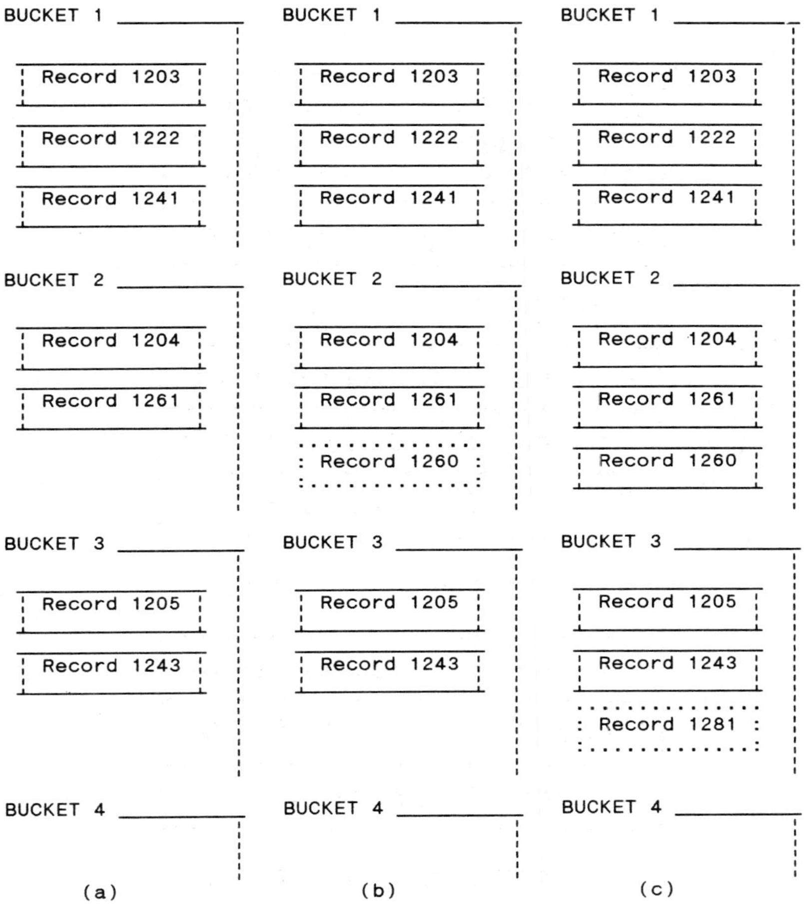

Figure 2.12 Handling overflow—1

When we are searching in this manner, an empty space means 'here's a gap, so the record you want cannot exist, otherwise it would be in this gap.'

We can illustrate this by the section of a file shown in Figure 2.12. Initially, the file is at the state shown in diagram (a). Imagine that we want to add two new records—1260 and 1281—and that the hashing algorithm sends both these records to Bucket 1.

When we attempt to add record 1260, the file handling system goes to Bucket 1 only to find that it is full. So it goes on to Bucket 2 and, since there is room, places record 1260 there, leaving the file in the state shown in diagram (b).

Later, we attempt to add record 1281. In its search for free space, the file handling system goes to Bucket 1 only to find that it is full. So it goes on to Bucket 2 to find that it too is full. So it goes on to Bucket 3 and, since there is room, places record 1281 there, leaving the file in the state shown in diagram (c).

Such a method of handling overflow makes the process of retrieval slow. If we want to find record 1281, we must first go to Bucket 1 (its *home* bucket); since the record is not there and the bucket is full, we must go on to Bucket 2. Record 1281 is not here and the bucket is full, so we must go on to Bucket 3. We find the record in Bucket 3.

If we are looking for record 1319—whose home bucket is also Bucket 1—we must go first to Bucket 1. The record is not here and the bucket is full, so we must go on to Bucket 2. The record is not here and the bucket is full, so we must go on to Bucket 3. The record is not here and the bucket is full, so we must go on to Bucket 4. The record is not here but the bucket is not full, so we know that record 1319 does not exist.

Here's something to think about: what happens if we delete a record, say we delete record 1222 and remove it from Bucket 1? How will this affect our search for, say, record 1281?

Unfortunately, as all the buckets become filled, we might get to a stage where we have to read through most of the buckets and most of the records in the file in order to find the one we need. Furthermore, this situation is aggravated by the fact that we cannot remove deleted records from the file.

A better solution is to link in another page (or pages) of storage to the end of the bucket and carry on using this *overflow* area just as if it belonged to that bucket. This is illustrated in Figure 2.13 where we see the situation described above but this time on a system which attaches overflow frames to each bucket, as necessary.

When a bucket is filled, a marker is set and this tells the file handling system which page it should go to next in order to find the overflow.

The various file handling systems treat the overflow pages in different ways: some allocate a separate overflow to each bucket (as illustrated here); some use the same overflow area for all buckets; others create a new bucket and add this to the index. In all cases, the linkage between the buckets and the overflow frames is taken care of entirely by the file handling system. Although these physical aspects of

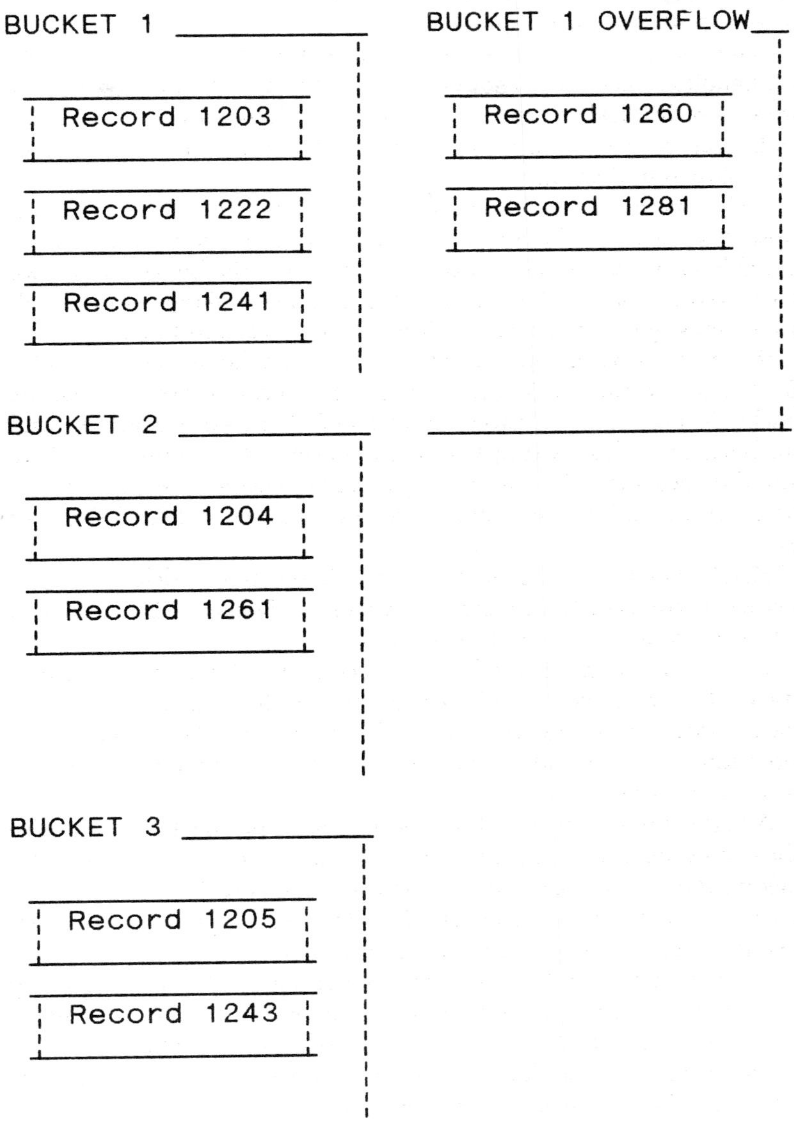

Figure 2.13 Handling overflow—2

file handling are outside the control of the systems analyst and the programmer, it is the analyst's responsibility to ensure that there is sufficient space to accommodate the data held in the file and that the file is properly organized. If there are a great many overflows, then the file handling system will become very slow as it becomes necessary to perform several disk read operations—from page to page—in order to find a single record.

Secondary keys

There may be occasions when we need to be able to access a record by more than one piece of data, or by means of an attribute other than the key.

In Question 4, we saw that Ivan identifies the components by the suppliers' code and may want to know how many DA/182/4646 there are in the warehouse; Barbara uses the product type and may want to know when the 0.5 OHM RESISTORS were ordered. Because we have decided to use the number in the company's sales catalogue to identify the various products, neither the suppliers' code nor the product type is the key for the components records. In another situation, a furniture company may hold records relating to the items of furniture which they produce. On one occasion, they may want to process all the records relating to CHAIRs, on another occasion they may need to process just the LEATHER furniture. Neither of these attributes—CHAIR or LEATHER—is the key for the furniture records. There will be many CHAIRs on the furniture file, and there will be many LEATHER items of furniture.

If our records contain an attribute which may (sometimes) be required to identify the record but which does not uniquely identify the record, then this piece of information is known as a *secondary key*.

To avoid confusion, the unique identifying key which we met earlier is sometimes known as the *primary key*.

Quite clearly *any* attribute can be thought of as a secondary key. It all depends how the data is to be used and the nature of the enquiries which are to be made about the data. In general, a secondary key is based upon data which has the same value in several records on a file, and where that piece of data can take one of a number of *discrete* values. Typical examples are colour (there may be several red items and several blue items), size (there may be small items, medium and large items), material (oak, wood, leather, plastic, and so on), type (chairs, tables, desks, beds) and category (products of type A, type B and type C).

It would be less common to find secondary keys based upon data which may take *continuous* values. For example, if we are designing a file to record the midday temperatures in Delhi, this may have any value from 0 degrees to 130 degrees Fahrenheit. Including fractions of a degree. As another example, the marks gained in an examination may have any value in the range 0% to 100%. There may be several students with, say, 85.5% but we are more likely to be interested in the *discrete* values such as Distinction, Pass 2, Pass 3 and Fail. Surnames, codes, descriptions and titles are particularly suitable for use as secondary keys.

Questions

A record relating to a bank account holds the following attributes: customer name, current balance, the town where the customer lives, the customer's post code, the account number, details of an overdraft limit, the customer's telephone number, the date when the customer opened the account.

12 How many primary keys are there? Identify the piece(s) of data which could be the primary key(s).

13 How many secondary keys are there? Identify the piece(s) of data which could be the secondary key(s). Suggest situations in which each secondary key might be useful.

14 Which of the following are continuous values suitable for use as secondary keys? Of those which you consider unsuitable, suggest some discrete values which might make them suitable.

(a) The height of the students. These would take values such as 165 cms, 179.7 cms, 159 cms and so on.

(b) The temperature in a laboratory. This is recorded with values such as freezing, cold, warm, hot.

(c) Students' qualifications. These would have values such as BSc, BSc (Hons), BSc 2.1, BA, MA, PhD.

(d) Car mileage recorded by salesmen as they travel around on their business. These would take values such as 100 miles, 200 miles, 17 miles, 37.5 miles.

Activity 4

Look again at the attributes on the files for the four college programs and indicate (or choose or invent) a suitable primary key for each of the data records which are used.

We have seen how a furniture company might need to produce a report about all their leather furniture, and for this reason we suggested that the *material* attribute be used as a secondary key. Suggest some attributes which might be used as secondary keys in the college system.

Inverted files

Each record is uniquely identified by its primary key: we use the primary key when we write the record to disk and we must have the record key in order to be able to find that same record again later. So how can we cope with secondary keys in practice?

An *inverted file* is one way in which we can access a file by means of a secondary key. For example, let us imagine that we have a file holding details of standby lecturers, with records such as those shown in Figure 2.14(a). There may be other attributes—the address, telephone number and so on—but we'll ignore these for our present purposes. There may be a need to access these records using the *surname* or the *subject* as a secondary key.

It would be possible to access this file using such a secondary key by means of the inverted files in Figure 2.14(b) and (c) which are organized according to the secondary keys: subject and surname of the lecturer. Each inverted file is constructed and maintained separately from the main file. The *primary key* of the records on the inverted file is the same data which makes up the *secondary key* of the records on the main file; the data in the records on the inverted file includes the primary keys of the records on the main file.

This may sound a bit complicated, but if you look at record 1101 on the STANDBY-LECTURER file which is for ARTHUR BARCLAY who lectures in STATISTICS, you will see that there are corresponding records on the inverted files:

1 on the SUBJECT file, there is a record with the key STATISTICS which contains data representing the records of *all the statistics lecturers*, one of which is 1101, the key of the STANDBY-LECTURER file record for ARTHUR BARCLAY.

NUMBER	NAME	SUBJECT
1101	ARTHUR BARCLAY	STATISTICS
2000	RITA LENNOX	CALCULUS
2003	JOHN BARCLAY	CALCULUS
3455	ETHEL LENNOX	STATISTICS
4511	HARRY BARCLAY	STATISTICS
6022	SHIRLEY MORRIS	CALCULUS

(a) STANDBY-LECTURER - main data file

SUBJECT	NUMBER
CALCULUS	2000 2003 6022
STATISTICS	1101 3455 4511

(b) SUBJECT - inverted file

SURNAME	NUMBER
BARCLAY	1101 2003 4511
LENNOX	2000 3455
MORRIS	6022

(c) SURNAME - inverted file

Figure 2.14 Inverted files

2 on the SURNAME file, there is a record with the key BARCLAY which contains data representing the records of *all the lecturers with the surname Barclay*, one of which is 1101, the key of the STANDBY-LECTURER file record for ARTHUR BARCLAY.

Let us imagine that we want to call in a statistics lecturer and need to know which lecturer(s) work in statistics. We can use the SUBJECT file to obtain the lecturer-number(s) for the lecturer(s) working in STATISTICS, and then use these value(s) (1101, 3455, and 4511) to obtain the appropriate record(s) from the LECTURER file. Similarly, if we need to make an enquiry about a lecturer called MORRIS, we can use the SURNAME file to obtain the lecturer-number(s) for MORRIS, and then use these value(s) (6022) to obtain Mrs Morris's record from the LECTURER file.

Without a DBMS, you would have to construct and maintain the SURNAME and the SUBJECT files yourself. Each time a record was added, changed or deleted on the STANDBY-LECTURER file, your program would have to make the corresponding changes to the inverted files. This can be quite an overhead, costing time and effort, but it is worthwhile if you (or the people who use your programs) need to do the sort of processing and make the sort of enquiries which can take advantage of these inverted files.

Questions

These questions are based upon the files shown in Figure 2.14.

15 Describe the actions which take place when we want to find and display the name of any statistics lecturer.

16 Describe the actions which take place when we want to find and display the name of all calculus lecturers.

17 Describe the actions which take place when we want to find and display the reference number of any statistics lecturer called Lennox.

Another way in which we might handle secondary keys is to hold within the records on the main STANDBY-LECTURER file—the key of the next record with that surname and also the key of the next record for that subject. The file might now look like that in Figure 2.15(a). So when we want to find a calculus lecturer, for example, having found the record for the first calculus lecturer (record 2000) we can follow the chain on to the next (3455) and then on to the next (4551) until we find the one we want.

All that we need is to know the key for the *first* record in each chain. This is held in an index (or indexes) as shown in Figure 2.15(b) and (c).

NUMBER	NAME	SUBJECT	NEXT SURNAME	NEXT SUBJECT
1101	ARTHUR BARCLAY	STATISTICS	2003	3455
2000	RITA LENNOX	CALCULUS	3455	2003
2003	JOHN BARCLAY	CALCULUS	4551	6022
3455	ETHEL LENNOX	STATISTICS	*	4511
4511	HARRY BARCLAY	STATISTICS	*	*
6022	SHIRLEY MORRIS	CALCULUS	*	*

(a) STANDBY-LECTURER - main data file

SUBJECT	START KEY
CALCULUS	2000
STATISTICS	1101

(b) SUBJECT index

SURNAME	START KEY
BARCLAY	1101
LENNOX	2000
MORRIS	6022

(c) SURNAME index

Figure 2.15 Indexed files

Questions

These questions are based upon the files shown in Figure 2.15.

18 How do we know when there are no more records in the chain?

19 Can you suggest any other ways of indicating the length of the chain?

20 Describe the actions which take place when we want to find and display the name of any statistics lecturer.

21 Describe the actions which take place when we want to find and display the name of all calculus lecturers.

22 Describe the actions which take place when we want to find and display the reference number of any statistics lecturer called Lennox.

This method does not take up quite so much disk space as the previous one. But it still requires the programmer to keep a tight check on the *next* fields when records are added to or deleted from the STANDBY-LECTURER file.

Some DBMS will maintain such inverted files and indexes automatically for you. They may also use these indexes when you need to retrieve a record.

Recap

In this chapter, we have looked at the ways in which files are accessed by the file handling system. A DBMS relieves us of the burden of knowing all about the work and the processing which it carries out on our behalf.

All the data of a database is held on magnetic disks. The DBMS (and the operating system) organize the disk storage into a set of numbered pages. A page may be 500, 1000 or 2000 bytes in size. A file is established with a specific number of pages and the records are placed on to these pages as they are written away.

Each record consists of a number of data attributes, and on each file, each record is uniquely identified by its primary key made up of one or more attributes.

To speed up the retrieval of the records, an index is normally maintained to show the keys of the records on each page. This might be a simple list showing which key is held on which page. We looked at the use of a binary search to speed up the task of finding an entry in the index, then we improved this by organizing the index as a B-tree. In a B-tree, the entries are sorted into groups and these are arranged in a tree structure, each group becoming a node of the tree. When searching the B-tree, you start at the root node and scan this—and the nodes linked on to it—until you find the record you need.

We introduced the idea of a hashing algorithm. This is a simple arithmetic calculation performed on the record key to decide which record goes into which bucket. When we want to read a record, we perform the same algorithm and then simply search through the correct bucket for that record. We looked at a simple hashing algorithm.

Secondary keys are non-unique data fields—such as surname or colour—which may be required to locate the records on a file.

An inverted file is one way of handling secondary keys. Each inverted file is constructed and maintained separately from the main file. The primary key of the records on the inverted file is the same data which makes up the secondary key of the records on the main file; the data in the records on the inverted file includes the primary keys of the records on the main file.

Secondary keys may also be organized as a series of chained records. Each chain consists of records with the same secondary key. Each record being a link in the chain and holding the key of the next record in the chain. An index must be maintained to show the start of each chain.

For secondary keys such as surnames, street names where it is possible to make spelling mistakes, the technique of Soundex indexing can be used. This encodes words in such a way that those which sound alike will have the same code.

Overflow is handled in many different ways. We looked at two methods: one which put a record into the next available bucket in which space could be found; the other linked on extra pages to a bucket if there was no room in the bucket to accommodate new records.

Answers

1 We may get two (or more) students with the same name. It might also be difficult (or time-consuming) to ensure that we type the student's name in correctly every time we need to find the student's record. For example: do we call Miss Sands by the name JENNIFER SANDS or J SANDS or J.SANDS or Jennifer Sands? And what about Bartholomew Featherstone-haugh?

2 For the reasons given earlier, we could not use the lecturer's name as the key. We could invent a fictitious lecturer reference number, or there may already be some unique identifier—such as payroll number or staff number—which we could use.

3 As before, we would not choose the title of the book, nor could we choose the ISBN number (unless we are sure that there will only be one copy of the same book). We could use the ISBN followed by an extra letter or number to make the key unique. For example: the copies of the book with ISBN

    0-434-91877-6

might have record keys:

    0434918776A
    0434918776B
    0434918776C

and so on. As with the lecturers in Question 2, we could invent a fictitious book identification number, or there may already be some unique identifier—such as book acquisition number—which we could use.

4 Unless we decide to invent a completely fictitious reference number, the product number in the sales catalogue seems the obvious choice. The suppliers' code is not necessarily unique (different suppliers may use the same code for different products) and the product type is certainly not unique (there will be many different transistors and many different resistors).

5 a) H635, b) H630, c) L200, d) L200, e) R152, f) S221, g) S354, h) S354, i) L152, j) W425.

6 Yes, otherwise you would never be able to find a particular record.

7 The size of (number of pages in) each bucket; the number of buckets; the page number of the first page in the file.

8 There is only one page in each bucket; there are 7 buckets in the file; the page number of the first page in the file is 2340.

9 If you said 'add the remainder to the number of the first page in the file' then this will only work when the bucket size is 1. You should have suggested a formula such as:

Page number = (Remainder × Bucket size) + First page number.

10 (a) ARTS
Hash total = 314 = 44 remainder 6 → Bucket 7 → Page 2346
(b) HUMANITIES
Hash total = 759 = 108 remainder 3 → Bucket 4 → Page 2343
(c) SOCIAL SCIENCES
Hash total = 1064 = 152 remainder 0 → Bucket 1 → Page 2340
(d) SOCIO-POLITICAL STUDIES
Hash total = 1676 = 239 remainder 3 → Bucket 4 → Page 2343
(e) C & G 417
Hash total = 428 = 61 remainder 1 → Bucket 2 → Page 2341
(f) C & G 714
Hash total = 428 = 61 remainder 1 → Bucket 2 → Page 2341.

11 This record is placed in the same bucket as the previous key. This is because both keys contain the same characters (only the order is different) and therefore produce the same results.

12 There is only one primary key for each record on a file. In this situation, the primary key would probably be the account number.

13 There may be any number of secondary keys. In fact, each attribute (except the account number which we have chosen as the primary key) could be a secondary key. Likely secondary keys are: the customer's surname (we might have had a letter from a Mrs Wilkinson and need to find details of her account), the town where the customer lives (we might want to send a publicity leaflet to all the customers who live in Accrington), the customer's post code (we might wish to send letters to all customers who live near a new branch which is to open shortly).

14 (a) The height varies continuously and is not suitable as a secondary key. The students could be graded as small, medium or large, or their heights could be divided into bands such as below 150 cms, above 150 but below 160 cms, and so on.
(b) Discrete values such as freezing, cold, warm, hot are suitable as secondary keys.
(c) The degree qualifications are suitable as secondary keys.
(d) The car mileage is unsuitable as secondary keys. It could be split into bands, as in answer (a) above.

15 We look for the keys of the records for the statistics lecturers in the SUBJECT file (record 1101, 3455, 4511) then, we read the first of these (since only want one lecturer) and display the name as required.

16 We look for the keys of the records for the calculus lecturers in the SUBJECT index (record 2000 2003, 6022). We then keep this list of keys and read each of these records in turn and display the name as required, until there are no more record keys in the list.

17 There are several possibilities here: we could read through all the statistics lecturers until we find one called Copley, or we could read through all the lecturers called Copley until we find one who teaches statistics, or (and this is probably the most efficient) we could take the two lists of keys (1101, 3455 and 4511 for statistics and 2000 and 3455 for Copley) and compare them to find a key which appears in both lists. This would be 3455 in this case. Then, having found the required record we can display the reference number or any other attributes which we might hold in the record.

18 When we come to a record which contains a dummy record (we used an asterisk) in the next field.

19 We could hold a number in the index entry showing how many records there are in each chain.

20 We look for the key of the record for the first statistics lecturer in the SUBJECT index (record 1101). Then, having found this record we can display the name as required.

21 We look for the key of the record for the first calculus lecturer in the SUBJECT index (record 2000). Then, having found this record we can display the name as required and then go on to find the key of the next calculus lecturer (3455). We read this record and display the name and then find the key of the next calculus lecturer (4551). We read this record and display the name and then find the key of the next calculus lecturer; this is the dummy key (an asterisk) and means that there are no more records, so we stop the processing.

22 There are two possibilities here: we could look for the key of the record for the first statistics lecturer in the SUBJECT index (record 1101), and then follow this chain until we find a lecturer called Copley. Then, having found the required record we can display the reference number or any other attributes which we might hold in the record.

The second possiblity is to look for the key of the record for the first lecturer called Copley in the SURNAME index (record 2000), and then follow this chain until we find a lecturer who teaches statistics. We would then process this record as required.

In practice, it would be more efficient to start with the shorter chain. That is why it might be valuable to hold the length of the chain somewhere in the index as we suggested in the answer to Question 19.

3: Data structure diagrams

Objectives

After reading this chapter, you should be able to:

- recognize the way in which one file can be logically related to another
- define the terms *entity* and *relationship*
- explain the difference between an *entity* and a file
- use the term *data structure diagram* and the abbreviation DSD
- describe and draw a data structure diagram
- recognize the alternative names for a DSD: entity-relationship model, logical model
- describe and identify entities and relationships
- describe and identify the various types of relationship which can exist between entities
- resolve a many-to-many relationship into two one-to-many relationships
- describe the term *optional relationship*
- describe the term *operational entity*
- describe the access paths of a data structure diagram
- use access paths to navigate through a data structure diagram.

In the simple files used by the four college programs which we met in Chapter 1, each file contains its own records and each record is identified uniquely by its record key. The real life situation is not quite like this. We have already seen that some pieces of data may be used by more than one program, but there is a further way in which files may be associated, one with another.

Most files do not exist in isolation. They may be related to other files in some way.

- A record on the file of students may hold information showing which subjects they are studying. The STUDENT file is related to the SUBJECT file.
- A record on a file of college departments may hold information about lecturers—this will enable us to find which lecturers work in

which departments. The DEPARTMENT file is related to the LECTURER file. We may also need to hold information on the LECTURER file about which department they work for.

In other situations:

- A file of sales ORDERs will hold information connected with the CUSTOMER file and also with the PRODUCT file.
- A BOOK file may contain information linked with the AUTHOR file, the SUBJECT file and the BORROWER file.

The relationships and associations which exist between one set of data and another is very important in many areas of knowledge:

- An understanding of the relationship between the size of a car engine and the power which it will produce enables us to design cars with a specific performance.
- An understanding of the connection between the earth's daily rotation, the moon's position in its orbit and the phases of the moon together with an understanding of the relationship between the moon and the tides enables us to predict the times at which the tide will come in and go out. Once we have identified these relationships, we can predict the times of high water and low water at any point on the coast.

and no doubt you can think of many more examples. Similarly, a knowledge of the associations between the data on our files is important if we are to make best use of the data. We shall see how some DBMSs use these relationships to find the information we need in our processing.

The actual physical data about the student may be held in different places on the computer's database. We may hold the student's name on one file, the course code on another file, and the course title on another file. For this reason, we cannot yet use the word *file*—we should not say the STUDENT file. Instead, we should say something like the STUDENT details or the STUDENT information. More precisely, we shall use the word *entity* and talk about the STUDENT entity, the LECTURER entity, the COURSE entity, and so on.

We shall define an entity as:

> An object or a concept—such as a person, a place, an event, a thing—which is meaningful to an organization and about which there is a need to record and hold data.

A college system might have entities such as STUDENT, LECTURER, SUBJECT, CLASSROOM, BOOK, EXAMINATIONS; a banking system might have CLIENT, ACCOUNT, LOAN, STANDING-ORDER, MORTGAGE; a library system might have BOOK, AUTHOR, CLASSIFICATION, REQUEST, RESERVATION.

Activity 1

List some of the entities which you would expect to find in the following situations:

1 A coach hire company organizes outings to various seaside resorts and inland beauty spots. The passengers make their reservations and pay their fares in advance.

2 A recruitment agency finds suitable employees for its client companies. The agency holds files of information about companies who are looking for employees, employees who are looking for jobs, newpapers in which to place advertisements, current pay rates for each job.

3 A doctor's surgery.

Data structure diagram

A useful way in which we can depict the entities and the relationships between them is by means of a *data structure diagram* or DSD. This is one of the most important tools when you are designing a computer system and you may already have met it in your studies of systems analysis and systems design. This is really a picture of the data encountered within a computer system, and allows us to study the effects of holding, and of not holding, the data which the users need. Since we can regard it as a model to study the way in which a computer system behaves, the data structure diagram is also known as a *data model* or a *logical model* or an *entity-relationship model.*

It is essential that you distinguish between the *logical model* of the data which is represented by the DSD and the *physical model* which represents the actual physical data when your logical model is *implemented* on a real DBMS. In almost all cases, you will have to make considerable concessions and modifications to your logical model in order to concede to the constraints and limitations which the DBMS imposes upon you.

Figure 3.1 shows a possible data structure diagram for the tutor allocation system.

Entities

This DSD tells us that we need to hold data about:

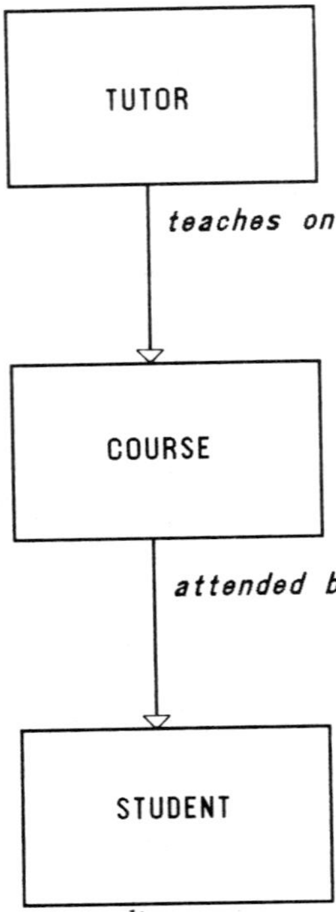

Figure 3.1 A data structure diagram

- *the tutors*
- *the courses*
- *the students.*

In a data structure diagram, each entity is represented by a box with the name of the entity, usually a singular noun, written inside it.

The information which we need to know about each entity are its *attributes.* A college's STUDENT entity might have attributes such as name, address, telephone number, enrolment date; a bank's ACCOUNT entity might have account number, account type, current balance, credit limit; a library's RESERVATION entity might have the date when the book was reserved, the title, the author, the borrower who reserved the book, the data by which the book is required.

We met the word *attribute* earlier, and we saw that it is really an alternative name for a *data field* or just a *field.* Some analysts use the names *data element* or *data item.*

Although you might need a little practice, it is important to recognize the distinction between an entity and an attribute: an entity is what you hold information about, an attribute is part of the information which describes an entity. *STUDENT* is an entity, the *Student Name* is an attribute of the *STUDENT* entity; *BOOK* is an entity, the *Book Title* is an attribute of the *BOOK* entity.

It is also important to distinguish between an attribute and a value: an attribute is something that describes an entity, a value is an actual *instance* of an attribute. The attribute *Student Name* can take values such as *SMITH* and *JONES*, the attribute *Book Title* can take values such as GONE WITH THE WIND or A DESCRIPTION OF THE FAMOUS KINGDOM OF MACARIA.

Some analysts write the names of the attributes alongside each entity on a DSD, as illustrated in Figure 3.2. As you see, the primary key which identifies each entity is underlined. Unfortunately, this can make a large DSD very confusing, so we shall not write the attributes on our DSDs.

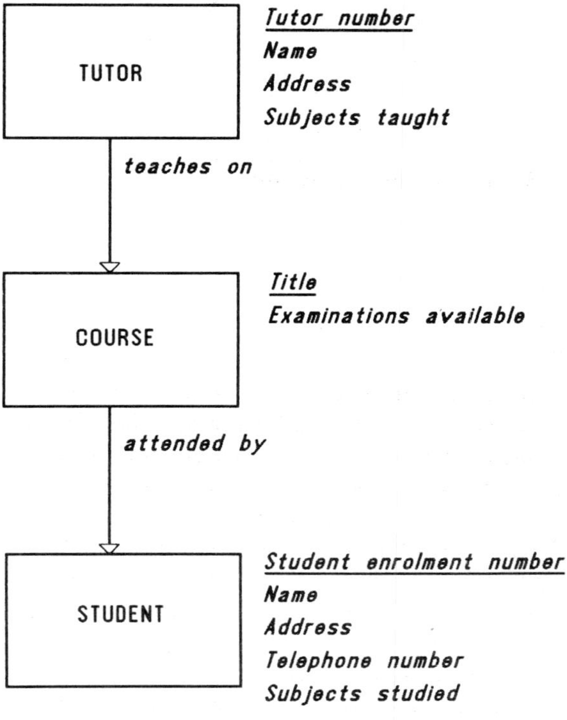

Figure 3.2 A data structure diagram showing attributes

Activity 2

1 For each of the entities which you identified in **Activity 1**, write down some attributes of that entity.
2 For each of the attributes, write down some possible values which instances (or occurrences) of the attribute might take.
3 For each of the following entities, write down some probable attributes, and some possible instances for those attributes.
   (a) CAR
   (b) HOUSE
   (c) EMPLOYEE
   (d) JOB
   (e) HOTEL

Relationships

An entity does not exist in isolation, but is associated with other entities by means of a *relationship*. On a DSD the entities are linked, one to another, by lines representing the relationships. Alongside the relationship there is a description of that relationship. The relationships in our DSD are:

- *teaches on*
- *is attended by*,

and these tell us several things about this particular situation:

- one tutor teaches on many courses and each course is taught by only one tutor;
- each course is attended by many students and each student attends only one course.

Note that the arrowed lines point from the *one* end to the *many* end: from the *one tutor* to the *many courses*, and from the *one course* to the *many students*.

Some relationships can be more complicated than this, but we'll talk about those later.

Activity 3

In the previous activities, you looked at the entities which you might encounter in certain situations. We list some possible entities here; add any others which you suggested. List some of the relationships which you would expect to find between those entities. Write your answers in a sentence such as:

'One tutor teaches on many courses'.

If you identify any relationships which you cannot express in this one-to-many manner, you should leave them and return to this activity later when we've looked at the other possibilities.

1 The coach hire company: destinations, routes, passengers, coaches, fares.
2 The recruitment agency: job titles, employers, employees, salary rates.
3 The doctor's surgery: patients, appointments, hospitals, medicines.

On a data structure diagram, we write a description of the relationship alongside the line. This description is an important feature when we are producing designs for use with certain databases. It doesn't matter how you describe the relationship, but you should choose descriptions which are meaningful and which are unique.

There are several different ways of drawing a data structure diagram: some systems analysts represent the entities by square boxes, others use ellipses or hexagons; some use arrowed lines to represent the relationships, some use forked lines called crows' feet, and others use lozenges with the description written inside. We shall use the simple boxes and arrows shown here.

Activity 4

1 Look up your notes on the student record part of the college system.
   (a) Make a list of the entities which are used there.
   (b) Make a list of the attributes which describe each entity.
   (c) Make a list of the relationships within the student record system.
   (d) Draw a DSD for the student record system.
   Repeat these activities for each of the other parts of the college system:
2 The Scientific Society system.
3 The Tutor Allocation system.
4 The Sports and Social Club system.

Your first attempt at a DSD may not be correct. This may be because, at the beginning of your investigations, you may not fully understand what the system is to do. Your understanding of the situation will develop and change as your systems investigation proceeds. In practice, the DSD is very useful in this respect because it makes you think and ask questions which might not otherwise have occurred to you. For example, in the above DSD when we were drawing the arrow from COURSE to STUDENT, this meant that one course could be attended by many students, but it also implied that each student could attend only one course. Before drawing the arrow we should think and check with the users that this is correct; in particular, we must ask

> 'Are we sure that there will never be more than one tutor on each course?'
> 'Are we sure that a student will *never* attend more than one course at the same time?'

If the answers we get from our users show that our assumptions were wrong, then the DSD would not be correct, and we must change it. The final version might look like that in Figure 3.3. Notice that we have

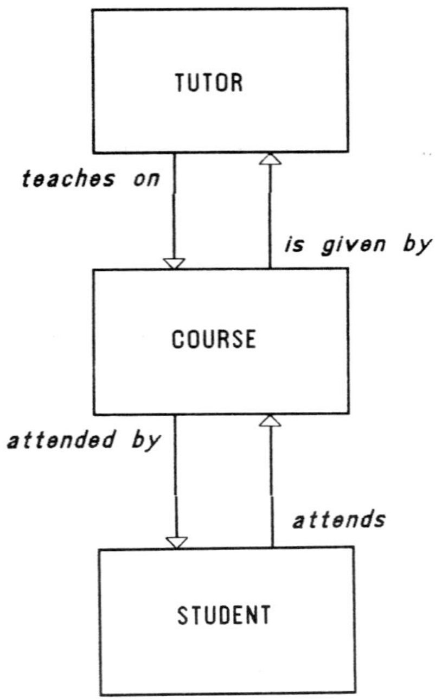

Figure 3.3 A simple data structure diagram—revised

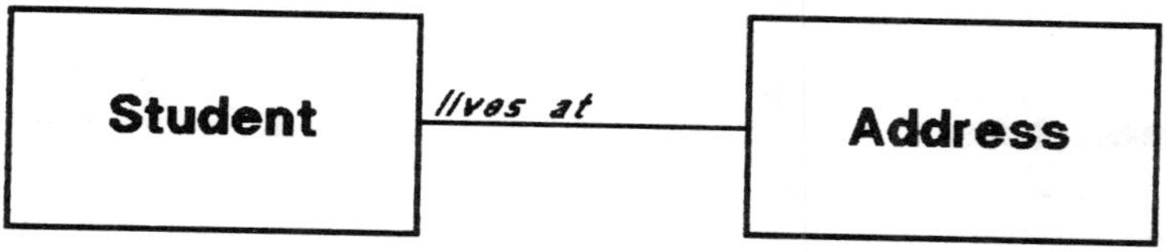

(a) Part of the DSD

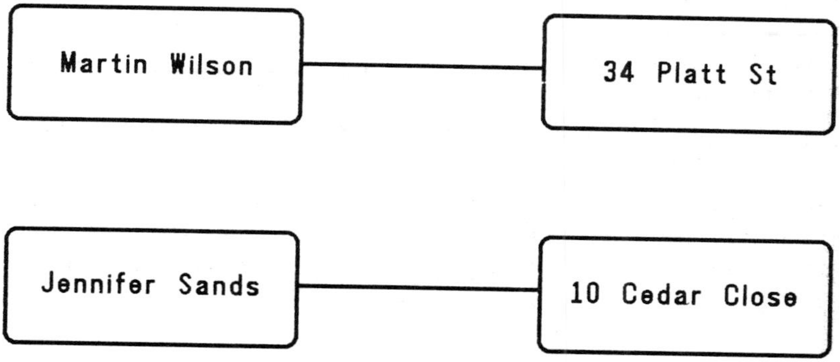

(b) Some instances

Figure 3.4   One-to-one relationship

added some further relationships. For clarity, the descriptions of the relationships are usually written towards the tail-end of the arrow.

Any errors, omissions and wrong assumptions which you may have made in drawing up a DSD will reveal themselves as the design for the system proceeds:

- If any entities or relationships have been omitted, then the system will not meet the needs of some of the users, and the DSD must be amended to meet these requirements.
- If too many entities or relationships have been introduced, then these will fall out of the picture as the design for the database is developed.

It an important feature of modern system design techniques that each of the various tools and diagrams act as a cross-check for the others. In this way, any mistakes you make at one point will generally be revealed at another place in your work.

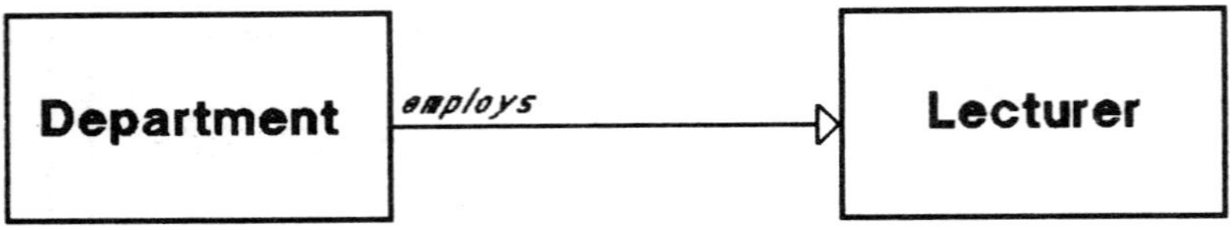

(a) Part of the DSD

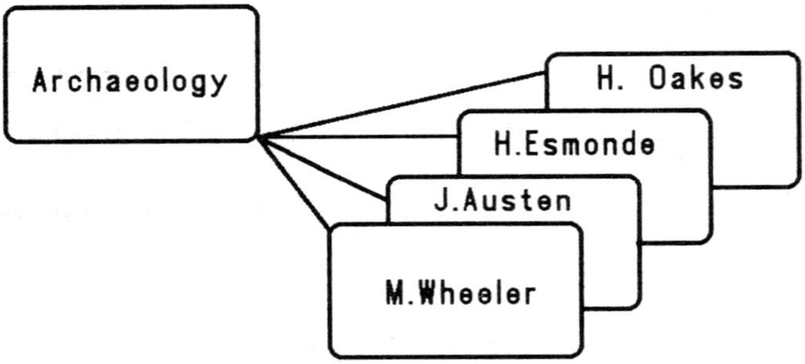

(b) Some instances

Figure 3.5 One-to-many relationship

Types of relationship

If we consider the relationships logically, we see that there are, at the most, four possible types:

1 one-to-one relationships
2 one-to-many relationships
3 many-to-one relationships
4 many-to-many relationships.

One-to-one relationships

One student may *live at* only one address, as shown in Figure 3.4. This may be recorded in your notes as:

Lives at: Student 1:1 Address

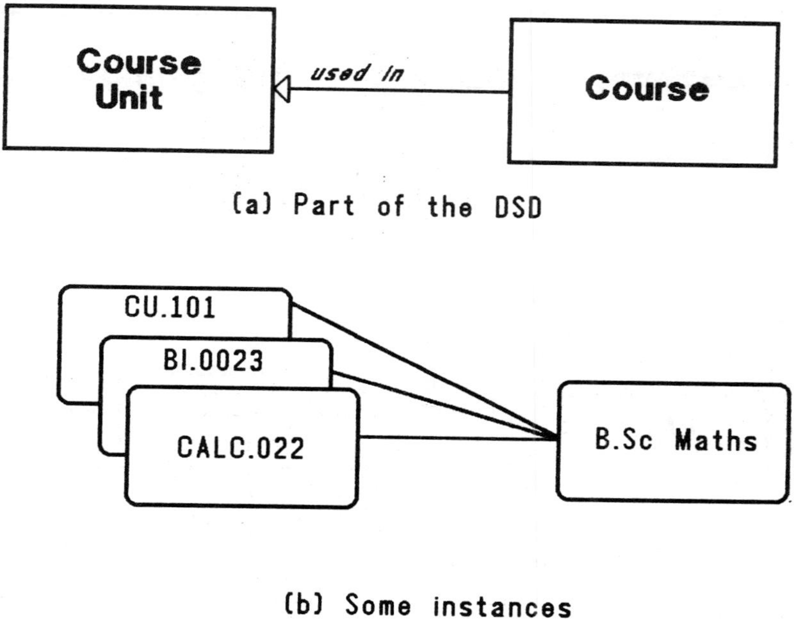

Figure 3.6 Many-to-one relationship

One-to-many relationships

One department may *employ* many lecturers, as shown in Figure 3.5.
Employ: Department 1: many Lecturer

Many-to-one relationships

Many course units may *be used in* one course, as shown in Figure 3.6.
Be used in: Course unit many: 1 Course

Many-to-many relationships

One lecturer may *teach* many students, and one student may be *taught by* many lecturers, as shown in Figure 3.7.
Teach: Lecturer many: many Student: *taught by*

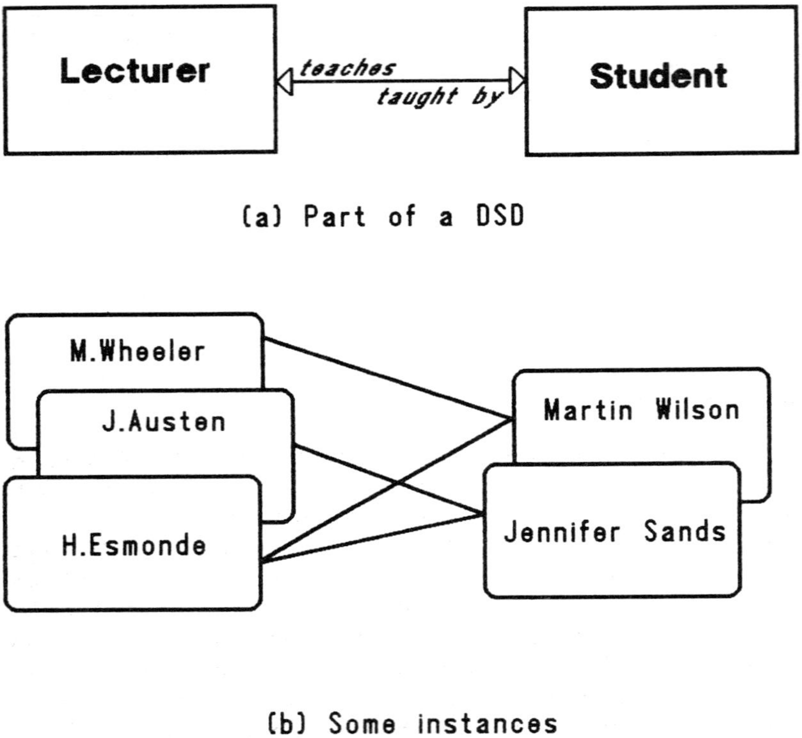

Figure 3.7 Many-to-many relationship

Activity 5

Draw a DSD for each of the following sets of relationships. Indicate clearly the names of the entities, and the nature and description of the relationship. If you do not have enough information, then you should make a valid assumption and write down the assumption which you are making.

1 There are several students living at one address.
2 Each football team plays the others.
3 There are several people with the same surname.
4 Each manager is in charge of just one department.
5 Each garage houses many buses and each bus covers any of a number of routes.

6 Each producer is in charge of several plays and there are several actors appearing in each play. At any one time, an actor may be involved with more than one play.
7 Each student may borrow a number of books, and each book may be used in several courses.
8 Each customer may send in several orders and each order may be for several products.

In practice, only *two* relationships need be used on data structure diagrams:

- one-to-one
- one-to-many

Many-to-one is really just another interpretation of one-to-many. A many-to-many relationship can be resolved into two one-to-many relationships by means of a third entity. Thus, instead of the many-to-many relationship shown in Figure 3.8(a), which tells us that one lecturer may teach many students, and one student may be taught by many lecturers, we would resolve this into two one-to-many relationships by the introduction of a third *link* lecturer-student entity, as shown in Figure 3.8(b). By simplifying the relationship in this way, we shall make it easier when we come to transfer this data model into a real database. Some types of DBMS, known as *hierarchical databases*, insist that we resolve our DSD into a structure made up of only one-to-many relationships. Other DBMSs demand that we simplify the DSD even further and do not permit an entity to be at the many end of more than one relationship. We shall look at this in Chapter 4.

Activity 6

A systems analyst has been looking at a library system in which a student may borrow many books and where any particular book may (throughout its life) be borrowed by several students.

1 Draw a small DSD representing this as a many-to-many relationship.
2 Give some fictitious occurrences, as in Figures 3.4 to 3.7.
3 Draw a second DSD which resolves this in the manner described. Think of a suitable name for the new link entity.
4 Revise your occurrences from part (2) to reflect the changes.

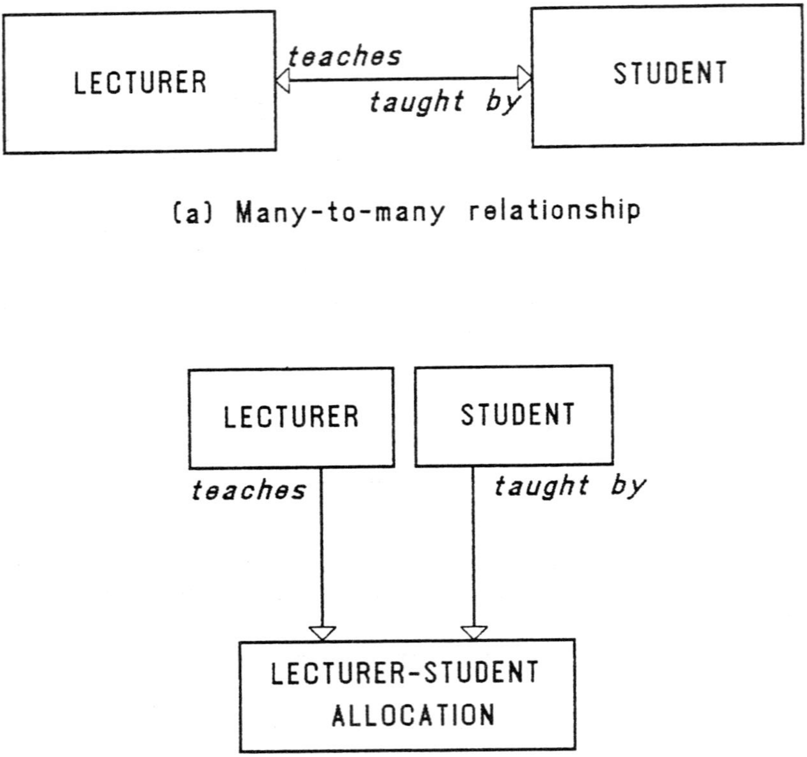

(b) Two one-to-many relationships

Figure 3.8 Resolving a many-to-many relationship

Some possible physical occurrences of the lecturer-student relationship are shown in Figure 3.9. Compare this with the many-to-many instances which we met in Figure 3.7.

Where possible, data structure diagrams usually show one-to-many relationships with the *many* end below that of the *one* end, as illustrated in our examples. The entity at the upper one end of a relationship (LECTURER and STUDENT in this last example) is called the *master* entity, and that at the lower many end is called the *detail* entity. Some analysts use the terms *owner-member* and *parent-child* as alternatives to *master-detail*.

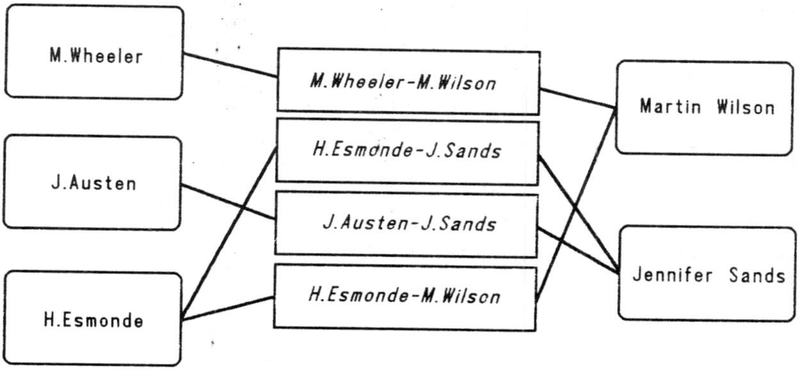

Figure 3.9 A link entity in practice

Activity 7

For each of the DSDs shown above write the names of the *master entities* and of the *detail entities*. Indicate which detail entity (or entities) belong to which master entity.

To recognize entities and relationships

The DSD is derived intuitively from the investigations which the systems analyst carries out. As a general rule, the systems analyst can recognize an entity whenever a *reference number* or a *code number* is encountered. For example:

Customer *reference*,
National Insurance *number*,
Department *number*,
Product *code*.

or when a *noun* is encountered. For example:

Order,
Client,
Student,
Depot,
Employee.

A relationship is implied whenever a *transitive verb* is encountered. For example:

- a lecturer *teaches* several students
- a sales order *contains* several order lines

- each student *attends* a course
- each employee *has* a manager.

or, when a *number* or a *repeating* idea is encountered. For example:

- a borrower may take out *up to three* books
- an order has *several* order lines
- a customer submits *a number of* orders
- an employee can have *several* job titles during his or her career
- we *keep adding* new books to the library.

As a systems analyst, you will quickly become experienced at recognizing such entities and relationships.

An entity cross-reference matrix

As a preliminary to preparing the data structure diagram, you might find it useful to record your findings about the entities and their relationships on an entity cross-reference matrix. This is a table in which each entity appears as a column-heading and as a row-heading. An asterisk is placed at the intersection of the row and the column if there is a relationship between the entity at the head of the column and the entity at the head of the row.

Let us imagine that you have discovered that in a library system

> Each borrower may borrow any number of books. The books are classified into various categories. There may be hundreds of books in each category. There may be several books by any author.

From this investigation, you will be able to identify entities: BORROWER, BOOK, CATEGORY, AUTHOR. You will also identify that relationships exist between: BORROWER-BOOK, BOOK-CATEGORY, BOOK-AUTHOR.

A possible matrix recording these relationships is shown in Figure 3.10(a). Since a relationship between, say, BORROWER and BOOK implies a relationship between BOOK and BORROWER we can reduce this matrix to the simpler version shown in Figure 3.10(b). Both matrices record the same information.

Notice that the matrix does not show the *descriptions* of the relationships, nor the type. Although, in place of the asterisk, you could write

	BOOK	BORROWER	CATEGORY	AUTHOR
BOOK		*	*	*
BORROWER	*			
CATEGORY	*			
AUTHOR	*			

(a) an entity cross-reference matrix - version 1

				BOOK
			BORROWER	*
		CATEGORY		*
	AUTHOR			*

(b) an entity cross-reference matrix - version 2

Figure 3.10 Entity cross-reference matrices

1:1

for a one-to-one relationship,

1:m

for a one-to-many relationship, and

n:m

for a many-to-many relationship.

Questions

1 A systems analyst has recorded the following conversation with Mr Kingsley, the manager of a large warehouse. What entities and relationships are implied by Mr Kingsley's remarks?

'We get the orders from the general office. Each order is sent in by a single customer, and each order may contain up to ten separate products. Each order is made up into one parcel and each parcel is delivered to just one address.'

'We have several warehouses and each warehouse holds a large number of products.'

2 Draw a cross-reference matrix showing which entities are related to others.

3 Draw a data structure diagram to represent the entities and the relationships.

Activity 8

Revise your DSD for the student records program in the light of this last discussion. Produce data structure diagrams for each of the other college programs: the Scientific Society, the Tutor Allocation program and the Sports and Social Club program.

Optional relationships

We must now clarify the significance of *one* and *many* which we have been using in our discussion of relationships.

The *many* end of a relationship includes the three cases: *none*, *one*, or *many*. Thus, the relationship depicted in Figure 3.11, where one student may be awarded many examination results, implies that a student may be awarded *no results*, *one result*, or *several results*. Note that this implies that there may be students who have *not been awarded any* results, this may be because they have not yet taken any examinations.

The *one* end of a relationship includes only one case: there must be one and only one occurrence at the *one* end. Thus, Figure 3.12 implies that any particular result is awarded to *one student*; a result cannot exist on its own, that is, there cannot be a result *without* a student to score that result.

In some situations, however, it may be possible for the detail entity to occur *without* the occurrence of an associated master entity. In the relationship shown in Figure 3.12(a), each school may have none, one or many persons attending it, and each person may attend only one school.

But there may be persons, such as babies and retired people, who do not attend any school. In this case, the many-to-one detail-master

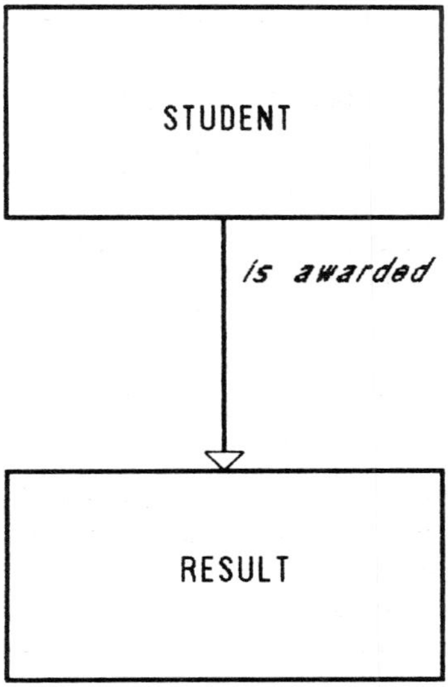

Figure 3.11 A one-to-many relationship

relationship is said to be *optional*, and is drawn as in Figure 3.12(b). The letter O along the relationship indicating that the person-school relationship is optional.

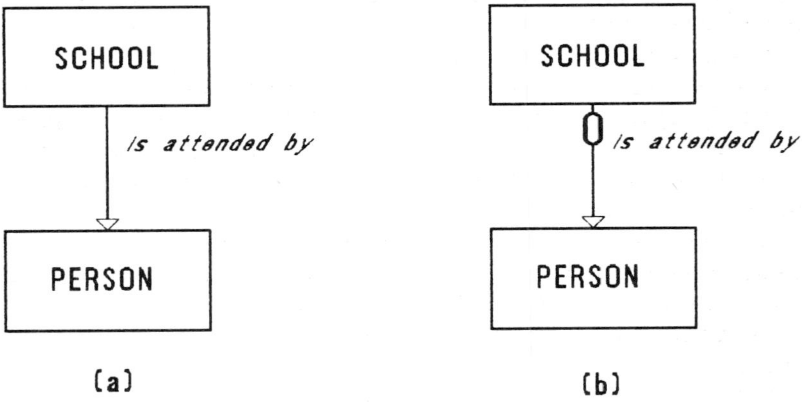

Figure 3.12 An optional relationship

Navigating through a data structure diagram

In any data structure diagram, it should be possible conceptually to *navigate* from entity to entity by way of the relationships. By doing this, we shall be creating paths by which the DBMS or our programs can access the data and use these paths to answer enquiries about the data. Let us look at the data structure diagram in Figure 3.13 and see what sort of questions we are able to answer.

If a diagram is laid out as shown here, with the relationships going vertically downwards, then, in general, the questions require us to navigate:

a) *down* the relationship in the direction of the arrow, for a given relationship we might wish to find all the details for a specific master: we might need to find all the lecturers employed in a given department; we might wish to know all the lessons which are taught by a given lecturer.
b) *up* the relationship for a given relationship, we might wish to find the master of a specific detail: we might need to find which lecturer teaches a particular lesson; we might wish to know which department employs a particular lecturer.

   The ease and elegance by which these access paths are traversed in the physical environment is a function of the database management system which we use. We shall look at this again later.

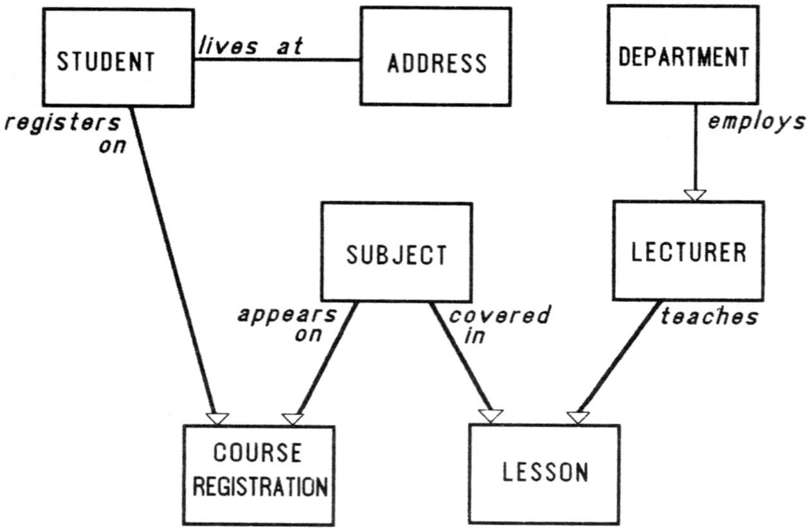

Figure 3.13 Navigating through a data structure diagram

We can only enter the diagram at a *specific* occurrence of any entity, that is when we know the key to a specific record and from there we can navigate along any relationship in either direction. This means that we must know the occurrence at which we wish to enter the diagram. In the illustrations below, we shall use the student number (possibly in a form such as 90/1022), the lecturer number (possibly BTC7760), the department name (possibly BIOLOGY), or the course code, as the identifier for that entity (or in physical terms, the *key* to the appropriate record on the files).

Typical questions which we might ask are:

1 What is the address of student number 90/1022? To answer this, we must go to the STUDENT entity and find the occurrence for student 90/1022 and then follow the *lives at* relationship to find his/her address.
2 To find which lecturers are employed by the BIOLOGY department, we must first go to the DEPARTMENT entity and find the occurrence for BIOLOGY and then follow the *employs* relationship to find all the lecturers employed by the BIOLOGY department.
3 To find the name of the department which employs lecturer BTC7760, we would enter the diagram at the LECTURER entity find the occurrence for lecturer BTC7760 Greenhead and then navigate up the *employs* relationship to find the department which employs that lecturer.
4 What subjects are being taken by student 90/1022? To answer this, we first obtain the information from STUDENT relating to student 90/1022, and then follow the *registers on* relationship to the COURSE-REGISTRATION entity to find all registrations for that student, and then finally navigate up the *appears on* relationship to find each of the subjects which he/she is studying.

Activity 9

Trace the access paths for these questions.

1 What subjects are taught by lecturer PW9021?
2 What are the addresses of all the students taught by lecturer BTC1022?
3 What are the subjects taught by lecturers working for the MATHEMATICS department?
4 What are the addresses of the students who are taught by staff of the PSYCHIATRIC MEDICINE department?

We could *not*, however, answer these questions if they were phrased as:

- What is Nathaniel Culverwel studying?
- What subjects are being studied by people who started college in 1989?
- Which lecturers live in Brighton?
- Which department does Mr Greenhead work in?
- Which students are studying science subjects?

We cannot answer such questions because there are are no entities which have the name (Nathaniel Culverwel), the year (1989), the town (Brighton) or the subject category (sciences) as their key. None of these pieces of information is the key field which we need to be able to enter the data structure diagram. If we want to access a data structure diagram by means of an entry point such as:

... started in 1989

then we must establish an *operational entity* which uses the *year* as the key, and we should need a further operational entity to answer questions about:

... students called Culverwel

as the section of the data structure diagram in Figure 3.14 illustrates:

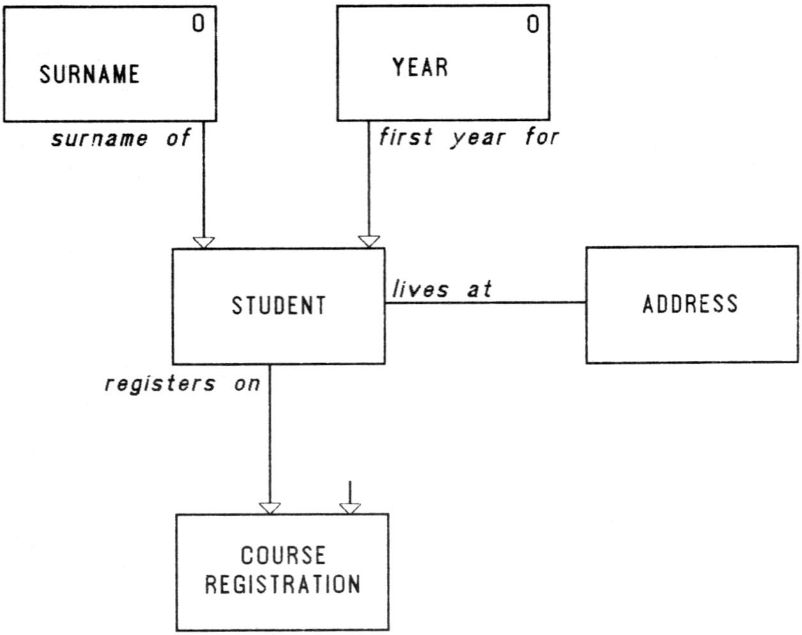

Figure 3.14 An operational entity

To highlight any such operational entities which have been added to our diagram for purely practical reasons, we write a letter O—for operational—in the *top right-hand* corner of the box.

You will probably have realized that an operational entity is simply a conceptual way of visualising the physical structure which we already know as *secondary keys*.

Recap

In practice, files do not exist in isolation. They are related to other files in some way. We now need to consider the logical meaning of the data and these relationships.

Because we are not yet concerned with the manner in which the physical data will be held (the files), we use the word entity to refer to an object about which we need to hold data. We also made the distinction between the words entity, attribute and value.

A data structure diagram or DSD is a convenient way of depicting the entities and the relationships between them and is a valuable means of constructing a model of the data encountered within a computer system. This allows us to study the effects of holding, and of not holding, the data which the users need.

On a DSD, an entity is shown as a named box, and a relationship is represented by a line joining two entities and bearing a description of the relationship.

The various DBMSs impose a number of constraints and rules which we must obey when we come to implement our logical data model as the true physical model on a database. Typically, only two relationships need be used on data structure diagrams: one-to-one and one-to-many. Many-to-many relationships are resolved into two one-to-many relationships by the introduction of a third link entity.

In a one-to-many relationship, the entity at the *one* end is called the master and that at the *many* end is called the detail entity.

We looked at the ways in which entities and relationships can be identified during the investigation and analysis stages of system development.

In a many-to-one and a one-to-many relationship there may be none, one, or several occurrences at the *many* end. In a many-to-one or one-to-many relationship there must be one and only one occurrence at the *one* end. If it is possible for there to be no occurrences at the *one* end of a relationship, then this is said to be an optional relationship, and a letter O is drawn along the line representing the relationship to indicate this.

In any data structure diagram, it should be possible to navigate from entity to entity by way of the relationships. By doing this, we shall be creating paths

	ORDER	CUSTOMER	PRODUCT	PARCEL	ADDRESS	WAREHOUSE
ORDER		*	*	*		
CUSTOMER	*					
PRODUCT	*					*
PARCEL	*				*	
ADDRESS				*		
WAREHOUSE			*			

(a) Entity cross-reference matrix - version 1

	ADDRESS	PARCEL	PRODUCT	CUSTOMER	ORDER
CUSTOMER					*
PRODUCT					*
PARCEL					*
ADDRESS		*			
WAREHOUSE			*		

(b) Entity cross-reference matrix - version 2

Figure 3.15 A cross-reference matrix for the entities

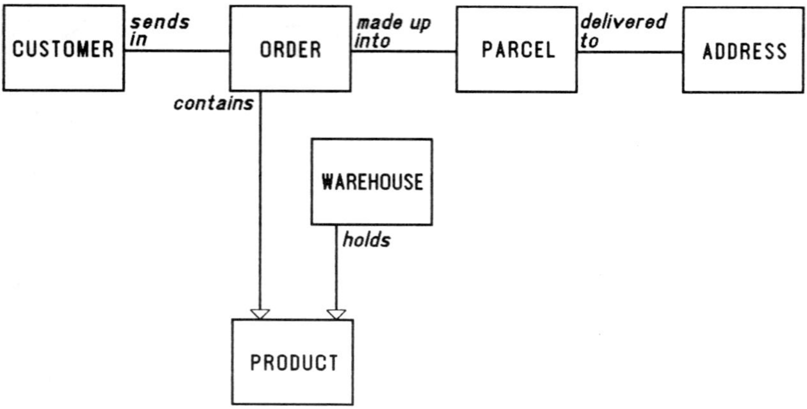

Figure 3.16 A data structure diagram for the warehouse system

by which the DBMS—or our programs—can access the data and use these paths to answer enquiries about the data. We saw some of the questions which this facility allows us to answer. If we want to access a data structure diagram by means of data which is not the identifier for the entity, then we must establish an operational entity which uses this data as its identifier. We have already met operational entities under the names secondary keys and inverted files.

Answers

1 Entities: Order; Customer; Product; Parcel; Address; Warehouse.
2 See Figure 3.15.
3 A possible solution is shown in Figure 3.16. You may have drawn the entities in some other arrangement. The important point is that the entities are joined by the correct relationship to other entities.

4: Physical data structures

Objectives

After reading this chapter, you should be able to:

- describe the way in which one file can be logically related to another
- describe how such a relationship can be represented by the data held on the files
- describe a *tree structure*
- identify the *root*, *parents*, *children* and *siblings* of a tree structure
- distinguish between a tree and a *plex* structure
- describe a *loop* structure
- describe some real instances of tree, plex and loop structures
- describe the significance of a *virtual field*, a *virtual record* and a *pointer record*.

In the previous chapter, we were concerned with the ways in which data and relationships between the data can be visualized and represented in logical terms. Now we want to look at the ways in which these relationships might be represented in physical terms.

In most cases, the DBMS will shield the user from the true physical representation of the data. Nevertheless, it is essential to understand the points which we shall make here. Even with a powerful DBMS, a knowledge of what is happening physically can be valuable and may help to remove many of the fears (and some of the dismay) which some systems analysts and programmers experience when they are first confronted by such a system.

Relationships

In the logical models, we were primarily concerned with the entities and the relationships between them. At the physical level, the entities are represented by *files*.

Because the record key uniquely identifies each record on a file, all we need to do in order to show the relationships which may exist between files is to arrange for each record to hold—as an ordinary data attribute—the key of the record(s) to which this record is related. This can be done in exactly the same way as we did when we wanted to link all the CALCULUS lecturers together and all the lecturers called LENNOX together.

Figure 4.1 shows how we might organize the data so as to associate the DEPARTMENT records with the LECTURER records. The DEPARTMENT records hold the keys (or keys) of the lecturers who work in that department, and the LECTURER records hold the key (or keys) of the department in which they work. Note that, in this illustration, we are using the lecturer number as the key to the LECTURER file, and the department name as the key to the DEPARTMENT file.

Although we have not shown it, the various records would contain other information: the LECTURER records might hold the telephone

NUMBER	NAME	DEPARTMENT
1057	DORIS MORE	LANGUAGES
3329	JANICE QUILLIAM	LANGUAGES
3418	RITA COPLEY	MATHEMATICS
3664	STANLEY ANDREWS	MATHEMATICS
4427	JOHN ANDREWS	MATHEMATICS
9813	LESLIE LINCOLN	FINE ARTS

(a) LECTURER file

DEPARTMENT	LECTURER
FINE ARTS	9813
LANGUAGES	3329 1057
MATHEMATICS	3664 3418 4427

(b) DEPARTMENT file

Figure 4.1 Showing relationships between files

number of each lecturer, their address, how much they are paid, and so on; the DEPARTMENT records might hold a count of the number of staff in the department, the number of courses offered, the departmental telephone numbers, the annual budget available, their expenditure, and so on.

It is convenient to visualize the data as a set of tables, as illustrated here. We can use these tables to answer questions such as:

'Who works in the languages department?'

To find the answer, we must look through the DEPARTMENT table to find the entry for the language department, then we find the reference numbers for the lecturers who work there, and then we use these reference numbers to look through the LECTURER table to find the name of each lecturer who works in the language department.

Earlier, we saw how we could answer the same sort of question by having chains of records linked together.

Activity 1

1 A new lecturer, Marie LePoint, joins the college. She will teach French in the languages department. Make the necessary changes to the tables in Figure 4.1. Her reference number is 8050.

2 The mathematics department teaches the subjects calculus, statistics, computing science and geometry. The fine arts department teaches painting and pottery. The languages department teaches French, German, Spanish, Russian and Chinese.

Create a table for the SUBJECT file and add the necessary data to show the relationships between the DEPARTMENT and the SUBJECT file.

Questions

1 Using the DEPARTMENT, LECTURER and SUBJECT tables, how would you find the names of the lecturers who work in the mathematics department?

2 How would you find the records for all the subjects taught in the mathematics department?

3 How would you find the name of the department in which lecturer 1011 works?

4 How would you find the telephone number of the department in which Ms Quilliam works? You may assume that the telephone number is held in the appropriate DEPARTMENT record.
5 How would you find the subjects taught in Mrs Doreen More's department?
6 How would you find the subjects taught by Mrs Doreen More?

Tree structures

We could depict the relationships between the DEPARTMENT file the LECTURER file, and the SUBJECT file, by means of a data structure diagram like that in Figure 4.2(a). Some specific instances of such records are shown in Figure 4.2(b). For clarity, I have underlined the record keys.

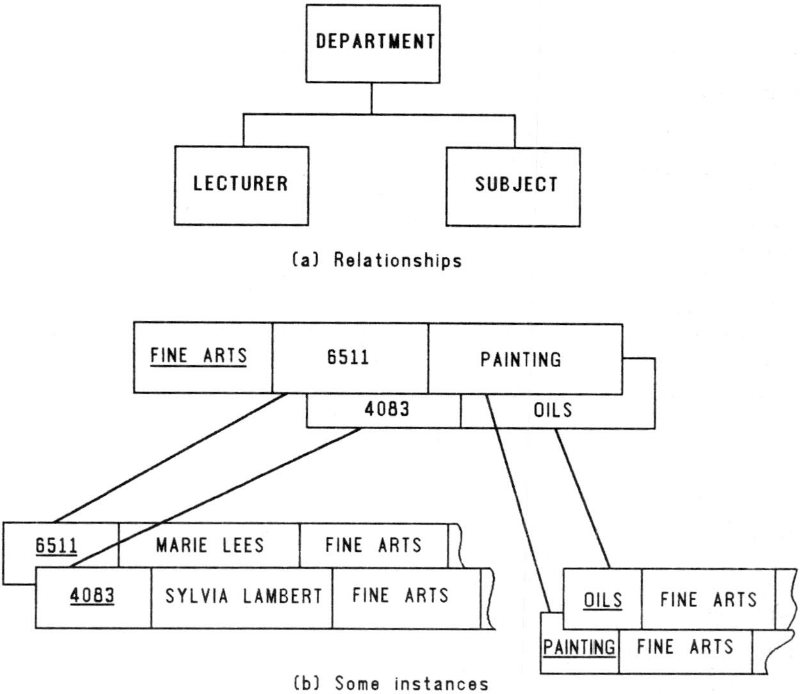

Figure 4.2 File relationships in practice

In Figure 4.2, I have depicted the files in a tree structure. The boxes representing the files are the leaves or the nodes of the tree. The node at the top of the diagram is called the root node or just the root of the tree —so it's really an upside-down tree! Every node (except the root node) is related to one and only one other node at a higher level: this is called its parent. A node can have only one parent. Any node may be related to one or more nodes at a lower level: these are called its children. Two or more nodes with the same parent are called siblings. You might also meet the words brother, sister or twin instead of sibling. You see that we don't bother about grand-parents and grand-children.

A part of a tree consisting of a parent and all its descendants is sometimes called a sub-tree.

Questions

Answer these questions about the tree in Figure 4.2.

7 What is the root node?

8 What is the parent of the LECTURER node?

9 What is the parent of the DEPARTMENT node?

10 Name the child or children of the DEPARTMENT node.

11 Name any siblings in the diagram.

12 We now wish to add to the diagram a new file, called SET-BOOK which we want to use to show which SUBJECT uses which set books. Draw a revised diagram to show where the SET-BOOK file would appear on the diagram.

13 We now wish to add to the diagram a new file called STUDENT which we want to use to show which SUBJECT is being studied by which student. Where would the STUDENT file appear on the diagram? Draw the revised diagram.

You may assume that each student studies only a single subject.

14 For each node on your final diagram, make a listing indicating the name of the node, whether it is the root node, the parents of the node, the children of the node, and the siblings of the node.

You could possibly think of other ways of arranging the boxes and the lines. You could even draw the tree the right way up. It is simply a convention to depict the data in this manner, and it is a convenient one which is encountered elsewhere. We shall see later that *hierarchical databases* also picture their data in just such a way—as a set of trees.

Plex structures

Let us imagine that we need to show that there is a relationship between, say, the records on the STUDENT file and those on the LECTURER file—we might wish to show which lecturer teaches which student, for example. It would be difficult to represent this as a true tree structure.

The difficulty arises because if we were to link the STUDENT node to the LECTURER node, as shown in Figure 4.3, then there would be two parents to the STUDENT: the SUBJECT and the LECTURER. This conflicts with the rules governing trees: *the nodes of a tree may only have one parent*. When any node in such a structure has more than one parent, the structure is called a plex structure, not a tree.

When we look at the ways in which the various DBMSs represent entities and relationships, we shall see that some handle tree structures more easily than they handle plexes. The systems analyst or the database designer would then have to resolve any plexes into a set of smaller trees in order to implement them.

We touched upon this need to simplify a data structure diagram when we looked at the ways in which we could resolve a many-to-many relationship in Chapter 3.

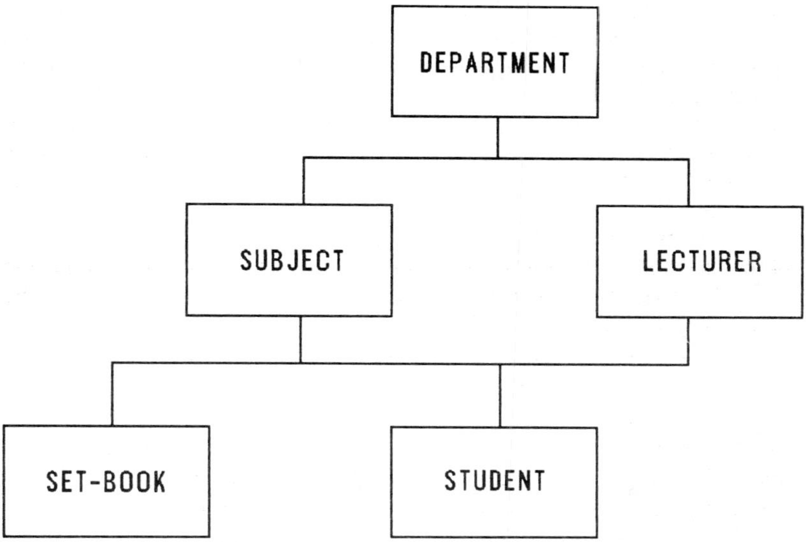

Figure 4.3 A plex structure

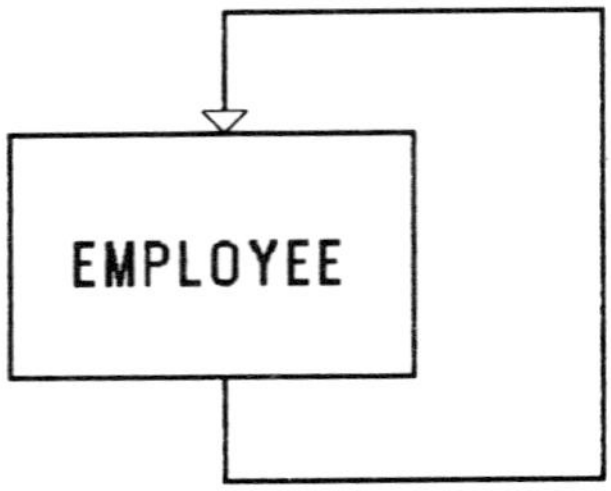

(a) Representation of a Loop structure on a DSD

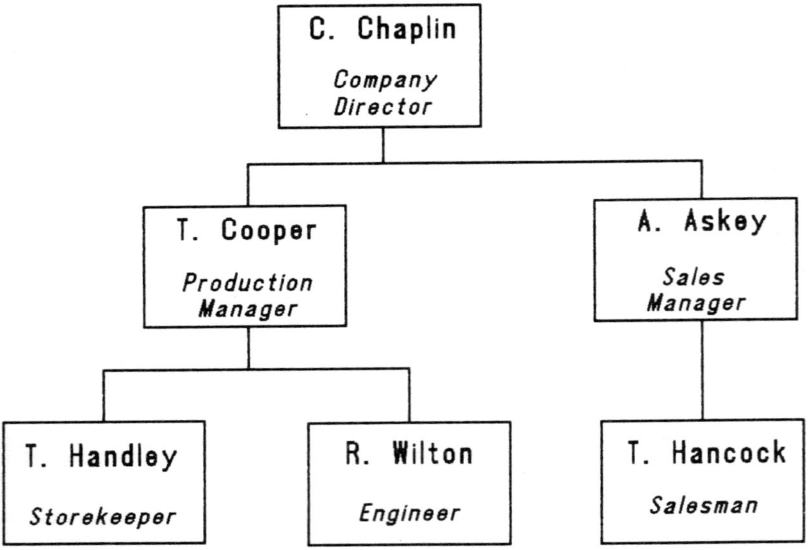

(b) A loop structure in practice - shown as a tree

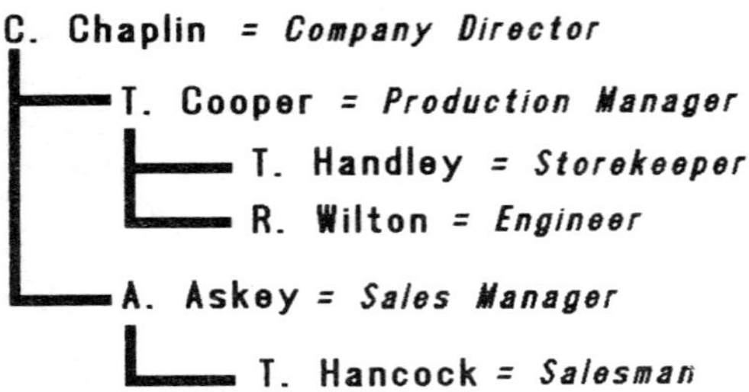

(c) A loop structure in practice - shown as a structured list

No	Name	Title	Senior	Junior
1200	C.CHAPLIN	COMPANY DIRECTOR		2273 3428
2273	T.COOPER	PRODUCTION MANAGER	1200	4224 5598
3428	A.ASKEY	SALES MANAGER	1200	4217
4224	T.HANDLEY	STORES KEEPER	2273	
5598	R.WILTON	ENGINEER	2273	
4217	T.HANCOCK	SALESMAN	3248	

(d) The records for a loop structure

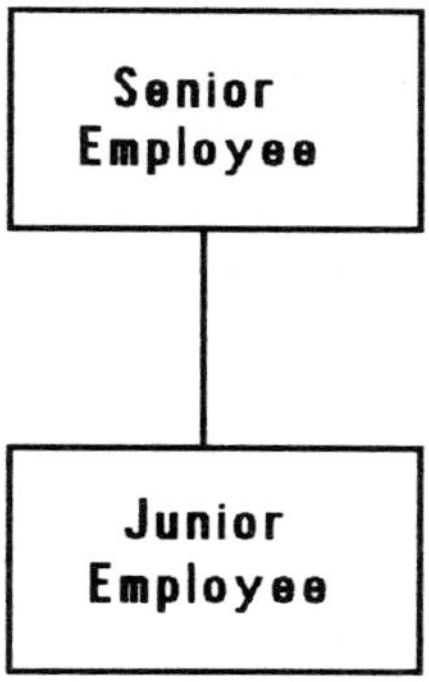

(e) a Loop resolved into a simple parent-child relationship

Figure 4.4 Loop structures

Loop structures

Finally, we shall look at another logical structure—the *loop structure* or *recursive structure*—which you may encounter, and one which is handled quite elegantly by some DBMSs.

We can illustrate it by a situation in which a EMPLOYEE file contains records relating to both managers and staff. The EMPLOYEE file holds only one type of record for both categories of employee: the managers' records contain a field pointing to the staff who report to them, and the staff records contain a field pointing to their manager. For the company directors, there will just be downward pointers (showing the senior management who are under them), for middle management, there will be upward pointers (to their manager) and downward pointers (to their junior staff), and for the junior employees there may only be upward pointers (to their manager or supervisor). These pointers are exactly like those which we saw in Figure 4.2 in which each record holds the key(s) of the record(s) to which it is related.

You can think of a loop structure as being a special case of a tree in which each node may be its own child and its own parent!

Some loop structures are illustrated in Figure 4.4. Figure 4.4(a) shows how we might represent this structure on a DSD showing that one employee is the manager of several other employees. Figure 4.4(b) shows how we might visualize an instance of this structure as a tree, and Figure 4.4(c) represents the same data as a *structured list*. Figure 4.4(d) shows some data records representing this structure, and Figure 4.4(e) shows how we might resolve this into a simple tree if our DBMS demands that we do so. In each case, the structure is simplified by duplicating one or more of the nodes.

Some further situations in which it is convenient to visualize the data as a loop structure are:

1 A catalogue of books might contain entries for the individual books together with entries for *collected works* and compilations, as illustrated by the data in Figure 4.5.

2 An engineering company uses a STOCK file with attributes showing which other (smaller) parts make up each large part. For example, a CAR may consist of a CHASSIS, DOORs, an ENGINE, WHEELs and a GEARBOX; a DOOR may consist of a WINDOW UNIT, an OUTER-SHELL, a LOCK, an INNER-FACING; a WINDOW UNIT may consist of a GLASS, a WINDING-MECHANISM; a

BOOK	TITLE	COMPRISING
2002	THE MERCHANT OF VENICE	
2003	ROMEO AND JULIET	
2004	HENRY IV - 1	
2005	HENRY IV - 2	
2006	HENRY V	
2007	OTHELLO	
2008	SHAKESPEARE, TRAGEDIES	2003 2007 2103
2009	SHAKESPEARE, HENRY PLAYS	2004 2005 2006
2010	SHAKESPEARE, COMEDIES	2076 2089 2104 2304 2305
2076	A MIDSUMMER NIGHT'S DREAM	
2089	MERRY WIVES OF WINDSOR	

Figure 4.5 A loop structure—book catalogue

WINDING-MECHANISM may consist of a HANDLE, a PLASTIC-BUSH, a RACK-AND-PINION-DRIVE, and so on. A loop structure would be useful here if we wanted to produce a list of all the parts we needed to produce, say, five WINDOW UNITs or twenty complete CARs. For this reason, the loop structure is often encountered in such *bill of materials* processing.

3 A route-planning program is used to work out the best car journey between two given places. The *map* covering the area may be held as a loop structure: the records for the shorter routes showing the distance and the average time required to make the journey; the records for the longer journeys being made up of references to a series of shorter routes.

4 A programmer may wish to have a file showing which of his programs use which subroutines, and in turn, which subroutines use other subroutines. A loop structure would be useful if he changed one of the subroutines and needed to know which other subroutines and programs would be affected by the changes.

A rough guide to recognizing a loop structure is

- Where all the records on the file are of the same type—in our examples, these were all employees, all parts, all routes, all programs
- There is an implied relationship between the records themselves—this may be a superiority or hierarchy amongst the records, some being more important than others or some being dependent upon others in some way.

Activity 3

Draw a tree structure or a structured list to represent the structure of the CAR as described in situation (1) above. Draw a circle around the sub-tree which represents the structure of the DOOR.

Activity 4

Try to think of some other instances where a loop structure might be useful.

Virtual records

Some DBMSs demand that we simplify a plex or a large tree structure, decomposing it into a set of smaller trees. This is done by duplicating one or more of the nodes in the structure. From our very first discussion of databases you will recall that duplication of data is one of the main situations which we want to avoid. We saw how inconsistencies may arise (and storage space will be wasted) if we hold the same information in more than one place.

Let us look at the diagram shown in Figure 4.6(a) where the SUBJECT entity is related to both the STUDENT and the LECTURER entities. If our particular DBMS does not allow a child to have more

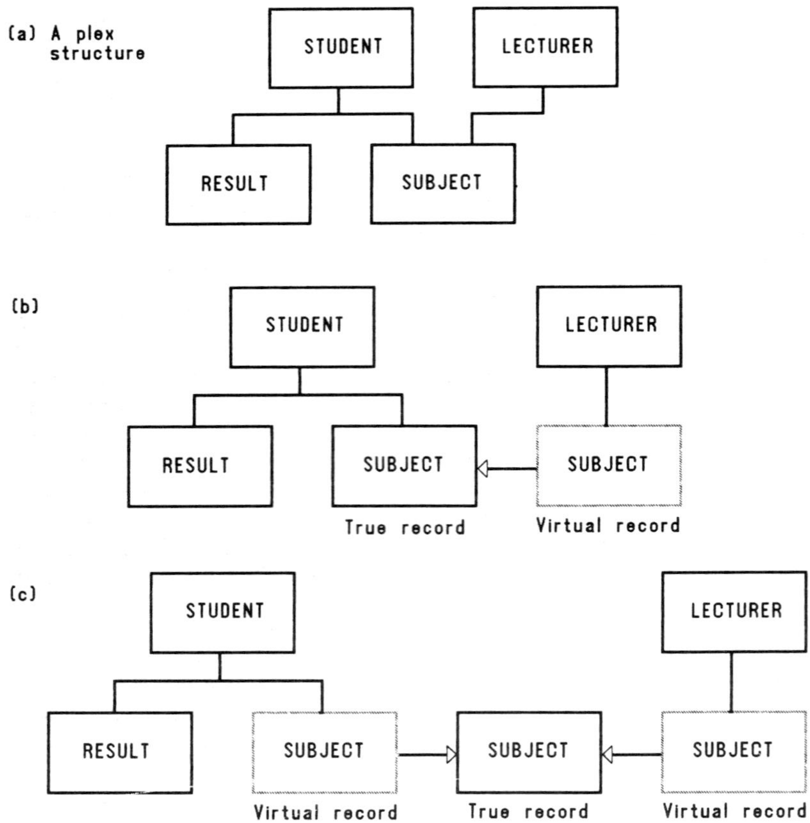

Figure 4.6 Virtual or pointer records

than one parent, then we could resolve the dilemma by introducing the concept of the *virtual* record, as illustrated in Figure 4.6(b). We could hold the true record in any position and refer to it from elsewhere. We could even hold it as a completely independent record which is always accessed by means of pointers, as illustrated in Figure 4.6(c).

If it is necessary to duplicate a single field, then the concept of a virtual field is also used in a similar manner.

Using this technique, we only hold each record once, but when we need to include the same record in several trees we include only the virtual record which points to the true record. For this reason, virtual records are sometimes called *pointer records*.

In physical terms, we could implement a virtual record by having a separate SUBJECT file and then holding the key within the LECTURER and STUDENT records.

Recap

Files and records do not exist in isolation: a student whose record appears on the STUDENT file may be studying subjects whose records appear on the SUBJECT file; a lecturer whose details are held on the LECTURER file may be the tutor to students whose details are held on the STUDENT file.

We can indicate these relationships or cross-references by holding the key of one record amongst the data of another. When we need to follow these cross-references to find details about the SUBJECTs which a particular STUDENT is studying, or to find details about the STUDENTs which a particular LECTURER is teaching, we can read the main record in order to find the keys of the related records and use these keys to retrieve the related records.

It is convenient to think of some data relationships being organized as tree structures. A tree consists of a number of nodes linked together in a series of parent-children relationships. The root node is usually shown at the top and each node may have one or more children at the lower level. In a tree structure, a node can only have one parent.

In a plex structure, a node may have more than one parent. In a loop structure, a node may be its own child and its own parent.

Both a plex structure and a loop structure may be resolved into a set of simpler tree structures by duplicating one or more of the nodes. Some DBMS demand that even simple tree structures be resolved into simple one-to-one structures.

The use of virtual records or pointer records avoids the problems which might arise as a consequence of duplicating nodes.

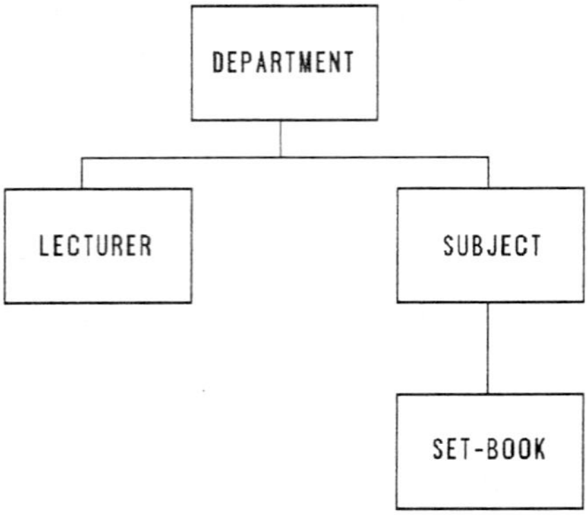

Figure 4.7 Tree structure—1

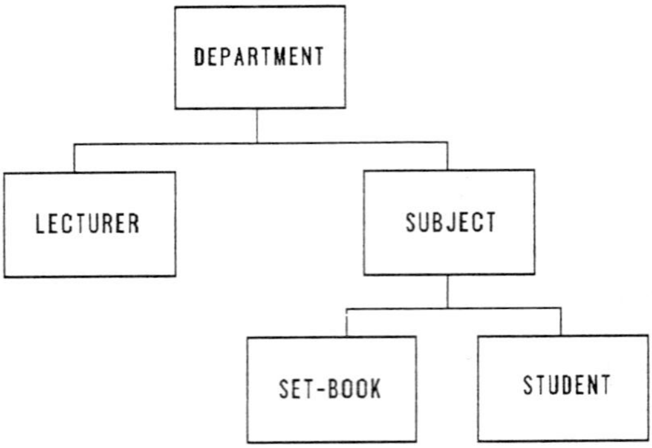

Figure 4.8 Tree structure—2

Answers

1 Look at the DEPARTMENT table and find the entry for the mathematics department; then find the reference numbers for the lecturers who work there, and use these reference numbers to look through the LECTURER file to find the name of each lecturer who works in the mathematics department.

2 Look at the DEPARTMENT table and find the entry for the mathematics department; then find the titles for the subjects taught there, and use these titles to look through the SUBJECT file to find the record for each SUBJECT taught in the mathematics department.

3 Look at the LECTURER table and find the record for lecturer 1011; then find the name of the DEPARTMENT where he/she works. If we want any

data held on that DEPARTMENT record, then we should have to go on to the DEPARTMENT table but we haven't been asked for that.

4 This is a little more complicated. We cannot go straight to Ms Quilliam's record (we can only read a record if we know its key and there is no index for a secondary key such as surname), so we must read through the entire LECTURER table until we find her record. Having done that, we can find the name of the department where she works and then use this to read the required record from the DEPARTMENT table, we should then be able to find the telephone number in that record.

5 You would have to find Mrs More's record (by scanning through the entire LECTURER file, as in Question 4); then you would find the department where she works; then you would have to use this department to find the correct entry on the DEPARTMENT file; finally you would read this record to find the subjects taught in that department.

6 The necessary information is not held on the files at present. So we cannot answer this question. The best we could do is that from the answer to Question 5.

7 The root node is DEPARTMENT.

8 The DEPARTMENT.

9 DEPARTMENT is the root node so there is no parent.

10 The SUBJECT and the LECTURER node.

11 SUBJECT and LECTURER are siblings.

12 See Figure 4.7.

13 See Figure 4.8.

14 Node: DEPARTMENT
  Parent: None
  Children: LECTURER, SUBJECT
  Siblings: None

  Node: LECTURER
  Parent: DEPARTMENT
  Children: None
  Siblings: SUBJECT

  Node: SUBJECT
  Parent: DEPARTMENT
  Children: SET-BOOK, STUDENT
  Siblings: LECTURER

  Node: SET-BOOK
  Parent: SUBJECT
  Children: None
  Siblings: STUDENT

  Node: STUDENT
  Parent: SUBJECT
  Children: None
  Siblings: SET-BOOK

5: Databases and users

Objectives

After reading this chapter, you should be able to:
- list the job titles of those people who are concerned with the use and maintenance of databases
- describe the ways in which these people interact with the database and the DBMS
- describe the meaning of a *view*
- recognize the difference between a view and an *instance*
- draw up some instances of views
- define the names *schema* and *sub-schema*
- draw up a hypothetical schema and sub-schemas
- describe the three-level model of the interfaces within a DBMS.

There are many people concerned with the DBMS and with the creation, maintenance and use of a database:

- The *systems analyst* performs the same role as in traditional data processing: determining the needs of the users and producing specifications for the processing to meet these needs.
- The *applications programmer* is responsible for developing the analyst's designs and implementing them as working programs. Like the systems analyst, the programmer must be fully conversant with the DBMS which he/she is using.
- The *database administrator* usually abbreviated to *DBA* is the chief coordinator of the database and the DBMS. He/she is responsible for:
  1 The security of the database and the authorization of access to the database,
  2 Monitoring the usage and the performance of the database,
  3 The manner in which the data will be stored,
  4 The control and coordination of how the data is held on the database,
  5 Ensuring that the database responds to the changing needs of the organization.

- There may also be a *database designer* who will work with the systems analyst to determine:
  1 The nature of the data to be held on the database,
  2 The relationships between the data,
  3 The users who will be responsible for providing the data,
  4 The users who will be allowed to use the data,
  5 The names by which each piece of data is to be identified.
  In many organizations, the duties of the database designer are performed by the database administrator, or they may be shared by the systems analysts and the DBA.
- The *end-users* are those people who use the computer system to process their data and to produce reports and results. In addition to the traditional end-users—clerks, typists, sales personnel, engineers, office workers and business people—the facilities offered on some DBMSs make them suitable for use by managers and others who need to use and manipulate the information which the system provides. In general, the end-users need not be aware that they are using a DBMS, although the last category—particularly those who will be using facilities such as query languages—could hardly be satisfied without an efficient database management system.

There are also a number of other people working behind the scenes: these are mainly software support personnel and those concerned with the operation of the hardware.

In this chapter, we are concerned with the end-users and their representatives, the systems analysts and programmers. Since both the end-user and the programmer will—at some time—sit at a terminal and interact with the programs and the DBMS, we shall employ the word *user* to include both end-users and programmers.

Views

The database allows each user to visualize the data in his or her own way. We can illustrate this by thinking of a database which is used in the personnel department of a company. A user who is (writing or) running a program to produce a telephone list may think of their data as being arranged as shown in Figure 5.1(a); the secretary of the company's chess club may think of the data as being arranged as in Figure 5.1(b). Another user who is responsible for sending correspondence to the employees may think of the data as being arranged as in Figure

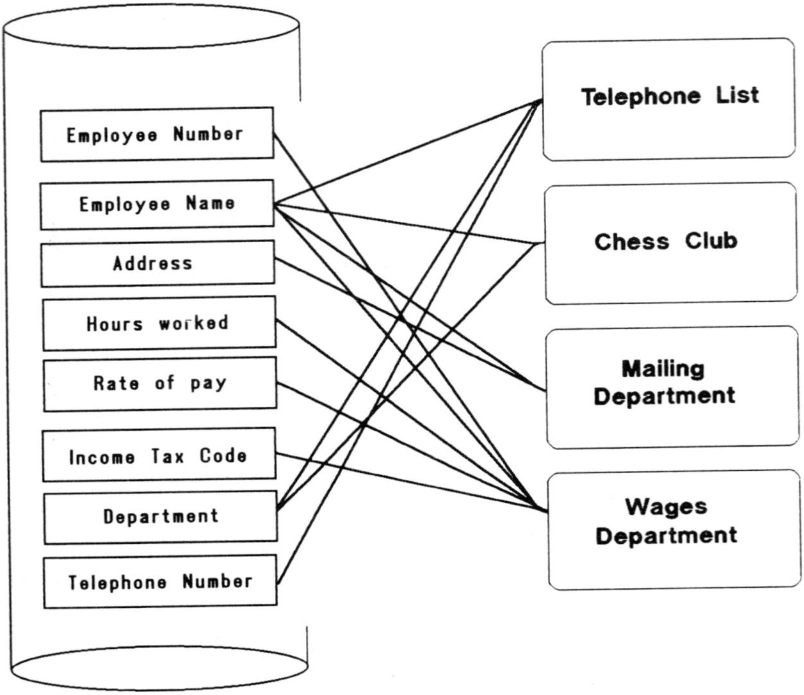

Name	Department	Telephone number

(a) the view used to produce the telephone list

Department	Name

(b) the view used by the Chess Club

Name	Address

(c) the view used by the mailing department

Employee number	Name	Hours worked	Rate of pay	Tax code

(d) the view used by the wages department

Figure 5.1 Some views of the data

Name	Department	Telephone Number
BARRIE	DESPATCH	2217
CHARLES	DESPATCH	2239
CHARLES	STORES	3260
GOSSE	LABORATORY	1287
GOSSE	STORES	3258
HARDY	FACTORY	9203
JAMES	LABORATORY	1281
JOHNSON	DESPATCH	2230
LEMMON	FACTORY	9255
LEMMON	STORES	3272
MALLORY	DESPATCH	2283
PALTOCK	LABORATORY	1291
SHAW	DESPATCH	2266
SHAW	STORES	3297
WILLIAMS	FACTORY	9262
WILLIAMS	OFFICE	4254
WILSON	FACTORY	9230

(a) the instance used to produce the telephone list

Department	Name
DESPATCH	JOHNSON
DESPATCH	MALLORY
FACTORY	HARDY
FACTORY	LEMMON
FACTORY	WILLIAMS
FACTORY	WILSON
LABORATORY	PALTOCK
STORES	CHARLES
STORES	GOSSE
STORES	LEMMON
STORES	SHAW

(b) the instance seen by the Chess Club

Figure 5.2 Some instances of the users' views

5.1(c). A third user who is responsible for calculating the employees' salaries may think of the data as being arranged as in Figure 5.1(d). Each user has his or her own *view* of the data. Each user's view will be just a small subset of the entire data within the database.

A single view will normally contain just a few of the many data fields which are available in the database, as illustrated in Figure 5.2(a) which shows the data included in the view used by the telephone list. A view may also contain a restricted number of records. This is illustrated in Figure 5.2(b) which contains just the employees who are in the chess club.

The actual data which falls within each user's view at any particular moment is known as an *instance* of the view. Whenever we change a data value, when we add a new record or when we delete an old record,

Employee number	Name	House number	Street	Town	Postcode	Telephone number

Hours worked	Rate of pay	Tax code	Department	Member of Chess Club	Date joined company

(a) First possibility

Employee number	Name	House number	Street	Town	Postcode	Telephone number

Employee number	Hours worked	Rate of pay	Tax code	Department

Employee number	Member of Chess Club	Date joined company

(b) Second possibility

Employee number	House number	Street	Town	Postcode	Telephone number

Employee number	Name	Member of Chess Club	Date joined company	Department

Employee number	Rate of pay	Tax code

Employee number	Hours worked

(c) Third possibility

Figure 5.3 Some of the possible schemas

the user's *view* stays the same but the *instance* changes if the changed data falls within that user's view.

To illustrate this, let us take another example of a university's student register. There are several users, and of these one user is working with the name, date of birth and address of a student, and another user is working with the name and qualifications.

- If a student moves house and changes his address, then only instances of the first user's view will change,
- If a new student enrols at the university, then both instances will change,
- If a new course is added to the database, then neither of these instances will change, although there will be other users whose instances are affected.

There may be any number of user views of the database and each view may be slightly different from the others. However, the *physical* arrangement of the data will usually be quite different from the ways in which the users view it. For example, Figure 5.3 shows some of the possible ways in which the data may be organized. This flexibility in the physical form of the data is a consequence of the data independence which the DBMS offers.

A diagram such as those in Figure 5.3 is called a *schema* or a *schema diagram*. This is a map of the entire database showing how and where the data is to be found. The schema is produced by the database designer working with the systems analysts, and is maintained by the database administrator. There may be several schemas, each relating to a particular part of the database. [Strictly speaking, the plural of *schema* is *schemata*. In the present book, however, we shall use the form *schemas*.]

The smaller maps representing those parts of the database which are involved in the views of the individual users are sometimes known as *sub-schemas*. We saw some sub-schemas in Figure 5.2. The sub-schemas and the contents of the views are allocated to the various users by the DBA.

Data which is not included in a particular user's view will be completely hidden from that user. The DBA is probably the only person who ever sees the entire schema, and any changes which the users wish to make to their views and sub-schemas will be authorized by the DBA. This is part of the data security features of a DBMS.

Look again at the instances in Figure 5.2. You will see that the view of the secretary of the chess club is that *only those employees who are members of the chess club* are included. However, the corresponding sub-schema does not show this restriction. If we also had a squash club, this too would probably use just the department and the name of the employees—that is the same sub-schema as for the chess club—but the view (and the instances of the views) would include only those people who were members of the squash club. This illustrates an important difference between a view and a sub-schema. As you can see in Figure 5.3, we chose to implement membership by having an extra data field—MEMBER OF CHESS CLUB—on the employee schema.

Activity

1 Copy out one of the schemas shown in Figure 5.3. Using four different coloured pens, indicate on the schema those fields which are involved in the four sub-schemas shown in Figure 5.1.
2 Draw sub-schemas for each of the four users of the college programs which we considered earlier.
3 Draw a possible schema for the college database as far as it concerns the views of your four users.
4 In your own words, describe the views of your four programs, indicating which fields are included and whether or not all the records are included.
5 Write down some (fictitious) instances of the views of your four users.

Questions

1 Indicate whether the following are true or false.
   (a) A user may look at any part of the database simply by changing his instance.
   (b) A view is the same as a schema.
   (c) The schema represents the entire database.
   (d) When a new instance of a data record is added to the database, the sub-schema will change.
   (e) A view may include specific fields from the database.
   (f) When an instance of a data record is deleted from the database, the view will change.
   (g) A user may add new data fields to his view whenever he wishes.
   (h) A sub-schema is the same as an instance.
   (i) When a new instance of a data record is added to the database, some of the instances may change.
   (j) The sub-schema represents the entire database.

(k) Some of the instances may change when the contents of the database change.
(l) When an instance of a data record is deleted from the database, the schema will be affected.
(m) The DBA may be required to add new data fields to the database.
(n) When an instance of a data record is deleted from the database, the schema will not be affected.
(o) When a new instance of a data record is added to the database, all the instances will change.
(p) A view is the same as the sub-schema.
(q) When a new instance of a data record is added to the database, the schema will change.
(r) An instance represents the appearance of the entire database at a particular moment.
(s) When a new instance of a data record is added to the database, all the sub-schemas may change.
(t) The DBA has access to the schema and can look at any part of the database.

2 Complete these sentences:
(a) the duties of the DBA include ...
(b) the schema is ...
(c) a sub-schema is ...
(d) a view is ...
(e) an instance is ...

3 The secretary of the chess club wishes to include the member's telephone number in the view used by the chess club program. Which of the following will change:
(a) the schema
(b) the sub-schema,
(c) the view,
(d) the instance?

4 Using the information shown above, draw the revised version of the schema/sub-schema/view/instance which are affected by the changes made in Question 1.

5 A new employee—Mrs Scott—joins the company to work in the office. She will be on telephone number 4258. She does not wish to join the chess club. Which of the following will change:
(a) the schema
(b) the sub-schema,
(c) the view,
(d) the instance?

6 Using the information shown above, draw the revised version of the schema/sub-schema/view/instance which are affected by the changes made in Question 3.

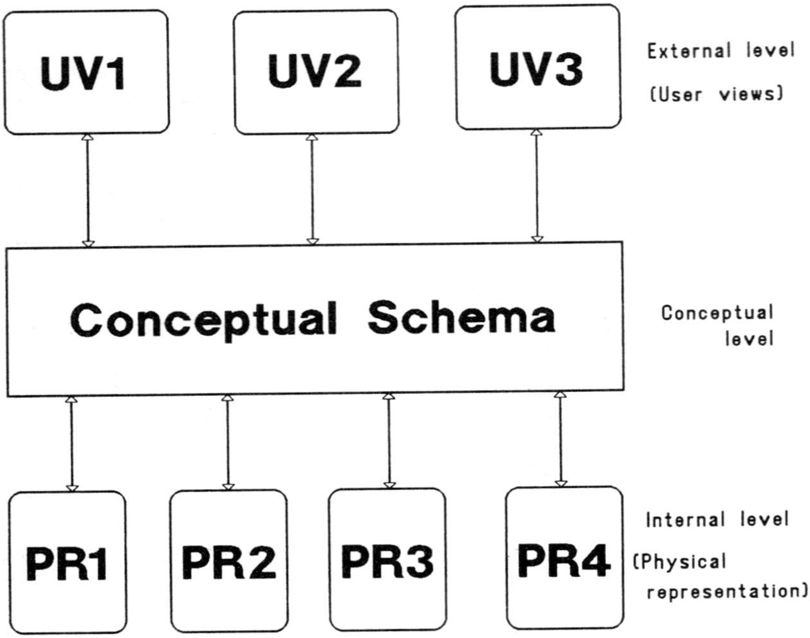

Figure 5.4 The three-level model

The three-level model

In the late 1970s, the Standards Planning and Requirements Committee (SPARC) of the American National Standards Institute (ANSI) proposed a standard model for the ways in which the various components of a DBMS should interface with each other. This *three level model* is illustrated in Figure 5.4.

At the top level (called the *external level*) are the user views—UV1, UV2 and so on—which the individual users have of the system. At the next level (the *conceptual level*) are the entities within the system—this is the view seen by the systems analyst and represents the *logical* picture of the database. At the lowest level (the *internal level*) is the *physical representation* of the system which maps each piece of conceptual data (of the conceptual schema) to a particular file on a particular disk PR1, PR2 and so on.

It was the SPARC concern that each of these levels should be independent of the others, and that there should be standards for the interfaces (represented by the arrows) between the various components.

Recap

Of the people involved with the database, the most important are the users amongst whom we include the programmers who act on their behalf and the database administrator. The DBA is responsible for coordinating and monitoring the use and performance of the database.

The DBMS allows each user to visualize the data as being organized in the way which he/she requires. Data which is not needed by this user can be ignored. Each user has his or her own view of the data. This view can consist of just certain parts of all the records on the database, or just certain parts of certain records on the database.

The actual data which makes up each user's view at any particular moment is called an instance of that view.

The data contents of each view may be described by a sub-schema.

The data contents of the entire database is described by the schema. The DBA is probably the only person who ever sees the entire schema.

The schema rarely changes.

The sub-schema and the associated view will change whenever a user requires to change the data which he/she is working with.

As the data on the database changes—as values are changed, records are added and records are deleted—an instance of a view will change if the changed data falls within that view.

In order to standardize the way in which the database serves its various users, the SPARC committee proposed a three-level model comprising the external level (as seen by the users), the conceptual level (as seen by the systems analysts) and the internal level (as seen by the database administrator).

Answers

1 (a) False
  (b) False
  (c) True
  (d) False
  (e) True
  (f) False
  (g) False, new fields may only be added when the DBA authorizes it
  (h) False
  (i) True
  (j) False
  (k) True

(l) False
(m) True
(n) True
(o) False, some instances may change, but not necessarily all
(p) False, a view may imply criteria by which the data is selected. As in the view which contained only those employees in the chess club
(q) False
(r) False, an instance represents just a single view at a particular moment
(s) False
(t) True

2 Your answer should include these main points:
(a) the duties of the DBA include: the monitoring of the usage and the performance of the database; the control and coordination of how the data on the database is held; the control of the security of the database and the authorization of access to the database. In some cases, he/she may also be responsible for the design of the database and the schema.
(b) the schema is the map which describes the contents of the database.

Department	Name	Telephone Number

(a) the revised schema

Department	Name	Telephone Number
DESPATCH	JOHNSON	2230
DESPATCH	MALLORY	2283
FACTORY	HARDY	9203
FACTORY	LEMMON	9255
FACTORY	WILLIAMS	9262
FACTORY	WILSON	9230
LABORATORY	PALTOCK	1291
STORES	CHARLES	3260
STORES	GOSSE	3258
STORES	LEMMON	3272
STORES	SHAW	3297

(b) the new instance

Figure 5.5 Revised schema and instances for the chess club.

(c) the sub-schema is the map which describes the view seen by any user or group of users. A sub-schema contains a specified number of fields from the data in the database.
(d) the view is the section of the database seen by any user or group of users. A view contains a specified number of fields from a specified subset of the data in the database.
(e) the instance is the actual occurrences of data which fall within a single view at a particular moment.

3 The following will be affected:
(a) the schema is a map of the entire database and will not change since the telephone number is already held in the database;
(b) the sub-schema will change to reflect the new view, as shown in Figure 5.5(a);
(c) the view will change to include the name, department and telephone number;
(d) the instance will change to include the new data, as shown in Figure 5.5(b).

4 See Figure 5.5.

Name	Department	Telephone Number
BARRIE	DESPATCH	2217
CHARLES	DESPATCH	2239
CHARLES	STORES	3260
GOSSE	LABORATORY	1287
GOSSE	STORES	3258
HARDY	FACTORY	9203
JAMES	LABORATORY	1281
JOHNSON	DESPATCH	2230
LEMMON	FACTORY	9255
LEMMON	STORES	3272
MALLORY	DESPATCH	2283
PALTOCK	LABORATORY	1291
SCOTT	OFFICE	4258
SHAW	DESPATCH	2266
SHAW	STORES	3297
WILLIAMS	FACTORY	9262
WILLIAMS	OFFICE	4254
WILSON	FACTORY	9230

Figure 5.6 The new instance used to produce the telephone list

5 The effects of adding a new data record will be:
   (a) the schema is a map of the entire database and will not change. The schema is not changed by the contents of the database.
   (b) the sub-schema will not change.
   (c) the view will not change.
   (d) the instance will change to include the new data, as shown in Figure 5.6.

6 See Figure 5.6.
   Your answer would be correct if you had chosen to put the new information about Mrs Scott elsewhere in the table.

6: Databases and software

Objectives

After reading this chapter, you should be able to:

- name the three main types of database
- describe the general manner in which each organizes and views its data
- describe the functions of the various pieces of the software which support a database
- describe the role of a *data description language*, a *data manipulation language* and a *query language* in data processing
- describe some other types of software which are available for use with DBMSs
- describe the security provisions which a DBMS must provide
- describe the nature of *transaction logging*, and use the terms *roll forward* and *roll back*.

The first database management system was the Integrated Data Store which was designed by Charles Bachman for the American General Electric company in 1961. Since that time, there has been a great deal of work done by a many different organizations in the design and development of DBMSs and also in the design of the languages which support the DBMS.

Today, there are many different DBMS commercially available. Each visualizes the data in a slightly different way from the others, although there are essentially just three main models:

- network databases
- hierarchical databases
- relational databases.

and they all use the underlying logical model of entities and their relationships which we met in Chapter 3.

In this chapter, we shall introduce these three types. We shall look at each in detail in the later chapters. We shall also look at the software which is needed to support the database. It is this software which constitutes the *database management system*.

Some work has been done towards producing a *canonical* database, that is one which supports two or more of the above data models, but in general, the various DBMS are not compatible, and data which is organized for use with one DBMS must be reorganized if you wish to use it with another DBMS. As we shall see later, each DBMS requires a different set of commands and program statements to describe the structure of the data records and to process them.

There are many software interfaces available. These are sometimes called *servers* and will allow you to process one type of database as if it were another type. For example, the IDMS network DBMS implemented by Cullinet Software has been extended, in a version known as IDMS/R, to allow the user to process a network database as if it were a relational database.

It seems possible that future trends will be away from a specific implementation-oriented design for the database to an *object-oriented* design. Object-oriented DBMS products such as VBASE from Ontologic Inc., GEMSTONE of Serviologic, and ORION from MCT Corporation allow the user to visualize his/her problems in their own terms without having to restructure the data artificially so as to fit in with the requirements of the DBMS. In many ways, this move to object-oriented DBMSs is similar to the move from machine language and assemblers to Cobol and Fortran which allowed the businessman and the engineer to express his/her problems in a language that they could understand. Research and development on these and similar products is continuing and when it has stabilized, we shall be able to include object-oriented DBMSs in a future edition of this book.

Network databases

A network database organizes its data as a series of records linked one to another within their relationships. It is a very close to our data structure model of the relationships which we discussed in Chapter 3.

As Figure 6.1 reminds us, the network model is based around a plex structure, and allows each set of data to have a relationship with another other set of data. Compare this with Figure 6.2 which shows how similar data might be organized for a hierarchical database.

The network model and the programming languages which support it were originally defined by the CODASYL committee, the people who gave us Cobol, and consequently, it is often known as the Codasyl network model. Extensions have been made to Cobol, Fortran and a number of other languages to allow them to manipulate a network

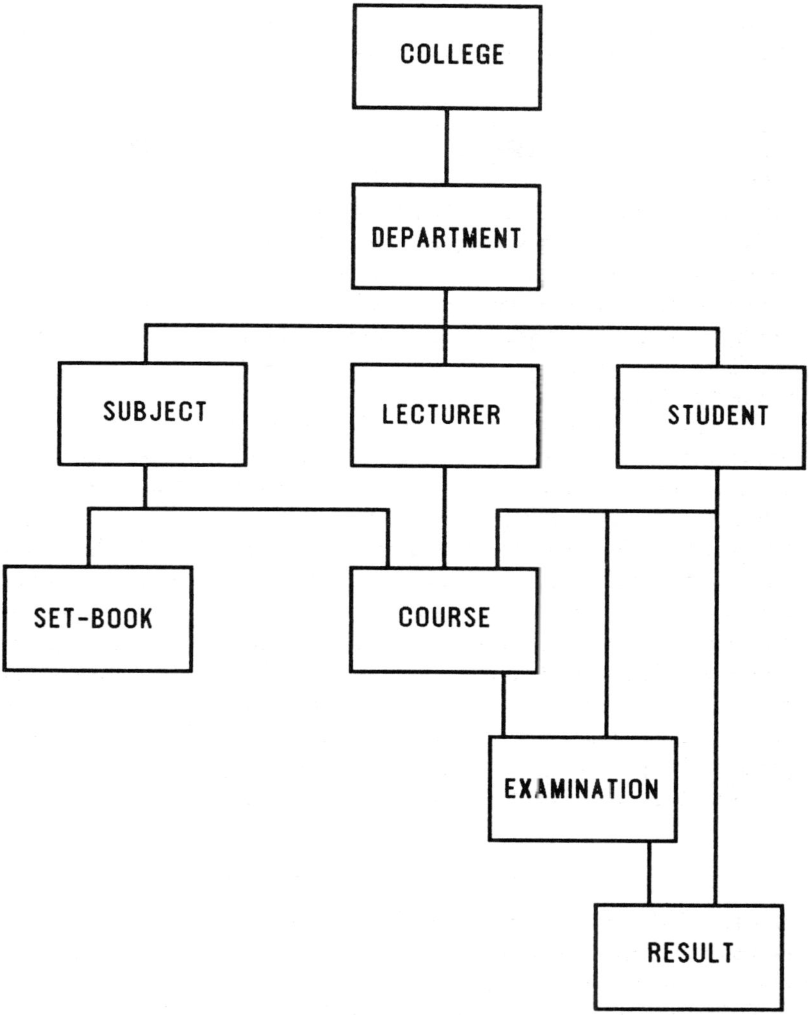

Figure 6.1 Network database—plex structure

database in a manner which closely aligns with the logical models we met earlier.

Network database models form the basis for a number of commercial DBMSs. We shall take a detailed look at network databases in Chapter 7.

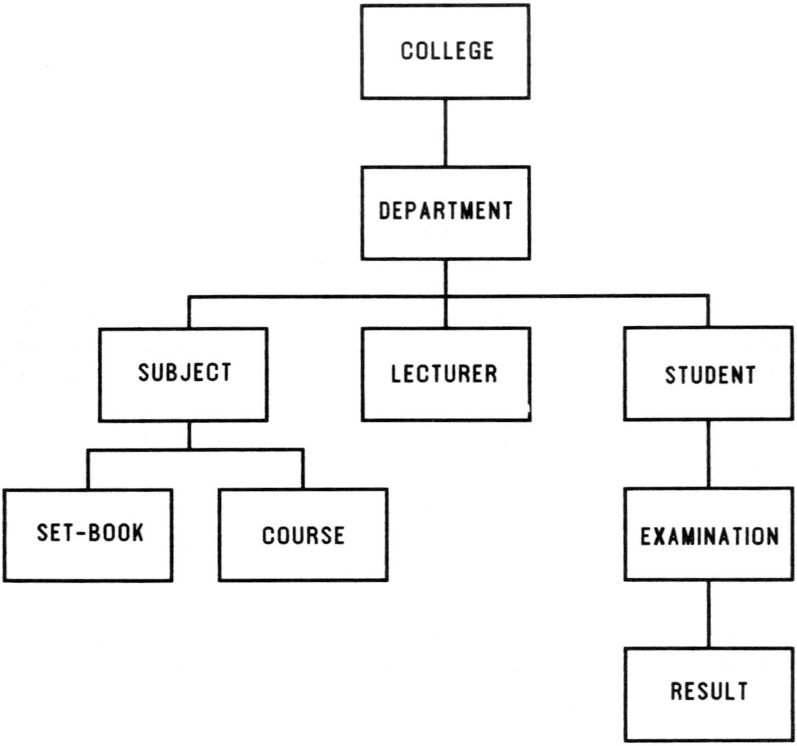

Figure 6.2 Hierarchical database—tree structure

Hierarchical databases

A hierarchical database organizes its data as a *tree-structure*. As Figure 6.2 reminds us, these may be visualized in exactly the same way as we saw in Chapter 4. Compare this with Figure 6.1 which shows how similar data might be organized for a network database.

We shall take a detailed look at hierarchical databases in Chapter 8.

Relational databases

The relational model was introduced in the early 1970s by an American called Ted Codd. It differs from the other two models in that it emerged as a formal mathematical representation of data, whereas the others came about much earlier as models of particular commercial applications.

A relational database is organized as a set of tables of data and a mathematical language called *relational algebra* is available to manipulate the data of the relational database. The abbreviation RDBMS is used for a relational database management system. We shall take a detailed look at relational databases in Chapter 9.

Database software

We have seen how data within the database is organized and accessed physically, and we have looked at the ways in which the data can be visualized in logical terms. But what does all this mean when we are using a DBMS and how does a DBMS affect the work of the programmer?

There are primarily three sets of software used in connection with a DBMS:

1 A *data description language* which allows the database designer and the database administrator to tell the DBMS how the data is structured and what security restrictions are to be applied;
2 A *data manipulation language* which allows the programmer to write application programs to process the data held in the database;
3 A *query language* which allows the users to make enquiries about the data held in the database. The provision of a query language means that it is not necessary to write a special application program for simple (or even quite complex) reports based upon the contents of the database.

We shall look at the general principles of each of these here. When we look at the various types of database in more detail, we shall see some particular illustrations of the software.

Data description languages

Recall that the DBA has the responsibility for the maintenance of the database. For this reason, the database administrator will be the main user of the data description language—DDL. The DDL is used to define those features of the database which are universally applicable and which do not apply just to one or two programs. The DDL is used to:

1 Describe the schema within the database and to specify the security controls for the data.

2 Describe the sub-schemas within the database, and to specify the users whose views they represent.
3 Describe the relationships which exist between the various entities represented by the database.
4 Define the physical location of various data attributes saying which piece of data is held on which disks. The definitions would also include the indexes which are to be maintained and used, and the hashing algorithms which are used.
5 Describe the physical appearance of the data: whether an attribute will hold alphabetic or numeric data; whether a numeric field is to be held in binary, decimal or packed decimal form; how many decimal places there are to be in a numeric field.

In some situations, these various tasks may be carried out by separate pieces of software within the DBMS. Nevertheless, their combined functions cover all the above requirements.

The data definitions and the descriptions of the relationships may be held separately from the processing statements of the programs, in much the same way that Cobol holds its ENVIRONMENT DIVISION and DATA DIVISION separately from the PROCEDURE DIVISION. In some DBMSs, they may be held outside the program completely and thus remain invisible to the programmers.

You may find that some people use the names *data definition language* and *storage definition language* for what we shall call the data description language.

Activity

Refer to the three-level data model of the interfaces within the DBMS, as discussed in Chapter 5, and indicate how this relates to the five points mentioned here.

Data dictionary

Much of the information concerning the data is specified by means of a *data dictionary*. The data dictionary is an important feature of a DBMS and acts as a general reference tool describing all the data held on the database.

In many situations, particularly the query languages which we shall look at later, there may be a data dictionary for each file, with one entry in the data dictionary for each piece of data on the file. Typically, each entry in the data dictionary will include:

- the name of the field
- the width of the field on the output reports
- the format of the field (integer, character or decimal)
- the location of that field within each data record.

Some DBMSs support a more extensive data dictionary which covers the entire database and defines the the schemas, sub-schemas, relationships and data structure. This might also include:

1 The access authority, the programs or users who are authorized to use each part of the database.
2 The update authority, the programs or users who are authorized to update each part of the database.
3 The processes which use each part of the database.
4 Synonyms, the names by which each data item and each part of the database is known to the users. This is important in a large organization where the same piece of data may be known as the PART NUMBER in one department, as the PRODUCT CODE in another department, whilst a third department might know it as the REFERENCE KEY.
5 A text description of each data field.

All those involved in the design and development of a computer system—especially the systems analysts and the programmers—will find the data dictionary of great value in their work. It can be used to avoid misunderstandings which may arise between the various users and the technical staff working on a large project. By its very nature, the data dictionary will be on-line and will act as a central clearing house for all designs and decisions made about the proposed system.

The actual format of the entries in the data dictionary will depend upon the precise nature of the DBMS. We shall meet some data dictionaries which are very formal and their contents are used by the DBMS when it is locating data and formatting data for output. Others may be quite informal and simply hold their information on a text file in a fairly free format. The latter sort of data dictionary can be used to advantage *even in computer environments which do not use a DBMS.*

Some more formal data entries in a dictionary might look like those shown in Figure 6.3. This shows the format of each data attribute: for example, *Description* and *Product-code*. It also shows the structure

```
Description = 25 {character}

Product-code = 4 {digit}

Product-record = {Product-code} + {Description} + {Location}
     + {Quantity-in-stock} + {Product-price} + {Movement-
     date} + ITERATIONS OF {Supplier-code}

Movement-date = {date}

Invoice-record = {Invoice-number} + {Client-code} +
     ITERATIONS OF ( {Invoice-entry} + {Payment-flag} ) +
     {Date-ordered} + {Invoice-total}

Invoice-reference = {Invoice-number}

Location = {Bay-number} + "/" + {Shelf-number}

Charge-rate = {Product-price} OR {Special-price}
```

Figure 6.3 Data dictionary entry—1

and contents of the records in terms of these atributes: for example, *Product-record* and *Invoice-record*.

On some DBMSs the data dictionary may be more comprehensive. A typical entry for a single field (or attribute) on a product information file might look like that shown in Figure 6.4.

Despite the implications of the name, the data dictionary may contain much more information than that relating simply to the data. It can also be used as a general repository to hold details of both the data and the programs for an application system. A typical data dictionary entry for a processing routine is shown in Figure 6.5.

The data dictionary may even hold the diagrams, data flow diagrams and data structure diagrams produced and developed by the systems analyst during the development of a computer application.

When the data dictionary is applied to these extended areas, its value to the organization becomes immense. Its value spreads to the operational aspects of the system and well into and beyond the implementation and live running phases.

Data manipulation languages

It is the *data manipulation language DML* which the programmers use to write their programs.

The DMLs fall into two broad categories:

1 Those which extend a conventional *host* language—such as Cobol

```
DATA-ITEM:...................... QUANTITY

TYPE:........................... ATTRIBUTE

DESIGNED:....................... 10 APR 1990
LAST UPDATED:................... 10 APR 1990

LOCATION:....................... LM34/V/9

FILE:........................... PRODUCT.MASTER
ATTRIBUTE:...................... 3

PASSWORD:....................... ABS445
UPDATE AUTHORITY:............... HEINE

DESCRIPTION:

     This field indicates the current stockholding of the
     item which is physically present in the warehouse.

     It does not include any incoming stock which has been
     ordered but not yet received.

     It does not include any outgoing stock which has been
     ordered by clients but not yet issued.

FORMAT:

    NUMERIC
    INTEGER
    MAXIMUM VALUE:.............. 9999999999
    LEADING ZEROES:............. NONE
    DISPLAYED:.................. RIGHT JUSTIFIED

SYNONYMS:

    QTY
    QUANTITY-IN-STOCK
    HOLDING
    STOCKHOLDING

THE DATA IS USED BY THE FOLLOWING PROGRAMS:

     CREATED:.................... MB1001

     READ:....................... MB1003
                                  MB1004
                                  MB1034
                                  VALN0001

     DELETED:.................... MB1003
                                  MB1002
```

Figure 6.4 Data dictionary entry—2

```
ROUTINE NAME: STOCKPROGRAM

LANGUAGE: COBOL

LAST UPDATED: 09:30:56  10 APR 1990

UPDATE AUTHORITY: HEINE

DESCRIPTION:

     This program is used to invoke the general
     processing routines for the main stock control
     system.

THE ROUTINE IS CALLED BY:

     STOCK001P     STOCK005P

THE ROUTINE CALLS:

     STOCK05           STOCK08            PG0010000
     STOCK06           STOCK33            PG0010300

THE ROUTINE USES THE FOLLOWING VARIABLES:

     ATTRNO            LAST.HEAD          PAGENO
     CLEAR.REST        LINES              VAR.END
     FILENO            LST.SUB.NO         VAR.LIST
     FILES             NUMERIC            VAR.NAME
     FUNC              NUMS               VARS
     HEADER            PAGE.LIMIT         ZERO.REC

THE ROUTINE USES THE FOLLOWING FILES:

     LOGIC - READ
     LOGIC2 - READ / WRITE
     LOGIC3 - READ / WRITE / DELETE
```

Figure 6.5 Data dictionary entry—3—process description

or Fortran or PL/1—to allow it to interact with the DBMS and thereby process the data on the files. We shall see how special subroutines and new Cobol statements such as FIND and GET allow a program to locate records by exploiting the relationships between the files, rather than by using the explicit key of the records.

2 Those which are completely new languages (often peculiar to one particular DBMS) replacing the traditional programming media.

In some cases, these may simply be a procedural version of the query language which the DBMS offers.

Some of the query languages—such as QBE and SQL—which we discuss in Chapter 10 include facilities for adding records, changing records and deleting records from the database.

We shall look at examples of these languages when we look at the various DBMSs in the next few chapters.

Query languages

A *query language* allows the users to make enquiries about the data on the database without writing a special program. Typically, query languages are used to find the answers to questions such as:

> 'What is the name and address of the student with enrolment number 92/7714?'
> 'What do our red leather gloves cost and where do we get from?'
> 'How many invoices are still unpaid after 60 days, what is the total value and who are offending customers?'
> 'Which products are selling well at the Bond Street shop?'
> 'Give me a list of the names, ages and salaries of all the employees in the company and group them together into the respective departments.'

The use of a query language can reduce much of the workload involved in the design and production of routine reports and on-line enquiries. If the language is sufficiently user-friendly and simple to use, it can be

STAFF NUMBER....	STAFF NAME................	STAFF AGE	STAFF ADDRESS...........
0551	MCINTOSH, C	52	391, HIGH ST
1002	WILSON, L	33	92, BROWN RD
1166	BROWN, F	39	689, BROAD AVE
1922	SMITH, J.A	42	34, HIGH STREET
2298	GREEN, W	29	49, HIGH GROVE
2378	GREEN, A	27	49, HIGH GROVE
2437	ANDERTON, J	26	93, CHERRY RD
2831	WILSON, C	23	276, BROAD RD
3351	ANDREWS, C	24	642, SMITH GROVE
4016	WILSON, W	25	19, BROWN AVE
4960	MACKEY, L	34	87, GREEN CLOSE
5342	LIVINGSTONE, R	33	572, WESTON RD
5664	CALLAGHAN, I	24	45, WILSON AVE
6069	BROWN, P	37	45, SMITH AVE
6073	LIVINGSTONE, E	48	5, WILSON GROVE

Figure 6.6 Query language report

```
WHAT IS THE DATABASE CALLED:  STAFF

WHICH FIELDS ARE TO BE DISPLAYED:  STAFF-NUMBER, STAFF-
     NAME, STAFF-AGE, STAFF-ADDRESS
```

Figure 6.7 Query language dialogue—1

offered to the end-users as a medium for generating *ad hoc* reports and for making one-off enquiries such as the examples above.

Many query languages take the form of simple English sentences such as:

> LIST ALL OVERDUE INVOICES SHOWING NAME DATE-DUE TOTAL AMOUNT
> PRINT THE NAME DATE AND BALANCE OF ACCOUNTS WITH DATE BEFORE "31/12/88"
> SUM AMOUNT FOR INVOICE = "UNPAID"
> LIST STAFF-NAME STAFF-AGE AND STAFF-ADDRESS

The last query might produce a report such as that shown in Figure 6.6.

```
WHAT IS THE FILE CALLED?

      1)      CLIENTS
      2)      DEPOTS
      3)      PRICES
      4)      PRODUCTS
      5)      SALARIES
      6)      SALES
      7)      STAFF

ENTER YOUR SELECTION: 7

WHICH FIELDS ARE TO BE DISPLAYED?

      1)      STAFF-ADDRESS
      2)      STAFF-AGE
      3)      STAFF-DATE-OF-BIRTH
      4)      STAFF-DATE-OF-JOINING
      5)      STAFF-LOCATION
      6)      STAFF-MANAGER
      7)      STAFF-NAME
      8)      STAFF-NUMBER
      9)      STAFF-REVIEW-DATE
     10)      STAFF-SALARY
     11)      STAFF-SALARY-HISTORY

ENTER YOUR SELECTION: 8 7 2 1
```

Figure 6.8 Query language dialogue—2

STAFF NUMBER	STAFF NAME	STAFF DEPT	STAFF AGE	STAFF JOIN DATE	STAFF ADDRESS
P.	P.		33		P.

(a) QBE request

```
STAFF        STAFF                         STAFF STAFF
NUMBER....   NAME................            AGE ADDRESS...........

1002         WILSON, L                        33 92, BROWN RD
5342         LIVINGSTONE, R                   33 572, WESTON RD
```

(b) Output report

Figure 6.9 Query by example

Other languages take the form of a series of questions asked of the user by the query language processor. For example, the report in Figure 6.6 might have been invoked by a sequence such as that shown in Figure 6.7.

Alternatively, the query language processor might display a list of possible answers, and the user will then make a selection from the available choices, as shown in Figure 6.8.

An extension of this last form is known as QBE—query by example. When using this language, the language processor will display a list of the available data fields as shown in Figure 6.9(a). The user will then enter the code P. alongside those fields which are to be displayed. If specific records are to be selected, then the selection criteria will be entered in the appropriate columns. The illustration would display the report shown in Figure 6.9(b), showing the staff-number, name, age and address for all employees aged 33.

Some form of data dictionary is used to define the various fields which are used in the enquiry sentences. In order to handle a sentence such as:

LIST STAFF-NAME STAFF-AGE AND STAFF-ADDRESS

the dictionary must hold definitions for STAFF-NAME, STAFF-AGE and STAFF-ADDRESS. Some query languages have a facility to *learn* the vocabulary which the users employ in their sentences, and even to modify their own data dictionary accordingly. For example, let us imagine that a user types in a statement such as:

LIST NAME AND AGE

```
It is not clear what you mean by NAME.

Is it one of the following?

      1)      PRODUCT-NAME
      2)      DEPOT-NAME
      3)      CLIENT-NAME
      4)      STAFF-NAME
      5)      SUPPLIER-NAME

Enter one of these names, or press <ESCAPE> to abandon:
```

Figure 6.10 Query language dialogue—3

and the language processor is unable to recognize the identifier NAME. The response by the query language may look like that shown in Figure 6.10.

When the user has clarified the requirements and, possibly, indicated that the STAFF-NAME is to be used, the processor might then ask if the user wishes to identify NAME with STAFF-NAME in future. In this manner, the query language processor builds up its vocabulary of file names, data names and the relationships between them.

Whatever the precise nature of the query language, in general, they offer a realistic and cost-effective way of producing reports and enquiries. Indeed, in some environments, the query language may be so powerful that an application programmer need never write a report program.

On many occasions, a systems analyst may be asked to produce a special report which cannot be handled by the query language: it may require some unusual formatting or some special layout of the figures on the printed page. In such cases, it may be worth talking the user into accepting something simpler and less complicated which can be produced much more easily and more cheaply by the standard query language software rather than by writing a special one-off application program which would take much longer to write and which would cost much more than a simple enquiry.

So what are the pros and cons of query languages?

- They are simple to use.
- They provide a facility whereby the end-user may interrogate a database directly.
- They are flexible in the format and content of the report, allowing the user:

1 To display any or all of the data fields of a record (as permitted by the security controls),
2 To sort the lines of the report into any specific order,
3 To select records according to one or more specific conditions,
4 To generate and display sub-totals and totals for specific fields,
5 To produce control breaks within the report,
6 To specify the format of the report, headings and footings.

- They may be appropriate for both ad hoc enquiries and longer reports.
- They allow enquiries to be made more quickly and without the long gestation period which is necessary when writing a standard program in, say, Cobol.
- They are easier to use than a third generation language, such as Cobol. A typical enquiry can often be specified in one line of typed input.
- If the user makes a mistake in the syntax or the logic of his enquiry, this will be detected and immediately rejected by the processor.
- They allow a process of trial and error in the enquiry. If a user finds that a particular query produces a large volume of output, then it may be reworded to reduce the size of the report.

On the other side of the argument:

- Query languages are generally used only for making enquiries on the contents of the database—for data retrieval. Standard programs still have to be provided to update and maintain the data.
- They may make considerable demands on the design of the database:
  1 They may demand that data be held in certain formats. For example, a date which is to be accessible by means of a query language may have to be held in a meaningful form such as 31/12/88 or 311288 instead of a more efficient internal or compacted form.
  2 They may require considerable support from the standard programs which are written to update the database, requiring the programs to establish and maintain entry points and other links within the database.
- If users are unfamiliar with the structure of the data, they may make inappropriate demands with their enquiries, causing the query language to be be inefficient when answering the enquiry, thereby wasting time and incurring expense.
- By allowing anyone to look at any part of the database, they may

put the security of the data at risk or demand additional security checks to be provided and maintained as the data is accessed.

A query language may be used as a development tool for producing a standard report program. The users can play around with the language until they have derived the sort of report which they want and then this can be rewritten as a possibly more efficient program in one of the usual third generation languages, such as Cobol, PL/1 or whatever.

Some query languages such as QBE and SQL, also include data manipulation facilities, allowing the users to add records, change records and delete records from the database.

Questions

1 Complete each of these sentences using one of: data description language, data manipulation language or query language.
  (a) the ___________ language is used to specify the sub-schemas.
  (b) the physical location of the data is described by means of the ___________ language.
  (c) the ___________ language may be an extension of a normal programming language such as Cobol.
  (d) the entities and their relationships are defined in the ______________________ language.
  (e) the security is imposed on the files by means of the ______________________ language.
  (f) a ______________________ language is used for one-off enquiries.
  (g) the programmer will write his/her programs using the ___________ language.

2 The secretary to the Dean of the College needs to be able to look at and change any field on the student record files. Describe some situations in which you think that the following security restrictions may be applied to the student record files.
  (a) user A may not look at or change the contents of the files.
  (b) user B may look at and change the contents of the files.
  (c) user C may look at but not change the contents of the files.
  (d) user D may look at some fields on a record but not look at other fields on the same record.
  (e) user E may look at some records on the file but not look at other records on the same file.

Indicate whether you would use a data description language, a data manipulation language or a query language in each of the following situations.

3 A manager at the head office in Glasgow wants to know how many leather jackets there are in the Bolton branch of a fashion shop.
4 The Westshire bank produces its customers' statements every Monday morning.
5 The police want to look through their database for a report about a stolen car.
6 We need to change the security to allow users in the stores to update the prices of products in the warehouse.
7 The credit limit for John Smith and Company has been changed from 200,000 to 2 million pounds.
8 The format of the credit limit is to be changed from hundreds of pounds to millions of pounds.
9 A pension manager needs to produce a regular report about the values of the stocks and shares owned by the company. All the necessary information is held on the database.

Other software

In later chapters, we shall look at the languages which are used to manipulate and generate reports about the data held on the database.

In addition to DBMSs, modern business uses a large number of other pieces of software: spreadsheets, word processing packages, graphic processors, and many others. Most DBMSs have some means of capturing their data and transporting it to or from such pieces of software. We shall look at some of these, here:

- The software which allows you to format the output reports,
- The software which allows you to interact with the contents of the database organized as a spreadsheet,
- The software which allows you to produce charts and graphs based upon the data on the database.

You may find it useful to refer back to this section later, after you have become familiar with the languages described in Chapter 10.

Forms and reports

In addition to the primary requirement of answering enquiries, some query languages offer a means of producing the output in the format of reports and forms. Thus, instead of having a simple report showing a list of the data on the file, that data may now be formatted to produce:

COMPANY	STREET	TOWN	POSTCODE	IN	NAME	TITLE
DARROW COUNCIL	PARK ESTATE	DARROWBY	DY77 9LL	B	WILLIAM	MR
ABC UK LTD	LANDSDOWN RD	LOUGHTON	ESSEX	G	ANDREWS	MRS
COMPUWARE	ARROWTON ST	BURY	IP99 9UU	T	BEESLEY	MR
KY ASSOCIATES	3 STATION RD	COVENTRY	CV99 2GT	K	JOHNSON	MS
DENTON LTD	REDSTONE WAY	BRISTOL	BS99 0BD	J	DENTON	MR
WHEELS LTD	TIVERTON RD	DERBY	DY3 9GN	G	KERNOW	MISS

(a) A simple report

```
MR B WILLIAM,          MR T BEESLEY,          MR J DENTON,
DARROW COUNCIL,        COMPUWARE,             DENTON LTD,
PARK ESTATE,           ARROWTON ST,           REDSTONE WAY,
DARROWBY,              BURY,                  BRISTOL,
DY77 9LL               IP99 9UU               BS99 0BD

MRS G ANDREWS,         MS K JOHNSON,          MISS G KERNOW,
ABC UK LTD,            KY ASSOCIATES,         WHEELS LTD,
LANDSDOWN RD,          3 STATION RD,          TIVERTON RD,
LOUGHTON,              COVENTRY,              DERBY,
ESSEX                  CV99 2GT               DY3 9GN
```

(b) Name and address labels

```
Mrs G Andrews,
ABC UK LTD,
Landsdown Rd,
LOUGHTON,
ESSEX

Dear Mrs Andrews,

We have pleasure in announcing a new venture which is sure
to be of interest to everyone living in your part of Essex.

Please return the enclosed postcard for more details.
```

(c) A printed letter

Figure 6.11 Not just a simple list

- Name and address labels,
- Printed letters,
- Invoices,
- Student Reports.

and many other documents which are used in business and commercial data processing.

In many cases, the special formatting is achieved by having an additional piece of software which interacts with the query language to format the the data in the required form. Some examples of such output are shown in Figure 6.11.

Spreadsheets

A spreadsheet is an accounting tool which organizes data—balance sheets, profit and loss accounts, budgets and the like—as a grid made

```
    .........1]........................2].....3]
 1
 2
 3 STOCK        DESCRIPTION                      PRICE
 4
 5 1000         DESK, GREEN-BLUE, WOODEN         56.00
 6 1111         STOOLS, GREEN, PLASTIC           20.00
 7 1200         DESK, GREY, WOODEN               56.00
 8 1234         CHAIR, RED, STEEL                10.00
 9 1500         CHAIR, ORANGE, PLASTIC           25.00
10 2000         SETTEE, YELLOW, STEEL           100.00
11 2200         SETTEE, BROWN, STEEL             10.00
12 2222         DESK, BLUE, STEEL                56.00
13 2500         TABLE, GREEN, LAMINATE           50.00
14 2936         SETTEE, GREY, STEEL               7.00
15 3000         SIDEBOARD, BLUE, WOODEN         130.00
16 3200         SIDEBOARD, NEUTRAL, WOODEN      130.00
17 3333         CHAIR, WHITE, LAMINATE           25.00
18 3500         STOOL, WHITE, PLASTIC            20.00
19 3579         SIDEBOARD, GREY, SPECIAL        130.00
20 4000         DESK, BLACK, SPECIAL             56.00
21 4200         SETTEE, GOLD, WOODEN             10.00
22 4444         SETTEE, BLACK, WOODEN            10.00
23 4500         CHAIR, RED, LAMINATE             25.00
24 4545         SETTEE, BLUE, SPECIAL            10.00
25 5000         SETTEE, ORANGE, WOODEN           10.00
```

Figure 6.12 A spreadsheet

up of rows and columns and data. Figure 6.12 shows a section of a simple spreadsheet which was produced with the aid of a package called Compusheet. This software is available on the Pick operating system and uses English language sentences very similar to those of the Access language which is provided by that operating system. We shall meet Access again in Chapter 10 when we look at query languages.

The particular example shown here was generated by means of the sentence:

SPREAD STOCK DESCRIPTION PRICE

and the Compusheet processor then consulted the data dictionary to locate the fields identified by the names DESCRIPTION and PRICE and then scanned through the STOCK file and produced the spreadsheet with three columns, one each for the stock-number, the description and the price, respectively—as directed by the SPREAD sentence—generating one row for every record on the STOCK FILE.

STOCK.....	MATERIAL..	VALUE
	ASH	42600.00
	LAMINATE	9859.00
	MAPLE	5698.00
	OAK	19920.00
	PINE	6860.00
***		84937.00

(a) A printed report chart

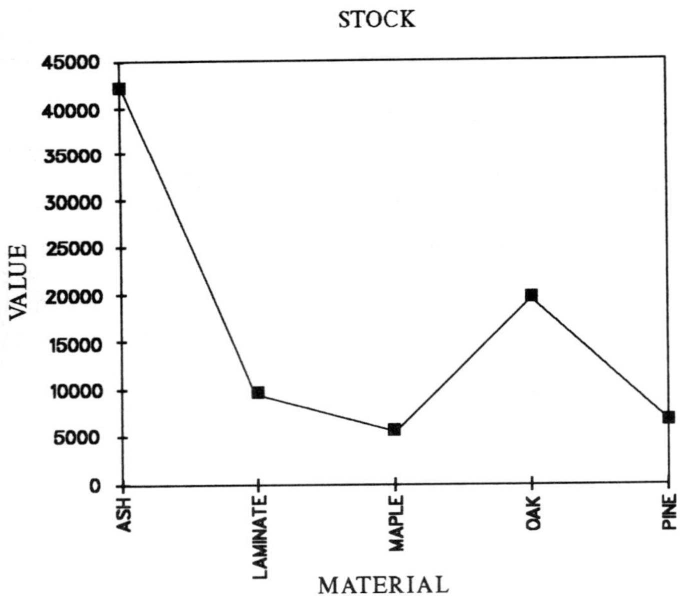

(b) A graph

Figure 6.13 Graphical output

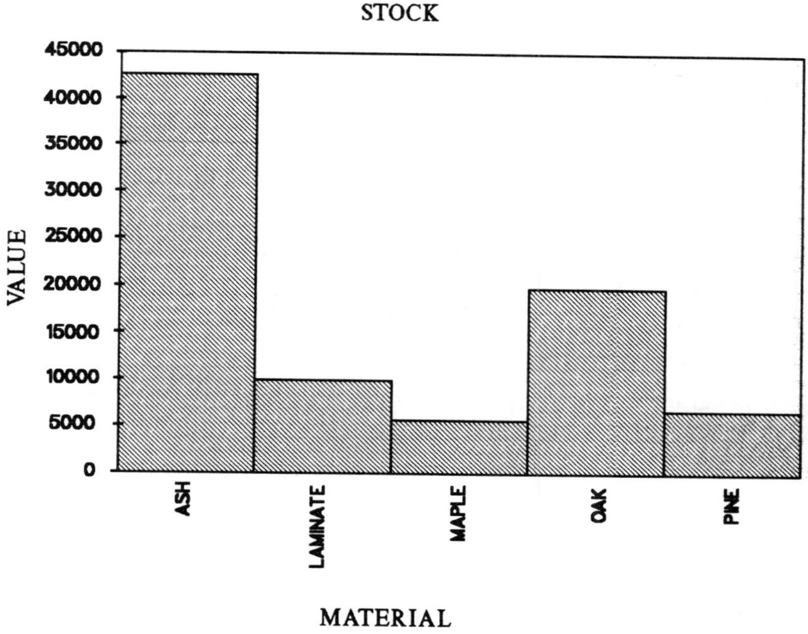

(c) A bar chart

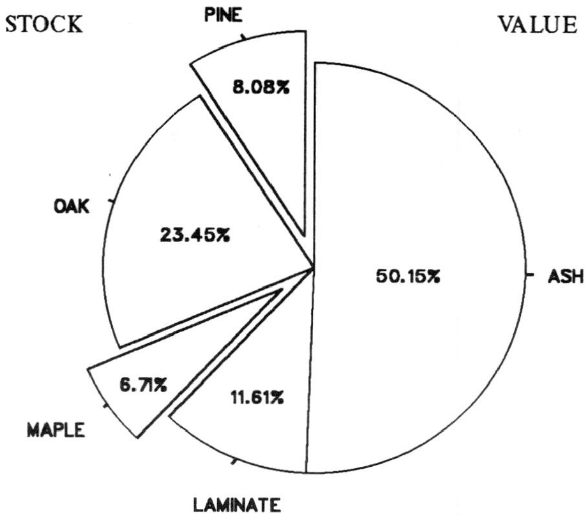

(d) A pie chart

Graphics software

As an example of graphics software, we take a package called Accuplot. Like Compusheet, this is available on the Pick operating system and uses English language sentences very similar to those of the Access query language.

Figure 6.13 shows how it is possible to present the data on a file in several ways:

1 Diagram (a) shows a simple report produced by means of the Access query sentence:

    SORT STOCK BY MATERIAL DESCRIPTION BREAK-ON MATERIAL TOTAL VALUE

2 Diagram (b) shows a simple graph produced by means of the Accuplot PLOT command in the sentence:

    PLOT STOCK BY MATERIAL BREAK-ON MATERIAL TOTAL VALUE

  Each peak of the graph represents the total value of products which are made of the material indicated along the bottom axis.

3 Diagram (c) shows a bar chart produced by means of the Accuplot PLOT command in the sentence:

    PLOT STOCK BY MATERIAL BREAK-ON MATERIAL TOTAL VALUE

  Each vertical bar represents a particular material, and the height of the bar represents the total value of products which are made of that material.

4 Diagram (d) shows a pie chart produced by means of the Accuplot PIE command in the sentence:

    PIE STOCK BY MATERIAL BREAK-ON MATERIAL TOTAL VALUE

  Each slice of the pie represents a particular material, and the size of the slice represents the total value of products which are made of that material.

Immediately before Accuplot produces its output, we are asked for details about the size of the chart, whether it is to be a graph or a bar-chart, and so on. In the pie chart, for example, we asked that all those slices of the pie above a certain size be exploded.

Accuplot—and indeed most graphical packages—offer many other facilities in addition to those illustrated by these examples:

- Plotting graphs

- Drawing several graphs and charts on the same axes. We could, for example, have asked to show the value, the cost and the profit of various products on the same graph
- Use coloured inks or coloured display.

Look at the charts and compare their contents with the simple Access report in Figure 6.13(a). You will see how graphical output has more visual impact than a printed report, although charts do not always carry the same detail of information.

Software and security

We have seen that a DBMS must take care of the security of the database, preventing access by unauthorized users. It is the DBA and some component of the data description language (rather than the data manipulation language) which allow these security constraints to be imposed. The actual range of security control varies according to which DBMS you use, but typically the DBA can control:

- *Who* is authorized to access the database,
- *Which files* a user may access,
- *Which fields* of the files a user may access,
- *What activities* a user may perform on the fields: add new files/ fields/records; look at fields; amend the contents of fields; delete files/fields/record,
- *Which programs* a user is allowed to execute.

The ways in which this is achieved in practice can become very complicated (and rightly so). You may find that one particular DBMS uses one or more of methods such as:

- Giving each user a unique code which is to be used to log on to the computer and start using the database,
- Giving each user a unique password,
- Organizing the users into groups. One group may never access the files belonging to another group,
- Giving each user a *security level*. Users with a higher security level may access more of the database than the other users,
- Tying each user to a specific terminal/location,
- Controlling the time of day when access is permitted.

The combined effects of these precautions is to prevent each user from accessing those pieces of data which he/she is not authorized to handle.

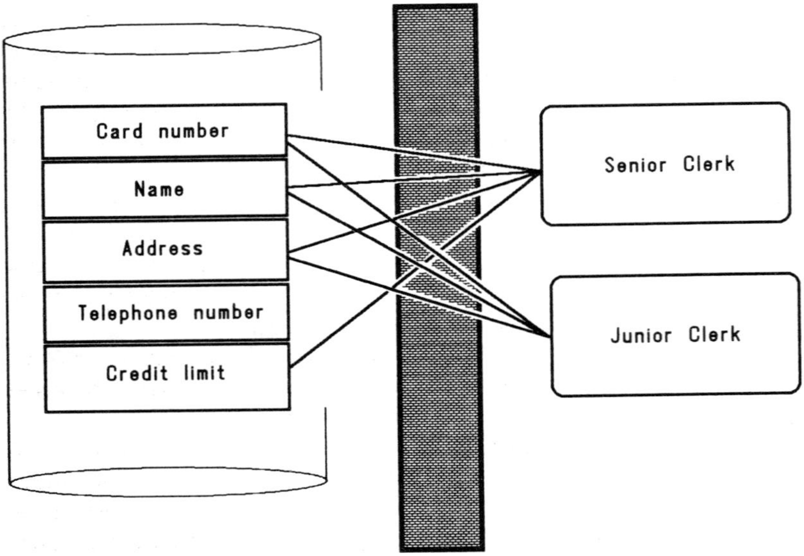

Figure 6.14 User views and security

Indeed, in many cases, the DBMS will leave each user completely unaware of the existence of any data to which they have no access. This is another aspect of the user views which we introduced in Chapter 5.

For example, if a senior clerk in a credit card company is concerned with the name, address and credit limit of the clients, then when she asks for all the details of client 12345, the name, address and credit limit will be displayed. However, a junior clerk may only be authorized to access the name and address of the clients; when he asks for all the details of client 12345, only the name and address of that client will be displayed. If, suspecting that there may be data other than just the name and address held on the database, the junior clerk asks for the credit limit or even the telephone number of client 12345, he will be told that the information is not available, or that he does not have the authority to look at that data. This is illustrated in Figure 6.14.

In many commercial applications, the access authority can be very complicated. For example:

- A keyboard operator who processes the credit card sales vouchers must be able to add data about transactions to the database (she must be allowed to write to the database), but she will not be able to look at details such as the client's current balance or his home telephone number (she is not permitted to read from the database).

- Someone who handles clients' questions on the telephone must be able to look at a client's record (read from the database), but she will not be able to change any information, such as the current balance (they cannot write to the database).
- A visitor to the computer centre may be able to look at his own name and address (read from one small part of the database), but he/she must not be able to look at other clients' details, not be able to change any part of the database (they have restricted powers to read from the database, and they cannot write to the database).
- A visitor who does not have a credit card with the company will not be able to look at or to change any information whatsoever (they cannot read or write to any part of the database).
- The general manager of the credit card company will be able to look at any part of the database—to resolve any unusual problems which may arise—and he/she will also be able to change any errors or mistakes which cannot be rectified by the standard processing routines and programs. He/she will have complete authority to read from and to write to the database, although even these special operations will be monitored and recorded by the DBMS.

It is the responsibility of the DBA to set these complex access patterns, and it is the work of the DBMS to enforce them.

Software and integrity

All computer systems have some sort of backup facility so that, in the event of any problems such as a system failure, lost data can be restored to its state at the time that the backup was made. The backup procedure usually involves making a copy of the data and dumping it on to a magnetic tape. But what happens to the data which was processed between the time that the backup copy was made and the time that the system went down? A DBMS should be capable of providing for recovery in the event of the computer failing in the midst of a job.

There are several possible solutions:

- Keep a record of all the transactions which are made and then, in the event of any problems, restore the backup copy of the system and then process the transactions again. This usually means reprocessing all the documents again manually. A better solution is to ...

```
Get the details of the sales order
START-TRANSACTION
    Process the order
    Update the customer record
    Update the stock levels
    Update the despatch record
    Produce the despatch documents
END-TRANSACTION
```

(a) START-TRANSACTION / END-TRANSACTION

```
Get the details of the sales order
START-TRANSACTION
    Process the order
    Update the customer record
    Update the stock levels
    Update the despatch record
    Produce the despatch documents
    Ask the user if he/she wants to cancel
    If YES then ROLLBACK
END-TRANSACTION
```

(b) ROLLBACK

Figure 6.15 Transaction logging and rollback

- Log the transactions on some form of off-line storage—typically magnetic tape—and then, in the event of any problems, restore the backup copy and then roll forward by processing the logged transactions through the system once more.
- Dump all the changed records to magnetic tape and then, in the event of any problems, restore the backup copy and then replace the changed records from the tape dump. If you can also dump copies of each record before and after each change, you would provide an excellent *audit trail* to keep your auditors happy.

One difficulty with these methods is that a single *transaction* may involve changes to several different files. For example, the processing of a sales order may require a change to the amount owing on the customer's record, a change to the quantity held on stock on the stock records, and a new record on the stock despatch file. If only one or two of these changes have been logged by the time that the failure occurred, there may be inconsistencies in the data restored from the log: if we log the changes to the customer's account but not those to the despatch file, then—when we restore the logged records—the customer will be charged for goods which have not been sent. This is a threat to the integrity of the database.

The requirement to cope with such situations has led to the concept of *transaction boundaries*. Records will only be logged when they and all the records within the same transaction boundary have been processed successfully.

In programming terms, we can think of a transaction boundary informally as shown in Figure 6.15(a).

When the logging process is taking place, all changes after the START-TRANSACTION will be noted by the DBMS but they will not be logged on the magnetic tape until the END-TRANSACTION is encountered. You can think of the START-TRANSACTION as a *recovery point* which indicates the moment and the state to which the system can return and still maintain consistency between the various data records.

Such a system has a further advantage in that it greatly simplifies the situation if a user needs to cancel a transaction. Let us imagine that towards the end of a transaction the keyboard operator realizes that he/she has input the wrong quantities and wants to start again. All that the DBMS has to do is to reject the details of the current transaction. Since no changes have been logged, there cannot be any inconsistencies in the database. Undoing a transaction in this manner is known as *rolling back*. This may be represented by the sequence shown in Figure 6.15(b).

Activity 2

Using the informal language in the manner illustrated in the text, together with the statements START-TRANSACTION, END-TRANSACTION and ROLLBACK, design a simple program which will allow a user to call up and display a client record, and then change the client's name. The program should ask the user if he/she wishes to proceed with the change or to cancel it.

Recap

There are many different DBMS commercially available, each modelling the data in a slightly different way. We shall concern ourselves with just three main models: hierarchical databases, network databases, and relational databases. They all use the underlying logical model of entities and their relationships which we met earlier.

If we were to discuss the subject in greater depth, we might describe the relational model and the entity-relationship model as conceptual models (logical ways of visualizing the data) whilst the hierarchical model and the network model are structural models, physical ways of organizing the data. But the distinction made in the text is sufficient for our purposes.

There are three main categories of software used in connection with a DBMS: a data description language which allows the database administrator to define and control the database, a data manipulation language which allows the programmer to write application programs to process the data held in the database, and a query language which allows the users to make enquiries about the data held in the database with the need for a special application program.

A data dictionary is used to hold information about the schemas, sub-schemas, relationships, data structure and security of the data.

Finally, we looked at the ways in which the DBMS handles the security and integrity of the database. The concept of transaction logging enables the software to recover from potential loss of data and data integrity in the event of machine failure and similar breakdowns.

The DBMS does not exist in isolation. To enable the users to make the best use of the data resource, the DBMS will have facilities for transferring data to and from the database to other pieces of software: spreadsheets, word processing, graphics packages.

Answers

1 (a) the data description language is used to specify the sub-schemas.
(b) the physical location of the data is described by means of the data description language.
(c) the data manipulation language may be an extension of a normal programming language such as Cobol.
(d) the entities and their relationships are defined in the data description language.
(e) the security is imposed on the files by means of the data description language.
(f) a query language is used for one-off enquiries.
(g) the programmer will write his/her programs using the data manipulation language.

2 The following situations are amongst the numerous possibilities:
  (a) there may be no reason why someone in the library, say, should have any knowledge of the student record files.
  (b) we have already implied that the Dean's secretary is responsible for the data on the files and must therefore have complete access.
  (c) a student may be permitted to look at his/her examination results but there is no requirement for him/her to be able to change those results.
  (d) a student may be permitted check that his name and address are correct but not be permitted to look at the private comments which the lecturers or examiners made about his/her performance.
  (e) a student can look at his/her own record but not those of other students.
3 The situation implies that the manager needs to know the *current* stock, not the stock at the close of business yesterday. A query language would be more appropriate than a program written in the data manipulation language.
4 A program written in a data manipulation language.
5 A query language.
6 The DBA uses a data description language.
7 A program written in a data manipulation language would be needed to change the appropriate record.
8 A data description language would be used to change the definition of the credit limit field. The DBA might also need a program written in a data manipulation language to change the data occurrences in every case.
9 Since there are special processing requirements, it may be quite feasible to use a query language here instead of an application program written in a data manipulation language.

7: Network databases

Objectives

After reading this chapter, you should be able to:
- describe the features of a network database
- define and use the terms *record type, data item, area, set, set type, vector, repeating group, owner* and *member*
- describe a possible physical representation of a network database
- describe the way in which relationships may be represented by physical links maintained by the database
- describe the ways in which the data manipulation language allows the user to navigate through the DSD
- recognize the data manipulation statements which support a network database.

A network database organizes its data as a series of records linked one to another within their relationships. It is essentially a plex structure and represents a very close model of the relationships which we discussed in Chapter 3.

The network model and the programming languages which support it were originally defined in 1971 by the Data Base Task Group (DBTG) of CODASYL (the Conference On DAta SYstems Languages), the people who gave us Cobol, and consequently, it is often known as the Codasyl network model or the DBTG model. Codasyl gave no precise indication of *how* the requirements would be implemented in the physical environments. This was left up to the individual hardware and software suppliers. Like most committee work, the reports of the DBTG are continuing projects, and the brief summary offered here indicates the general features of a Codasyl database.

Extensions have been made to a number of standard programming languages to enable them to manipulate a network database in a manner which closely aligns with the logical models we met earlier. These languages called *host languages* include Cobol, Fortran and Pascal, and they all use similar commands to support network databases. The original CODASYL report used Cobol as the host language.

BOOK					
ACQUISITION NUMBER	TITLE	AUTHOR	CLASSIFICATION	DATE	PRICE

Figure 7.1 The record type—BOOK

There are many commercial implementations of network DBMSs: IDS II from Honeywell; DMS II and DMS 1100 from Unisys; DBMS 10 and DBMS 11 from DEC; IMAGE from Hewlett-Packard; IDMS from Cullinet Software.

The vocabulary for network databases

The data within a network database is organized into *records*, and records are grouped into *record types*. Each record type has a name. On a college database, for example, we might have record type STUDENT, record type COURSE and so on. The records are made up of *data items* (equivalent to fields or attributes). Figure 7.1 shows the record type BOOK which might form a part of the library database.

Any data item may have multiple values: for example, a student may have many books on loan. A data item with multiple values is called a *vector*. A set of repeated data items is called a *repeating group*. Figure 7.2 illustrates some instances of vectors for the record type STUDENT-LOAN and repeating groups for the data item EXAMINATIONS within the record type EXAM-RESULTS.

Any data item may be a *virtual data item*. This is equivalent to the *virtual fields* which we met in Chapter 4.

Relationships

All the data within the database is described by a *schema*. The various record types within the schema are are grouped together into *areas* (these are also called *neighbourhoods* or *realms*). Within any one schema, such as that of a large company, there may be several areas: a WAGES area—personnel, salary rates, pensions and job codes; an ACCOUNTS area—customers, orders, products, prices and invoices.

The word *set* is used to describe what we know as relationships. Most relationships are of the many-to-many and the one-to-many type and relationships between record types in any one area are described by

STUDENT-LOAN	
STUDENT	BOOKS-ON-LOAN
89/1911	192834
	293745
	463529

(a) BOOKS-ON-LOAN - a vector

EXAMINATION-RESULTS					
		EXAMINATIONS			
STUDENT	DEGREE	EXAM	DATE	RESULT	RESIT
89/1911	B.Sc	PT1	23/5/88	89	N
		PT2	22/5/89	44	Y
		PT2	13/11/89	69	N

(b) EXAMINATIONS - a repeating group

Figure 7.2 Repeating values

set types, exactly like those we met in our data structure diagrams. The *owner* record type is at the *one* end of the relationship and the *member* record type is at the *many* end. Note that the network handles many-to-many relationships without any need to simplify them by resolving them into two one-to-many with an artificial link record type.

To illustrate this, let us look at the data model for an ACCOUNTS area shown in Figure 7.3.

The record types are: CUSTOMER, SALES-ORDER, PRODUCT, and ORDER-LINE. These are shown in Figure 7.4. Note that each record type describes the structure of the records which fall within that record type.

It is convenient to use the same names for the sets as for the names of the relationships in the data structure diagram: SENDS-IN, CONSISTS-OF and IS-ORDERED-ON.

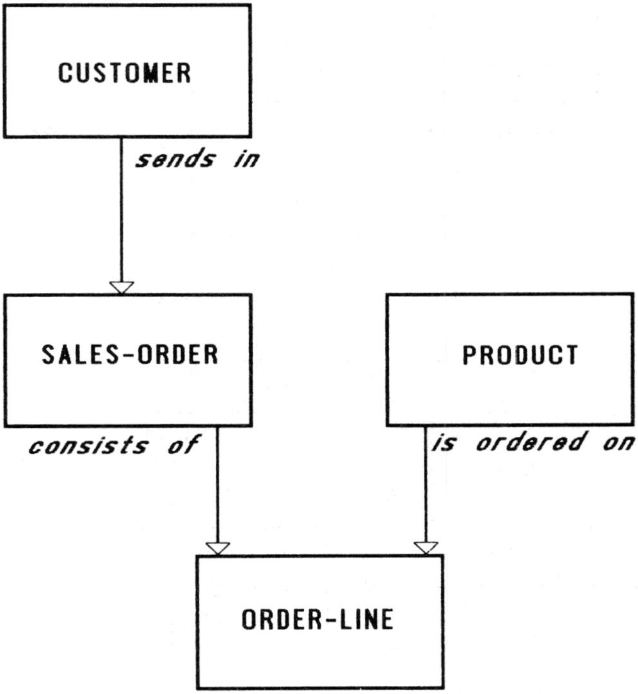

Figure 7.3 Data model for the ACCOUNTS system

Activity 1

Complete the following table to show the words which are used in connection with network databases and their equivalent in other areas of data processing:

Standard data processing	*Network databases*
File	
Record	
Field	
Relationship	
Repeating value	
Repeating group	

CUSTOMER		
Client-number	Client-name	Client-address

SALES-ORDER			
Order-Number	Order-Date	Delivery-Date	Order-Value

PRODUCT		
Product code	Product-name	Product-price

ORDER-LINE			
Order-Number	Product-Number	Order-Quantity	Line-Value

Figure 7.4 The record types for the ACCOUNTS system

Figure 7.5 illustrates the way in which a network database organizes its physical records to simulate the set (relationship).

a) Diagram (a) shows a single CUSTOMER record—that for CUSTOMER 1285. This is the *owner* of an occurrence (or instance) of the set SENDS-IN. As yet, there are no member records, so this is an *empty set.*
b) When CUSTOMER 1285 sends in a sales order—order number 1636—this will be linked in as a member of the SENDS-IN set. The DBMS maintains the necessary fields within the data records to link CUSTOMER 1285 to SALES-ORDER 1636, and this in turn is linked backed to the owner CUSTOMER, as shown in diagram (b).

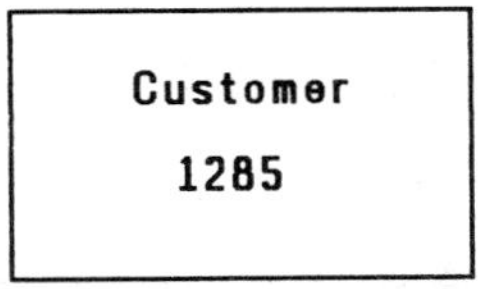

(a) : An empty set - SENDS-IN

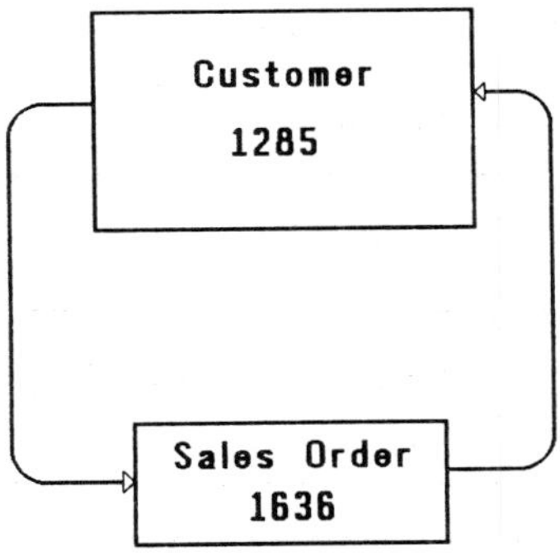

(b) : SENDS-IN with one member

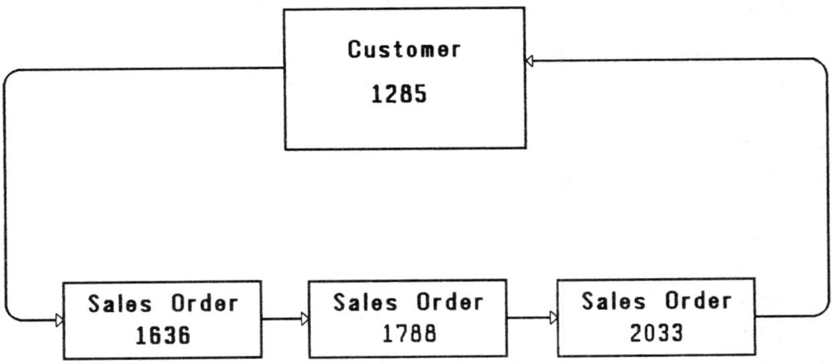

(c) : SENDS-IN with one member

Figure 7.5 Relationships as physical links *continued*

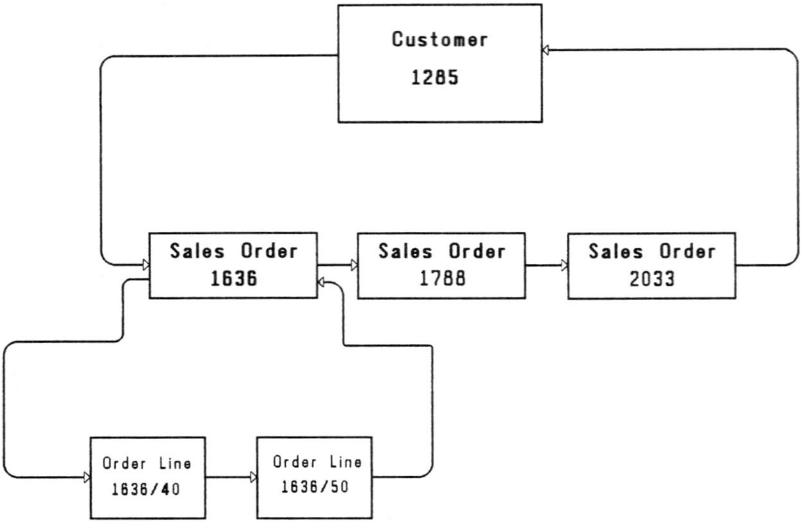

(d) : CONSISTS-OF for owner 1636

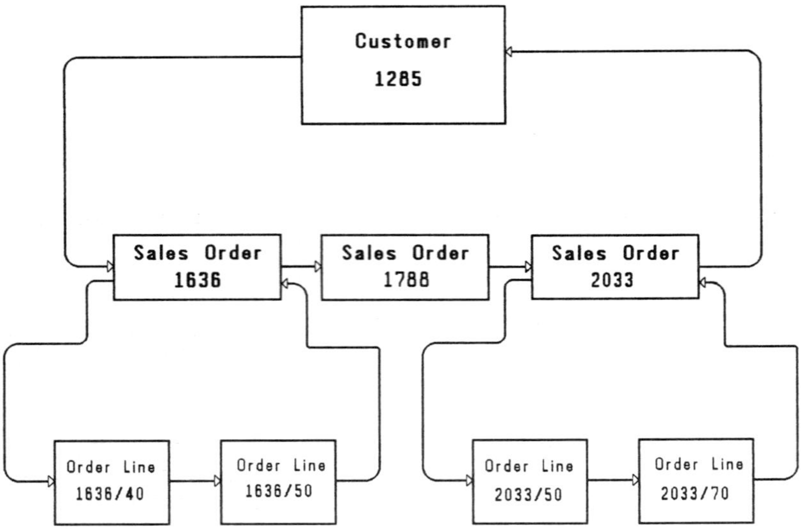

(e) : CONSISTS-OF - two occurrences

continued

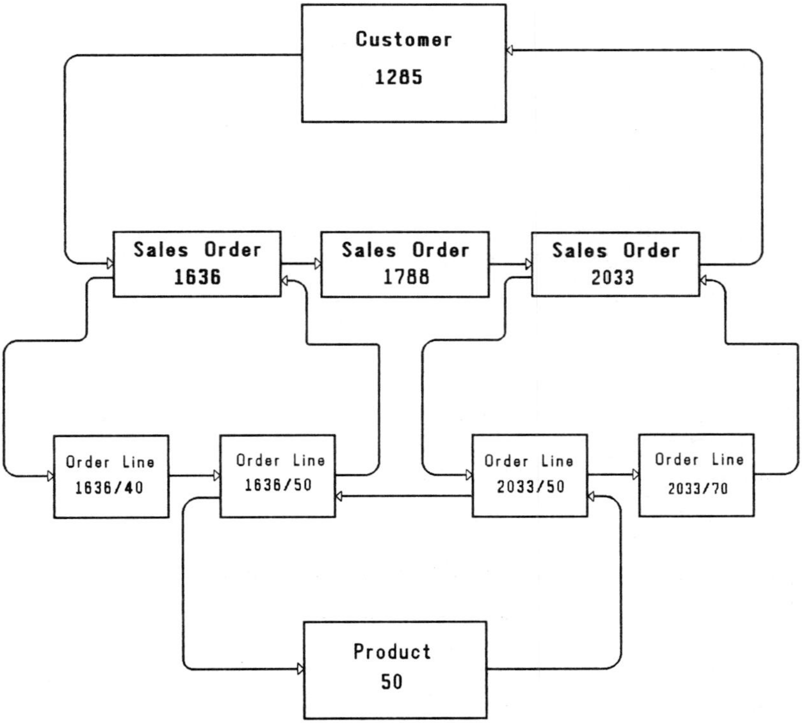

(f) IS-ORDERED-ON for owner 50

Figure 7.5 – *continued*

c) As CUSTOMER 1285 sends in more SALES-ORDER records, these too are linked in to the SENDS-IN set—first SALES-ORDER 1788 , then SALES-ORDER 2033, as shown in diagram (c).
d) But we must remember that each SALES-ORDER consists of a number of sales ORDER-LINEs. Let us imagine that order number 1636 contains two order lines: one for product 40 and one for product 50. Diagram (d) shows how ORDER-LINEs 1636/40 and 1636/50 will be linked into the CONSISTS-OF set, with SALES-ORDER 1636 as the owner and the separate ORDER-LINEs as the members of the set. For convenience, we have given identifiers such as 1636/40 to the order line to remind us that this order-line is for order number 1636 and for product number 40.
e) Diagram (e) shows further occurrences of the ORDER-LINEs linked into the set CONSISTS-OF, this time with ORDER-LINE 2033/70 as the owner and ORDER-LINEs 2033/70 and 2033/50 as the members.

f) Finally, in diagram (f), we remind ourselves that the order-lines are members of two sets: CONSISTS-OF and IS-ORDERED-ON. This means that all order lines for the same product are also members of the set IS-ORDERED-ON with PRODUCT 50 as the owner and ORDER-LINEs 1636/50 and 2033/50 as the members.

The DBMS will take care of all the necessary linkage between the various members of the sets:

- Linking all the SALES-ORDERs in as members of an occurrence of the set SENDS-IN with their appropriate owner CUSTOMER record,
- Linking all the ORDER-LINEs as members of an occurrence of the set CONSISTS-OF with their appropriate owner SALES-ORDER record,
- Linking all ORDER-LINEs as members of an occurrence of the set IS-ORDERED-ON with their appropriate owner PRODUCT record.

There will, of course, be a great many customers, each sending in a great many sales-orders, and these will in turn consist of a great many order-lines. Further, these order-lines will be members of the IS-ORDERED-ON set attached to the appropriate product record.

Activity 2

This activity concerns the CUSTOMER, SALES-ORDER, ORDER-LINE and PRODUCT entities shown in Figure 7.5. Add the following occurrences to the diagrams shown there.

1 Sales order number 1788 has two order lines: one for product number 40 and one for product number 70. Add the necessary members of the CONSISTS-OF set.
2 Add the IS-ORDERED-ON set which has product number 40 as its owner, and link in all the members of that set.
3 A new customer, number 3220 is added to the database. No orders have yet been received from this customer.
4 Customer 3220 sends in an order (number 6788) for products 40, 50 and 70. Add the required members and set occurrences.
5 Link all the members to their correct owners within the SENDS-IN, IS-ORDERED-ON and CONSISTS-OF sets.

A record type which is a member of more than one set as with the ORDER-LINE which is owned by relationships to both the SALES-

CUSTOMER

Client Number	Client Name	Client Address	SENDS-IN link

SALES-ORDER

Order Number	Order Date	Delivery Date	Order Value	SENDS-IN line	CONSISTS-OF link

PRODUCT

Product Code	Product Name	Product Price	IS-ORDERED-ON link

ORDER-LINE

Order Quantity	Line Value	CONSISTS-OF link	IS-ORDERED-ON link

Figure 7.6 Using link-fields to represents sets

ORDER (within the CONSISTS-OF relationship) and the PRODUCT (within the IS-ORDERED-ON relationship)—will have *several* sets of link fields to show these relationships.

Figure 7.6 shows what might be the true physical content of the records in an implementation of a network database. The various link fields are used to indicate the next member of the appropriate set.

Note that, since the DBMS maintains all the necessary linkage between the members of a set and the owner, it is not absolutely necessary to hold the product number within the order line record as we have done.

Because of the way in which the owner and the members of a set are linked together, the names *ring structure* and *multi-ring structure* are sometimes used to describe a network database.

Activity 3

You are involved in the development of a lending library system. A systems analyst has developed the DSD shown in Figure 7.7. The data held in each record type is shown in diagram (b) and some instances are shown in diagram (c).

Perform the following:

1 Draw a diagram, similar to that in Figure 7.5 showing how the records for student 90/1005 might be linked to the LOAN-HISTORY records within the BORROWING relationship.

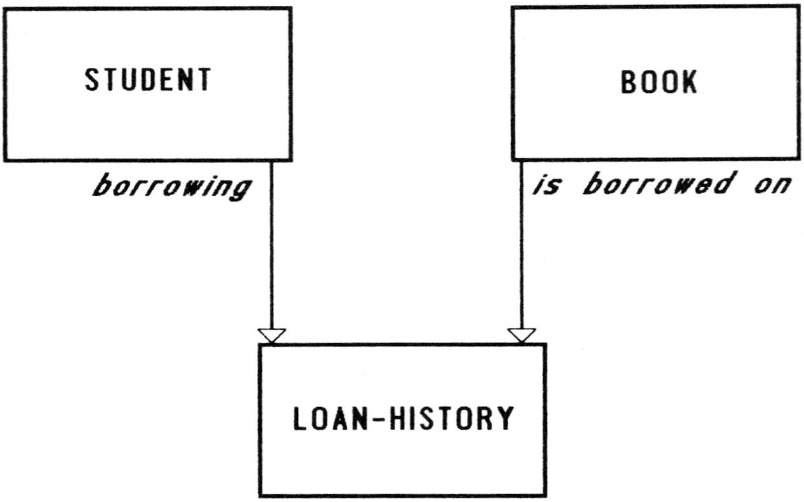

(a) Data structure diagram

Figure 7.7 Data model for a library system

2 Modify your diagram to include the BOOK records within the IS-BORROWED-ON relationship.
3 Repeat this to show the records for student 90/1006.

In this example, we have not included the student-number or the book-number in the LOAN-HISTORY records, since we are assuming that we shall be using a DBMS which will handle all the linkage for us, and in such cases it will not be necessary to hold this additional data in the record.

Clearly, the data description language and the data manipulation languages for a network DBMS have to describe and handle the various requirements in detail:

- The format of the record types,
- The relationships between them,
- The participants in the relationships,
- The manner in which new members are to be added to a relationship,

STUDENT

STUDENT REGISTRATION NUMBER	STUDENT NAME	DATE OF ENTRY

BOOK

ACQUISITION NUMBER	TITLE	AUTHOR

LOAN-HISTORY

LOAN SEQUENCE NUMBER	DATE BORROWED	DATE DUE BACK

(b) The entities

STUDENT

90/1005	SWIFT, J	09/10/89
90/1006	WALTON, I	09/10/89

BOOK

194432	DUNESHIFT	POE
192283	ON THE EDGE	WELDON
195622	PICKWICK PAPERS	DICKENS
203394	MIDNIGHT'S DAY	KING

LOAN-HISTORY

007816	26/05/92	09/06/92
007992	17/06/92	01/07/92
008003	19/08/92	02/09/92
008100	15/09/92	29/09/92
009002	05/10/92	19/10/92
009345	10/11/92	24/11/92

(c) Some instances

- What happens to the members if an owner record is deleted,
- Whether or not a member record can exist without being associated with a particular owner (an optional relationship),
- Whether or not a member can be moved from one relationship to another,

together with the security and other aspects which we identified in Chapter 1.

We shall not go into the detail of the data description language and the data manipulation languages here. The section of coding in Figure

```
SCHEMA NAME IS ACCOUNTS.
AREA NAME IS ORDERING.
RECORD NAME IS CUSTOMER WITHIN ORDERING.
    01 CUSTOMER-NUMBER PICTURE "9999".
    01 CUSTOMER NAME TYPE IS CHARACTER 20.
    01 CUSTOMER-ADDRESS TYPE IS CHARACTER 80.
RECORD NAME IS SALES-ORDER WITHIN ORDERING.
    01 ORDER-NUMBER PICTURE "9999".
    01 ORDER-DATE.
         02 ORDER-DAY PICTURE "99".
         02 ORDER-MONTH PICTURE "99".
         02 ORDER-YEAR PICTURE "99".
    01 DELIVERY-DATE ·
         ACCESS CONTROL LOCK FOR GET IS 'ABCXYZ'.
         02 DELIVERY-DAY PICTURE "99".
         02 DELIVERY-MONTH PICTURE "99".
         02 DELIVERY-YEAR PICTURE "99".
    01 ORDER-VALUE PICTURE "9999V99".
RECORD NAME IS PRODUCT WITHIN ORDERING.
    01 PRODUCT-CODE PICTURE "9999".
    01 PRODUCT-NAME TYPE IS CHARACTER 80.
    01 PRODUCT-PRICE PICTURE "999V99".
RECORD NAME IS ORDER-LINE WITHIN ORDERING.
    01 ORDER-LINE-NUMBER.
        02 ORDER-NUMBER PICTURE "9999".
        02 PRODUCT-NUMBER PICTURE "9999".
    01 ORDER-QUANTITY PICTURE "9999".
    01 ORDER-PRODUCT-NAME TYPE IS CHARACTER 80
       SOURCE IS PRODUCT-NAME.
    01 LINE-VALUE PICTURE "99V99".

SET NAME IS SENDS-IN
    OWNER IS CUSTOMER
         ORDER IS SORTED
    MEMBER IS SALES-ORDER
         ASCENDING KEY IS ORDER-DATE.
SET NAME IS CONSISTS-OF
    OWNER IS SALES-ORDER
         ORDER IS SORTED
    MEMBER IS ORDER-LINE
         ASCENDING KEY IS ORDER-LINE-NUMBER.
SET NAME IS IS-ORDERED-ON
    OWNER IS PRODUCT
         ORDER IS SORTED
    MEMBER IS ORDER-LINE
         ASCENDING KEY IS ORDER-LINE-NUMBER.
```

Figure 7.8 Data description language

7.8 shows an informal example of the data description language (sometimes called just DDL) for a Codasyl area. Such statements will be included in each program which manipulates the data in this area. See if you can identify the purpose of the various clauses in this coding.

Anyone who is familiar with Cobol will recognize much of the style of that language here.

The following parts of the program are of particular interest:

a) The section:

```
01 ORDER-PRODUCT-NAME TYPE IS CHARACTER 80 SOURCE
IS PRODUCT-NAME.
```

within the description of the ORDER-LINE record. This is the way in which the language handles *virtual records*, and indicates that the true data is held in the PRODUCT-NAME field of the PRODUCT record.

b) The clause:

```
ACCESS CONTROL LOCK FOR GET IS 'ABCXYZ'.
```

within the description of the SALES-ORDER record. This illustrates how the security controls—known in this context as *access control locks* and *access control keys*—are applied (perhaps not very realistically in this particular example) to the field DELIVERY-DATE. Whenever an application program attempts to read the ORDER record with a DELIVERY-DATE, there must a statement setting the required lock. Statements such as:

```
MOVE 'ABCXYZ' TO DB-ACCESS-CONTROL-KEY.
USE FOR ACCESS CONTROL ON GET FOR SALES-ORDER.
```

within the data manipulation language might do this.

Adding a member to a set

The data description language must also specify the way in which a new member is to be added to a set. This can be any of:

ORDER IS FIRST
: meaning that the new member is to be added at the front of the chain.

ORDER IS LAST
: meaning that the new member is to be added at the end of the chain.

ORDER IS SORTED
ASCENDING KEY IS ORDER-LINE-DATE

meaning that the new member is to be be sorted amongst the other members such that, in this example, their dates are in ascending order.

Further possibilities are to add the new member before or after a specific member of the set.

Activity 4

1 A network database used by a doctor's surgery contains a set called ATTENDS which represents a relationship between two entities, DOCTOR and PATIENT, such that a DOCTOR ATTENDS many PATIENTs. Using simple boxes such as:

Doctor: [LIVINGSTONE] Patient: [UNDERHILL]

to represent each record type, draw a diagram like those in Figure 7.5 to show the state of the set as each of the PATIENT records for five patients with the names:

ADAMS, WILSON, UNDERHILL, BAKER and MACKINTOSH

are added as members of the set of which DOCTOR Livingstone is the owner. The following specification is included in the schema:

ORDER IS LAST.

Repeat the previous Activity for each of the following specifications:

2 ORDER IS FIRST.
3 ORDER IS SORTED, ASCENDING KEY IS SURNAME.
4 ORDER IS SORTED, DESCENDING KEY IS SURNAME.

Inserting and retaining members

Two further facilities which the data description language provides, although we shall not illustrate them in our examples, are the specifications which describe how the members are of a set are to be added and retained within the set. This is achieved by clauses such as:

INSERTION IS AUTOMATIC

meaning that when a new member record is created, the DBMS is to link it in automatically to the set which it belongs according to the appropriate ORDER IS clause.

INSERTION IS MANUAL
meaning that the programmer will issue a CONNECT statement to link a member into the required set when he/she requires this to be done.

RETENTION IS FIXED
meaning that the member may only ever be attached to that one owner and may not be moved around to another owner of the same set type.

RETENTION IS MANDATORY
meaning that once it has been disconnected from its original owner, a member may be moved around to another owner of the same set type.

RETENTION IS OPTIONAL
meaning that, after it has been disconnected from its original owner, a member record may be held on the database without being attached to any particular owner.

Activity 5

Look at the DSD in Figure 7.3 and the equivalent section of the data description language in Figure 7.8. Now write down:

1 The entity names as they appear in the DSD and indicate how they are represented in the data description language.
2 The relationships as they appear in the DSD and indicate how they are represented in the data description language.
3 How the data description language indicates the order in which the records are added to the relationship.
4 How the data description language indicates which entities on the DSD are involved in each relationship.
5 How the record structure is specified in the data description language.

Currency

An important feature of the data manipulation language is the concept of *currency*. As a program executes, for each record type there will be a *current record*. This is the record of that type which was last located. For example, in the library system mentioned above, there will be a current record for the STUDENT record type, there will be a current record for the BOOK record type, and there will be a current record for the LOAN-HISTORY record type. There are also currency indicators for the different sets and for the different areas within the database. The DBMS uses this concept of currency to retrieve records and to navigate around the data structure.

The data manipulation language

The data manipulation language augments standard Cobol or indeed any other host language—with commands such as:

FIND
: to locate the position of a record on the database, thereby making it the *current record* for that particular record type, for the set and for the area.

GET
: to bring the current record into memory,

STORE
: to write the current record away to the database,

ERASE
: to remove the current record from the database,

MODIFY
: to modify specific data items within the current record,

CONNECT
: to link the current member record into a set,

DISCONNECT
: to remove the current member record from a set,

RECONNECT
: to remove the current member record from one set and link it into another set.

The short sequences in Figure 7.9 illustrates some features of the data manipulation language:

a) Diagram (a) lists the sort of commands which you would expect to find in a language which support network databases.
b) Example (b) illustrates how you might process the current orders for customer 1234. The processing would enter the data structure diagram at the CUSTOMER file looking for customer-number

1234. If this were successful, then it would descend the SENDS-IN relationship to find the first of the SALES-ORDERs which were linked to the CUSTOMER.

It might help to read this and the following section of coding in conjunction with the DSD shown in Figure 7.3.

c) Example (c) finds product, then all the ORDER-LINEs for that PRODUCT, then the SALES-ORDER to which that ORDER-LINE

```
CONNECT
DISCONNECT
ERASE
ERASE ALL
ERASE PERMANENT
ERASE SELECTIVE
FIND ... WITHIN ... USING
FIND ANY
FIND CALC ... {To use a record-key supplied by the program}
FIND CURRENT ... WITHIN
FIND DBKEY IS
FIND DUPLICATE
FIND FIRST .. WITHIN
FIND LAST ... WITHIN
FIND NEXT ... WITHIN
FIND NTH ... WITHIN
FIND PRIOR ... WITHIN
GET
MODIFY
RECONNECT
STORE
```

(a) Some data manipulation statements

```
MOVE '1234' TO CUSTOMER-NUMBER.
FIND ANY CUSTOMER.
GET CUSTOMER.
FIND FIRST SALES-ORDER RECORD WITHIN SENDS-IN.
GET SALES-ORDER.
PERFORM PROCESS.ORDER.RECORD.
```

(b) process order records.

```
MOVE '9002' TO PRODUCT-CODE.
FIND ANY PRODUCT.
GET PRODUCT.
FIND FIRST ORDER-LINE WITHIN IS-ORDERED-ON.
GET ORDER-LINE.
FIND OWNER ORDER WITHIN CONSISTS-OF.
GET ORDER.
FIND OWNER CUSTOMER WITHIN SENDS-IN.
GET CUSTOMER.
```

(c) find the customer who sent in an order for a given product.

Figure 7.9 Data manipulation language

belongs, then the CUSTOMER who submitted that SALES-ORDER. This is identical to the navigation which we saw in Chapter 3.

Query languages and networks

A network database differs from a relational database in a number of ways. One of the most significant is that the network DBMS processes one record at a time, whereas a relational DBMS allows us to process and interrogate the entire file (relation) at once. For this reason, the concept of query languages here is quite different from that which we shall encounter when we look at Access, dBASE, QBE and SQL on relational databases.

All queries on network databases must be resolved by means of a specially written program in the data manipulation which is available.

Questions

Answer these questions about network database management systems.

1 What is a host language?
2 Is there a data description language?
3 Is there a data manipulation language?
4 Are the data description language, the data manipulation language and the query language identical?

Recap

A network database organizes its data as a series of records linked one to another within their relationships. This can be visualized as a plex structure and allows us to represent our data structure diagram very accurately.

The network model and the programming languages which support it were originally defined by the Data Base Task Group of CODASYL and a network database is often known as the Codasyl network model.

The data within the entire database comprises a schema. The various record types within the schema are are grouped together into areas.

The word set is used to denote a relationship. The relationships are of the many-to-many and the one-to-many type and relationships between record types in any one area are described by set types. The owner record type is at the one end of the relationship and the member record type is at the many end.

Sets—the relationships between entities—are represented by a circular linked series of records, starting with the owner of the set and connecting each member record in the required sequence, finally returning back to the owner.

The DBMS maintains all the necessary linkage and pointer records to support the physical structure.

A record type may be a member of more than one set and there will be several link fields within the records to show these relationships.

Because of the way in which the owner and the members of a set are linked together, the names ring structure and multi-ring structure are sometimes used to describe a network database.

The data definition language DDL is used to describe the schema, the records and the sets, and to control the security aspects of the DBMS. The data manipulation language is used by the programmer to process the data on the database. The data manipulation language is made up of a number of extra facilities embedded within a host language such as Cobol, Fortran and Pascal. These allow the programmer all the usual file-handling capabilities as they apply to the newtork structure of the database.

We looked at examples of both languages.

Within the data manipulation language, there are very simple facilties for navigating through the data structure.

Queries on network databases are resolved by means of a specially written program in the data manipulation language.

Answers

1 This is a standard programming language to which special statements and routines have been added to support the database.
2 This is performed by means of the standard data and variable definition facilities of the host language.
3 Only by adding extra facilities to the host language.
4 Yes, they are all performed by the host language.

8: Hierarchical databases

Objectives

After reading this chapter, you should be able to:

- describe the features of a hierarchical database
- describe and use the terms *segment* and *segment type*
- resolve a plex structure into a tree structure.
- describe and use the terms *hierachical level* and *path*
- describe the meaning of *virtual child* and *virtual parent*.

A hierarchical database organizes its data as a set of *tree-structures*. These may be visualized in exactly the same way as the trees which we saw in Chapter 4.

IBM's Information Management System (IMS) and the Control Data Corporation's Multi-access Retrieval System (MARS) are two examples of commercial hierarchical database systems.

The vocabulary for hierarchical DBMS

The chief elements of a hierarchical DBMS are the *segment* and the *parent-child relationship*.

A segment is equivalent to the *node* of a tree structure, or to the entities which we encountered in our data structure diagrams. Segments are grouped into *segment types*, and each segment type has a name. On a college database, for example, we might have segment type STUDENT, segment type COURSE and so on. The segments are made up of *fields* or *data items*.

As you might have anticipated, a parent-child relationship is a one-to-many relationship between two segment types, exactly like those of our data structure diagrams. The *parent* segment type is at the *one* end of the relationship and the *child* segment type is at the *many* end.

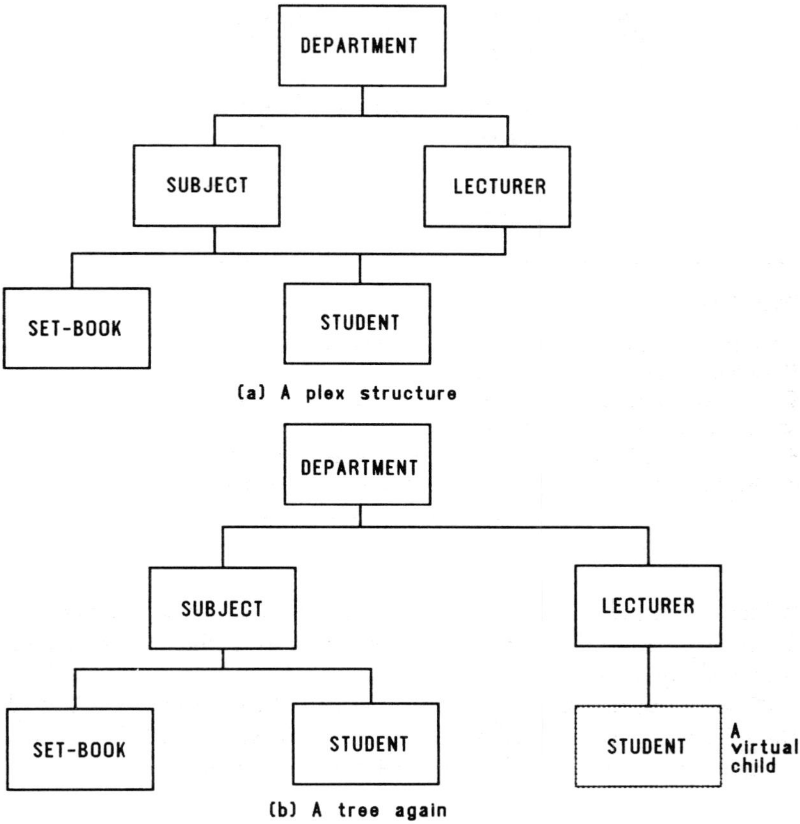

Figure 8.1 Resolving a plex structure into trees

In general, a segment may be the child of only *one* parent-child relationship, but it may be the parent in *any number of* (or no) parent-child relationships. In a moment, we shall see that there may be further constraints on the structure of the tree.

Activity 1

Complete the following table to show the words which are used in connection with hierarchical databases and their equivalent in other areas of data processing:

Standard data processing	*Hierarchical databases*
File	
Record	
Field	
Relationship	

Trees not plexes

The above rules mean that a hierarchical database cannot represent many-to-many relationships nor plex structures in which a child may have more than one parent. These must be simplified before they can be implemented by a hierarchical database. The solution is to resolve a plex structure into a tree. This can be achieved by duplicating a child node which is present in more than one relationship, as shown in Figure 8.1(b).

The potential duplication of data which this is implies is avoided by using virtual records or pointer records, as we discussed in Chapter 4. Such a record is then known as a *virtual child*. In Figure 8.1, we have shown the STUDENT which is the child of the LECTURER as a virtual child.

Activity 2

Look at the structures shown in Figure 8.2, and decided whether they are tree or plex structures. Write down your answer. For simplicity, we have used letters instead of names to identify the segment types.

If a structure is a plex, then resolve it into a tree and indicate any virtual children which your new structure would require.

If they are trees derived from plexes, then revert them to the plexes from which they might have been derived.

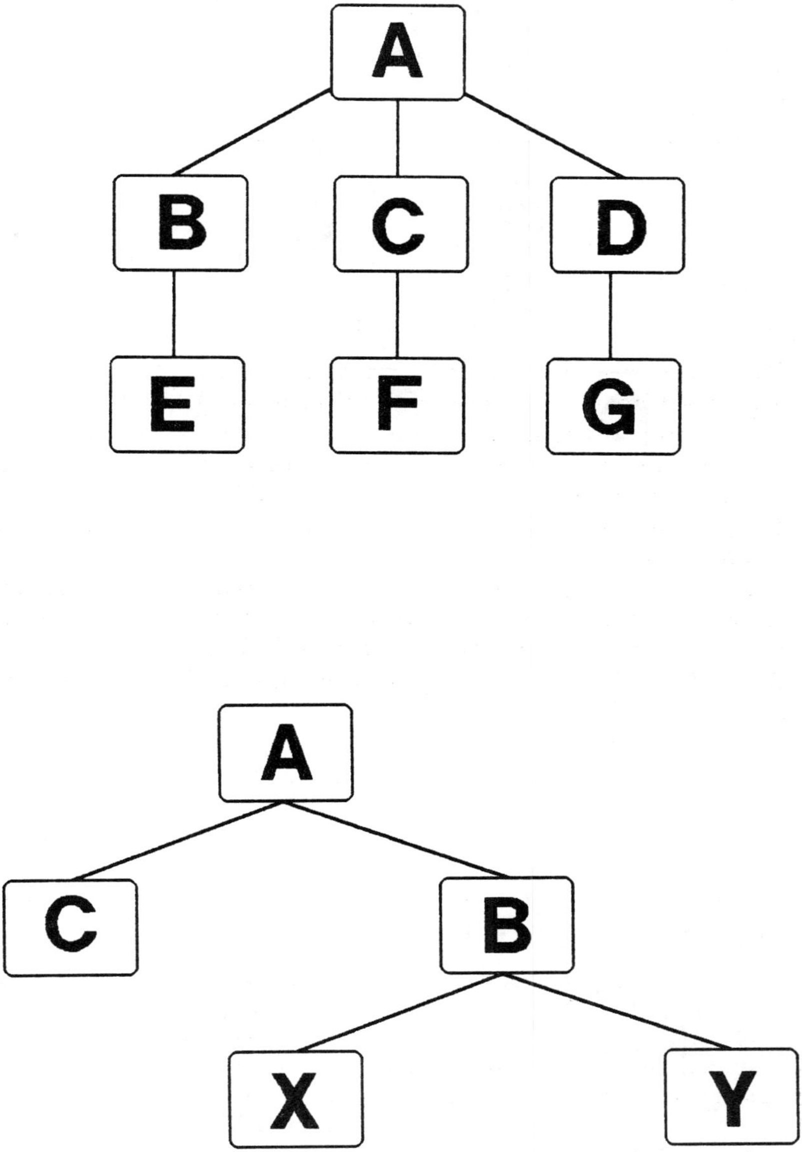

Figure 8.2 Trees or plexes?

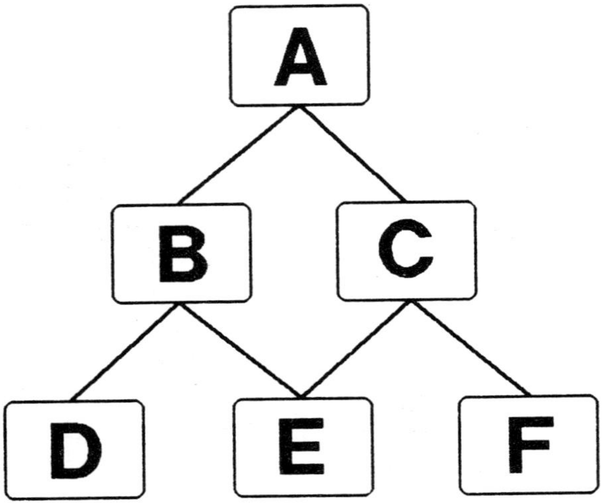
A
B
C
D
E
F

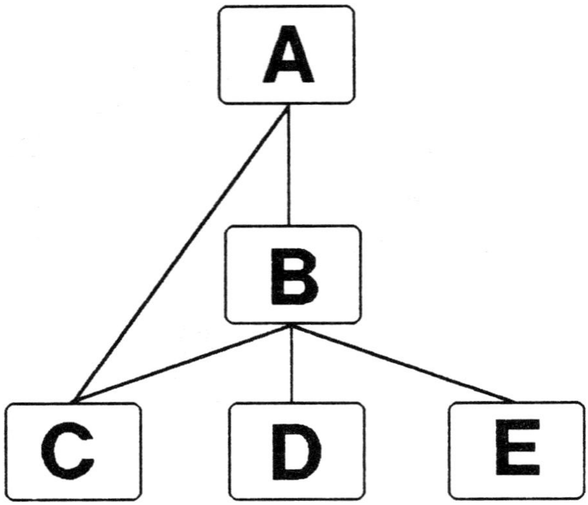
A
B
C
D
E

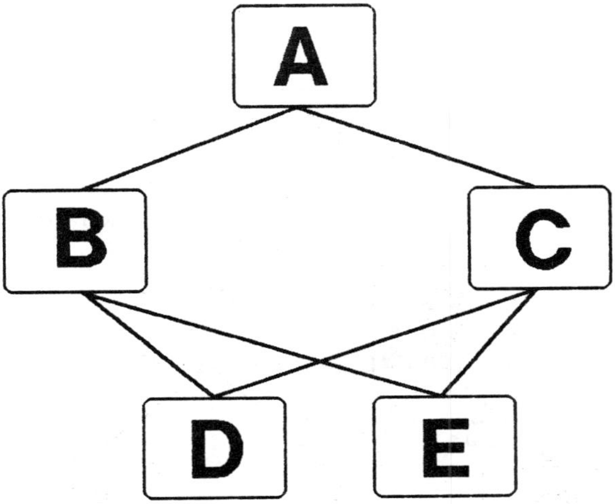
A
B
C
D
E

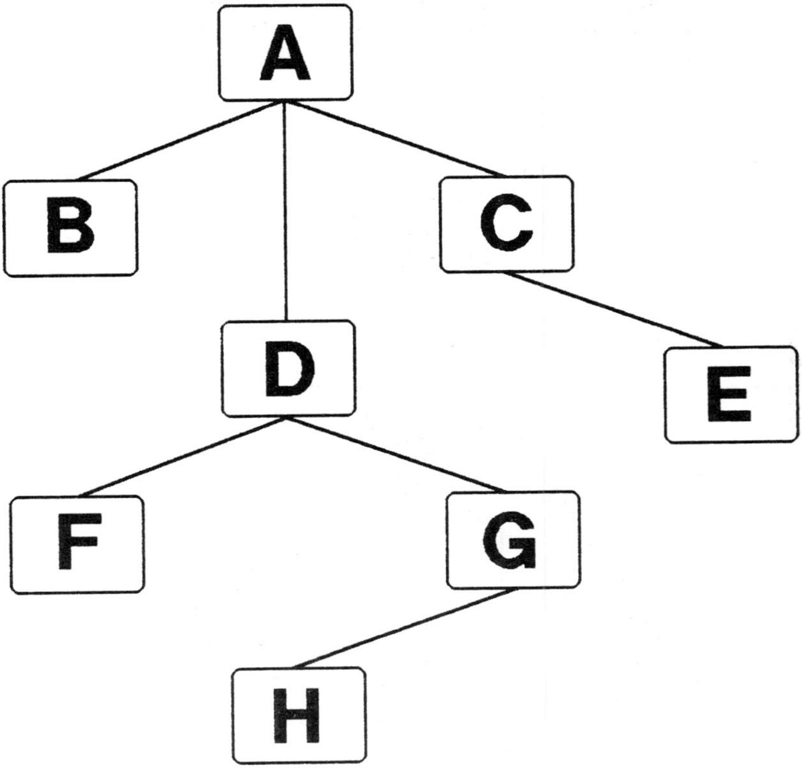
A
B
C
D
E
F
G
H

The number of segments which you pass going from the top to the bottom of a tree is the *hierarchical level*, or the *level* of that tree. The tree shown in Figure 8.1(b) has three levels, since we pass three nodes—DEPARTMENT, SUBJECT and SET-BOOK—in going down the *path* from the top (DEPARTMENT) to one of the bottom nodes (SET-BOOK) of the tree. If there are paths with several different lengths in a particular tree, then the longest path is usually taken to express the level of the tree.

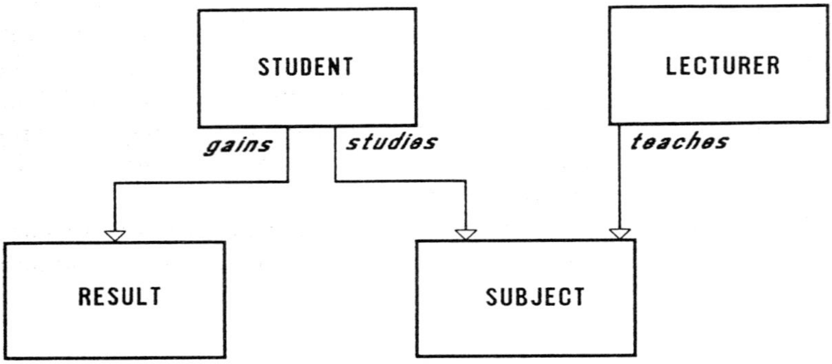

(a) The data structure diagram

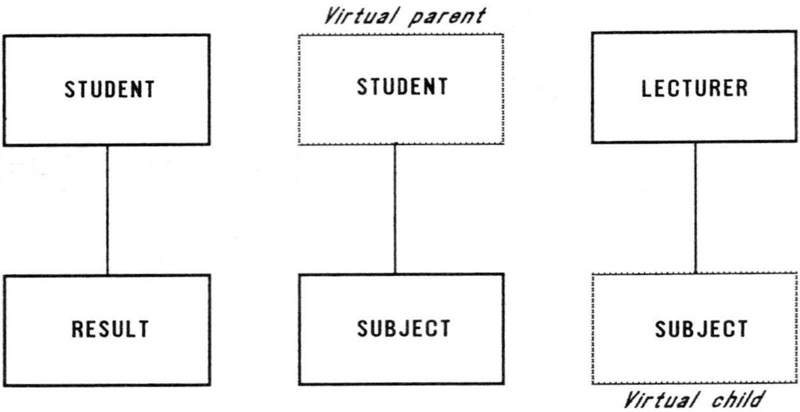

(b) Resolving for a hierarchical database

Figure 8.3 Simple two-level trees

Restrictions on the tree structure

Beyond insisting that the DSD be resolved into a tree structure, the DBMS normally imposes further restrictions on the relationships between the segments: some will handle trees of up to 15 levels; others restrict the number of children which a parent may have; some allow two or more children, as illustrated in Figure 8.1; others allow only structures with two levels, that is with one parent-one child. In such cases, both virtual children and *virtual parents* must be introduced.

We illustrate this is Figure 8.3 where the data structure diagram (a) shows the STUDENT as the parent of both the BOOK and the SUBJECT, and the SUBJECT as the child of both the STUDENT and the LECTURER. If we imagine that—on our particular hierarchical database—a child may have only one parent, and a parent may have only one child, we can resolve the situation with a virtual parent and a virtual child, as shown in diagram (b).

In addition to the restrictions on levels, the number of children and the number of parents, the various hierachical databases may impose

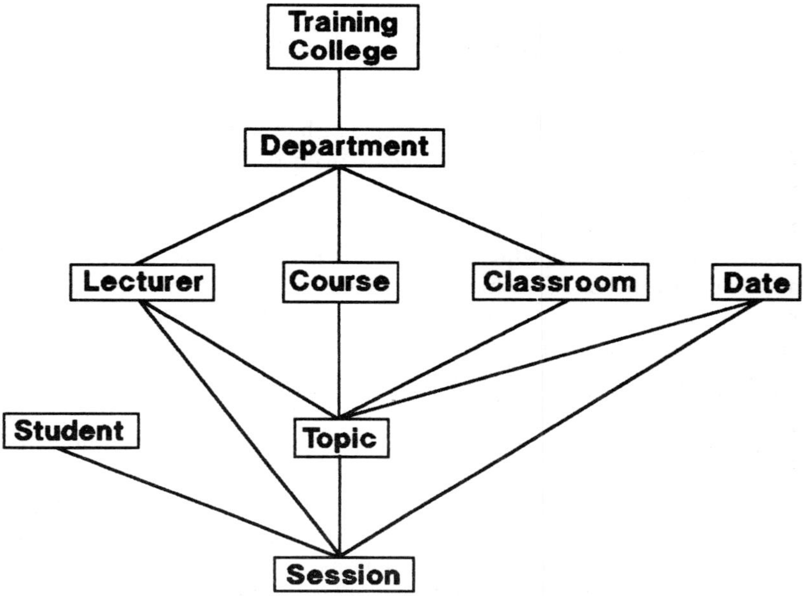

Figure 8.4 Simplifying a structure

other restrictions such as a maximum number of segment types and rules such as a virtual child may not itself have a virtual child. It is the task of the systems analysts, the database designer and the DBA to ensure that a logical data model is suitably organized so as to conform to the requirements of the particular DBMS which is being used.

Activity 3

This activity is based upon the structure shown in Figure 8.4.

1 Resolve the structure into a set of two-level structures in which the parent may have two (or more) children.
2 Resolve the structure into a set of two level structures in which the parent may only have one child.

The physical implementation

To see how hierarchical structures may be implemented, let us look at the data model shown in Figure 8.5(a). The hierarchical schema for this is shown in diagram (b). Some specific occurrences of records within the parent-child relationships are shown in diagram (c); for clarity, we have only shown the significant data items.

The precise way in which these structures are implemented varies according to the DBMS which you are using, and we shall not go into much detail here. As a first step, to visualizing the physical structure, it is convenient to think of the tree arranged as a *structured list*, and then put this into in a form such as you might find in the index to a book, as illustrated in Figure 8.6. The physical model then transposes this directly as a set of linked records. As with network DBMS, the hierarchical DBMS uses flags, pointers and link fields to associate one record with another. The DBMS also includes its own control information. One of the most important pieces of this information is that which identifies the segment type. This is used by the DBMS as it is searching through a hierarchical sequence such as that illustrated here. We show this in Figure 8.6(d).

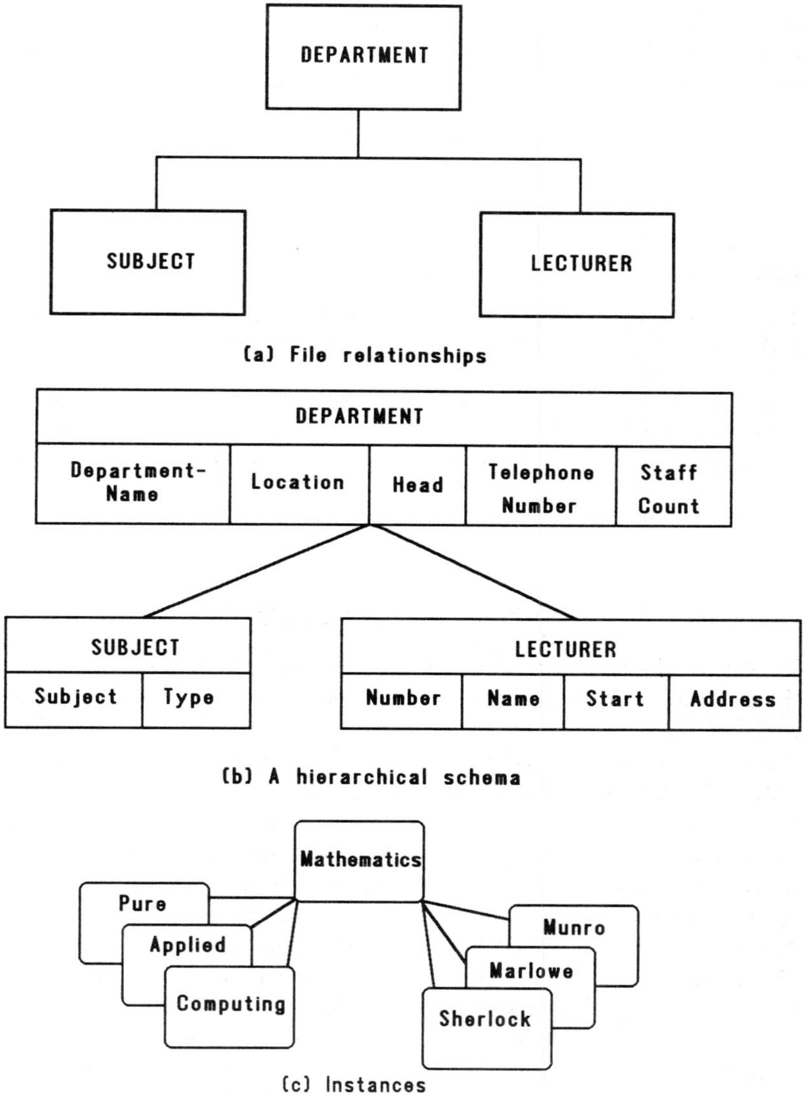

Figure 8.5 Hierarchical database

```
College
|
|______Department
|       |
|       |______Subject
|       |       |
|       |       |______Setbook
|       |       |
|       |       |______Student
|       |
|       |______Lecturer
|
|______Buildings
```

(a) The tree as a structured list

```
1    DEPARTMENT
     1.1      SUBJECT
     1.2      LECTURER
```

(b) A part of the structured list as a CONTENTS LIST

```
1    Mathematics
     1.1.1    Pure
     1.1.2    Applied
     1.1.3    Computing
     1.2.1    Munro
     1.2.2    Marlowe
     1.2.3    Sherlock
```

(c) the instances

Figure 8.6 Physical implementation of a relationship

Activity 4

You have been asked to look into the design of a database for a computer system for a package holiday company. The company arranges holidays in a number of resorts.

Your investigations have revealed the following relationships:

- Each resort is served by a number of flights.
- Each resort has a number of hotels.
- Each hotel has a number of rooms.

Perform the following steps:

1. Make a list of the entities concerned.
2. Draw a data structure diagram which represents these relationships.
3. Re-draw the data structure diagram so that it is suitable for implementation on a hierarchical database which has no restrictions on the number of levels. Indicate any virtual children or virtual parents which this requires.

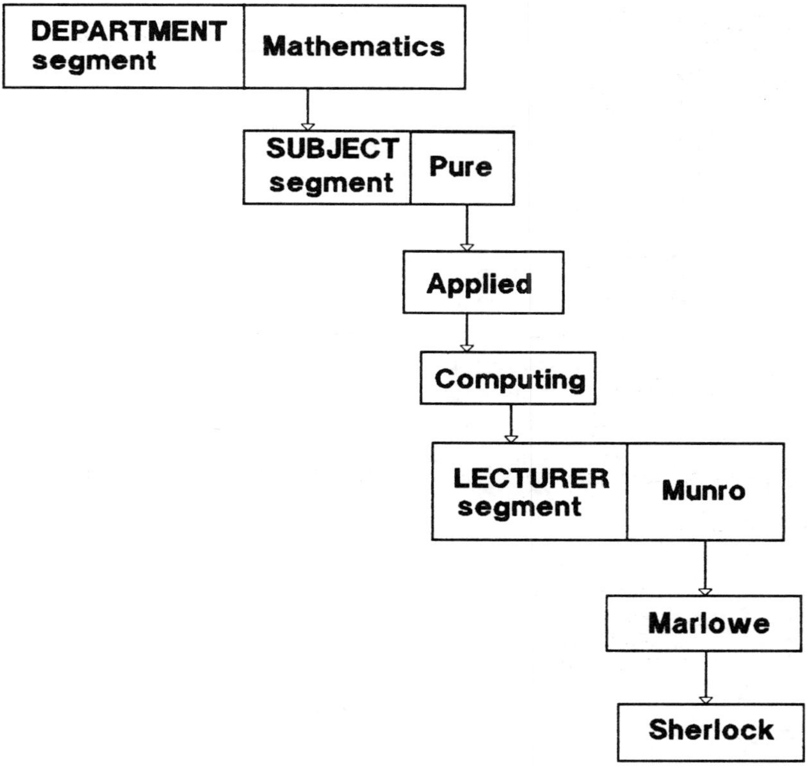

(d) The physical implementation

4 Based upon the information given in the text, show how the following instances might be implemented physically:

Resort: Kardamena
Flights: FG10293
DGF10293
DA3546
Hotels: Grand
Royale
Churchill
Rooms: 10, 20, 25, 26 at the Grand,
15, 27, 38, 199 at the Royale,
100, 101, 102 at the Churchill.

Data description language

The data description language and the data manipulation language of a hierarchical database are embedded within a host language. IBM's CICS and IMS database management systems have a language called DL/1 which performs both the data description and the data manipulation functions and allows the application programmer to embed subroutine calls within a program written in a language such as Cobol, Fortran, PL/1 or even Assembler language. The embedded statements are distinguished from the statements of the host language by preceding them with some identifier, such as a special character or keywords such as DBD and SEGM for the data description language and GET, INSERT and REPLACE for the data manipulation language.

To illustrate this, let us imagine that the data structure which we met earlier has (because of the demands of our particular DBMS) been re-organized into that shown in Figure 8.7. As you see, the physical implementation would eøect the *duplication* of the ORDER-LINE segment by means of *virtual records*.

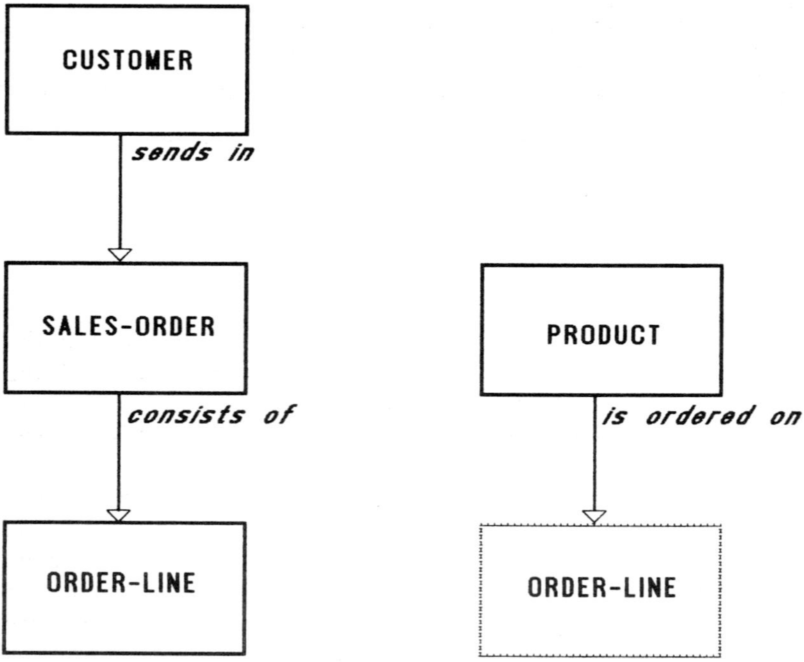

Figure 8.7 Organising a data structure

```
SEGM NAME=CLIENT, BYTES=104
FIELD NAME=CLIENT-NUMBER, BYTES=4, START=1, TYPE=P
FIELD NAME=CLIENT-NAME, BYTES=20, START=5, TYPE=C
FIELD NAME=CLIENT-ADDRESS, BYTES=80, START=25, TYPE=C

SEGM NAME=SALES-ORDER, BYTES=27
FIELD NAME=ORDER-NUMBER, BYTES=4, START=1, TYPE=C
FIELD NAME=ORDER-DAY, BYTES=2, START=5, TYPE=C
FIELD NAME=ORDER-MONTH, BYTES=2, START=7, TYPE=C
FIELD NAME=ORDER-YEAR, BYTES=2, START=9, TYPE=C
FIELD NAME=DELIVERY-DAY, BYTES=2, START=11, TYPE=C
FIELD NAME=DELIVERY-MONTH, BYTES=2, START=13, TYPE=C
FIELD NAME=DELIVERY-YEAR, BYTES=2, START=15, TYPE=C
FIELD NAME=ORDER-VALUE, BYTES=7, START=17, TYPE=C
FIELD NAME=CLIENT-NUMBER, BYTES=4, START=24, TYPE=C

SEGM NAME=ORDER-LINE, BYTES=17
FIELD NAME=ORDER-NUMBER, BYTES=4, START=1, TYPE=C
FIELD NAME=PRODUCT-NUMBER, BYTES=4, START=5, TYPE=C
FIELD NAME=ORDER-QUANTITY, BYTES=4, START=9, TYPE=C
FIELD NAME=LINE-VALUE, BYTES=5, START=13, TYPE=C
```

(a) Describing the segments

```
DBD NAME=ORDERING
SEGM NAME=CUSTOMER, PARENT=0
SEGM NAME=SALES-ORDER, PARENT=CUSTOMER
SEGM NAME=ORDER-LINE, PARENT=SALES-ORDER
SEGM NAME=PRODUCT, PARENT=0
SEGM NAME=ORDER-LINE-2, PARENT=PRODUCT, SOURCE=ORDER-LINE
```

(b) Describing the relationships

Figure 8.8 The DL/1 data description language

The left-hand structure in Figure 8.7 might be represented by the segment descriptions shown in Figure 8.8(a). Compare this with the equivalent CODASYL data description in Figure 7.8. The specification for the individual segments (identified by the keyword SEGM) describes the fields and the length and format of the data.

The physical database description (identified by the keyword DBD) showing the relationships between the segments for both parts of the data structure might be specified as in Figure 8.8(b). Notice how the SOURCE statement allows one part of the database to be accessed from more than one place. This is the way in which *virtual records* are implemented and allows the duplication of data to be controlled and handled consistently.

```
GET UNIQUE CUSTOMER
GET NEXT SALES-ORDER WITHIN PARENT
GET HOLD UNIQUE CUSTOMER
GET HOLD NEXT SALES-ORDER WITHIN PARENT
INSERT SALES-ORDER
REPLACE SALES-ORDER
DELETE SALES-ORDER
```

Figure 8.9 The DL/1 data manipulation language—some statements

---

Activity 5

Using the information shown in Figure 7.8 and the informal language illustrated in Figure 8.8, produce data description statements which would describe the right-hand structure shown in Figure 8.7.

Data manipulation language

Some of the statements which are offered by the DL/1 data manipulation language are illustrated in Figure 8.9. Those instructions which include the word HOLD allow one user to stop another processing the same record and illustrate how DL/1 handles the data concurrency problem. As you see, these resemble conventional Cobol statements and are identified by the keywords GET, INSERT and REPLACE.

Query language

DL/1 offers query language facilities by the use of calls to one of a series of subroutines embedded within the host language program. For example, a request such as:

> 'Produce a list showing the descriptions and prices of all the products which are out of stock and which were ordered more than 30 days ago.'

might by handled by means of a subroutine call such as:

```
CALL SUBDL1("GET", PCB00, IOAREA00,
  "DESCRIPTION","PRICE", "STOCK(LEVEL < '0')",
  "ORDERS(AGE > '30')")
```

We shall not discuss this in detail, beyond the comment that PCB00 and IOAREA00 are the names of variables which the subroutine is to use for program communications and input-output work areas.

Recap

A hierarchical database organizes its data as a set of tree-structures.

The chief elements are the segment and the parent-child relationship. A segment is equivalent to the node of a tree structure, and to an entity of a data structure diagram. Segments are grouped into segment types, and each segment type has a name.

A parent-child relationship is a one-to-many relationship between two segment types. The parent segment type is at the one end of the relationship and the child segment type is at the many end.

A segment may only be the child of one parent-child relationship, but it may be the parent in any number of (or zero) parent-child relationships.

This means that a hierarchical database cannot represent the plex structures in which a child may have more than one parent. The solution to the problem is to resolve a plex structure so that it looks like a tree, duplicating any child node which is present in more than one relationship.

Some DBMSs place further restrictions: for example, a child may only have two parents; the number of segments which you pass going from the top to the bottom of a tree is called the level of that tree—some DBMSs will handle trees of up to 15 levels, whilst others will only handle simple trees; some DBMSs will only allow trees with two levels; some will allow branching trees, whilst other will only allow non-branching structures. In all these situations, any complex relationships must be resolved into the simple permitted structures with the aid of virtual children and virtual parents.

Hierarchical structures are implemented physically as a set of linked records. As with network DBMS, the hierarchical DBMS uses flags, pointers and link fields to identify the segment type and to associate one segment type with another.

The data manipulation language of a hierarchical database is embedded within a host language. The embedded statements are distinguished from the statements of the host language by preceding them with some identifier, such as a special character or keywords.

The query language is represented by a series of subroutines embedded within the host language program.

9: Relational databases

Objectives

After reading this chapter, you should be able to:

- describe the relational model which is used to represent data
- write down some of the properties of relational databases
- recognize some of the constraints which are imposed upon relations
- recognize and use the terms *relation, tuple* and *domain*
- describe the logical meaning of *repeating values* within an attribute
- explain the meaning of *flat file* and *flat record*
- describe the way in which a relational database might be implemented
- recognize the term *foreign key*
- describe the fundamental operations of relational algebra: SELECT, PROJECT, JOIN, PRODUCT, UNION, INTERSECT and DIVIDE
- describe how these operations are used to answer questions about the data base.

The relational model was introduced in the early 1970s by an American called Ted Codd. It was the result of an attempt to produce a precise, formal mathematical representation of data, and has since become widely accepted as a means of modelling and representing data.

A number of commercial implementations of relational databases (RDBMSs) soon appeared: DB2(Database 2) from IBM; INGRES from the University of California, Berkeley and subsequently Relational Technology Inc; ORACLE; UNIFY; RBASE 5000; RIM; RDB; INFORMIX for use on Unix systems; PARADOX.

The vocabulary of relational databases

A relational database is organized as a set of tables of data and a mathematical language—called *relational algebra* is available to manipulate the tables.

Look at the table shown in Figure 9.1. In the context of relational databases, such a presentation of data is known as *a relation*. Each

PERSONNEL

STAFF NUMBER	EMPLOYEE NAME	AGE	EMPLOYEE ADDRESS
0551	MCINTOSH, C	52	391, HIGH ST
1002	WILSON, L	33	92, BROWN RD
1166	BROWN, F	39	689, BROAD AVE
1922	SMITH, J	42	34, HIGH STREET
2298	GREEN, W	29	49, HIGH GROVE
2831	WALKER, C	23	276, BROAD RD
4012	CALLAGHAN, W	38	411, BROWN AVE
4016	WILSON, W	25	19, DERBY AVE
5342	LIVINGSTONE, R	33	572, WESTON RD
5664	CALLAGHAN, I	24	45, WILSON AVE
6069	BROWN, P	37	45, SMITH AVE

tuples

attributes

Figure 9.1 A relation—PERSONNEL

relation has a *name*. Figure 9.1 shows an *instance* of the relation named PERSONNEL.

A relation is made up of a number of *tuples* (rows) and *attributes* (columns). Figure 9.2(a) shows two tuples of the PERSONNEL relation, and Figure 9.2(b) shows two attributes of the relation.

Activity 1

1 Complete the following table to show the words which are used in connection with relational databases and their equivalent in other areas of data processing. If any of the terms are not used in the context of relational databases, you should indicate this.

Standard data processing	*Relational databases*
File	
Record	
Field	
Relationship	
Repeating value	
Repeating group	

The rest of this Activity is based upon the relation shown in Figure 9.3.

1166	BROWN, F	39	689, BROAD AVE

4016	WILSON, W	25	19, DERBY AVE

(a) Tuples (or rows) of the PERSONNEL relation

STAFF NUMBER
0551
1002
1166
1922
2298
2831
4012
4016
5342
5664
6069

AGE
52
33
39
42
29
23
38
25
33
24
37

(b) Attributes (or columns) of the PERSONNEL relation

Figure 9.2 The components of a relation

STOCK

CODE	DESCRIPTION	PRICE	LOCATION	QTY
9000	SIDEBOARD, YELLOW, WOODEN	130.00	MN/14/70	99
5500	TABLE, YELLOW, PLASTIC	50.00	LS/15/77	15
2000	SETTEE, YELLOW, CHROME	100.00	DN/1/69	18
4500	CHAIR, RED, LAMINATE	25.00	MN/3/29	18
1000	DESK, GREEN-BLUE, WOODEN	56.00	LS/17/81	8
7000	DESK, WHITE, WOODEN	56.00	LS/20/49	70
3500	STOOL, WHITE, PLASTIC	20.00	DN/7/80	40
4200	SETTEE, GOLD, WOODEN	10.00	XN/19/35	55
2500	TABLE, GREEN, LAMINATE	50.00	LS/11/76	48
6000	SIDEBOARD, GOLD, CHROME	130.00	MN/3/66	0
8500	TABLE, ORANGE, LAMINATE	50.00	LS/5/50	57
5000	SETTEE, ORANGE, WOODEN	10.00	DN/19/3	24
1500	CHAIR, ORANGE, PLASTIC	25.00	MN/6/13	33
2200	SETTEE, BROWN, CHROME	10.00	DN/1/43	36
1200	DESK, GREY, WOODEN	56.00	LS/17/1	16
7500	CHAIR, BLACK, PLASTIC	25.00	MN/4/82	85

Figure 9.3 A relation—STOCK

1 Write down the name of the relation.
2 Write down two tuples of the relation.
3 Write down two attributes of the relation.

Domains

The values which can appear in each column are taken from the *domain* for that attribute. For example, we might have a STUDENT relation showing the NAME, AGE and the DEGREE QUALIFICATION for a set of university graduates:

- The AGE will be in the range 16 to 65, so the domain of the AGE attribute will be an integer in the range 16 to 65.
- The domain of the NAME attribute is the set of names of people and consists of an alphabetic surname followed by an initial.
- The domain of DEGREE QUALIFICATIONS is the set of all degree abbreviations of the form BA, BSc, PhD.

You can think of the domain as a *pool* or a *range* of possible values from which the instances of each attribute are drawn. Normally, each attribute is drawn from a different domain.

It is important to know the domain for each attribute so that the programmer—and the DBMS—can determine what is a valid value and what is an invalid value for that attribute.

Questions

Suggest the domain for each of the following attributes and give some typical instances.

1 Telephone numbers
2 National insurance numbers
3 Student names
4 College departments
5 Academic subjects.

The properties of a relation

A relation is defined precisely according to a number of rules. These tell us that:

1 Each relation has a name.
2 No two tuples of a relation can be the same.
3 The order in which the tuples are presented is not important.
4 Each attribute has a unique name.
5 The order of the attributes is significant.

It is possible to present a relation with the attributes in some other order. In this case, according to the strict definition of a relation, the two relations are considered to be different.

In general, however, and in most practical situations, the order of the attributes is usually not important.

6 At the intersection of any tuple and any attribute there is a single value. Because there is only one value, each value in a tuple is said to be an *atomic* (that is, indivisible) value.
7 The values in any one column are all from the same domain.
8 Each tuple is uniquely identified by a single attribute or by a combination of attributes. This identifying attribute(s) is the *key* of that tuple.

This is known as the *key constraint.*

9 The primary key must not be null, otherwise it would not be possible to identify the tuple. This is known as the *entity integrity constraint.*
10 If a value in one relation refers to a tuple in another relation, then the second tuple must exist.

To clarify this, let us imagine that a STUDENT relation contains an attribute which refers to the COURSE relation; then if a particular STUDENT tuple has a value referring to course BA, then there must be a tuple in the COURSE relation with the key BA.

This is known as the *referential integrity constraint.* In most practical situations, referential integrity is imposed by the application program, the programmer writing in checks to ensure that there is a tuple for course BA before creating a STUDENT tuple referring to this course.

A value in a tuple of one relation which is the key to a tuple in another relation is called a *foreign key*. Thus, in our example, the course code BA would be a foreign key within the STUDENT relation because it is the key to a particular tuple in the COURSE relation.

Activity 2

In your own words, describe the meaning of
1 the key constraint
2 the entity integrity constraint
3 the referential integrity constraint.

Degree of a relation

The number of columns in a table is a measure of the *degree* of the relation. A relation of degree 2 is called a *pair*. A relation of degree *n* is called an *n-tuple*. The above relation is of degree 3 that is, a 3-tuple. The number of tuples in a table is a measure of the *cardinality* of the relation. The PERSONNEL relation shown above has a cardinality of 11.

The schema which describes a relation

A relation can be described by a schema of the form:

PERSONNEL(Staff-number, Employee-name, Age, Employee-address)

this shows the name of the relation and the attributes which it contains. The key of which identifies the tuple is *underlined* and the attributes are enclosed in brackets.

If each tuple is identified by a *composite* key made up of more than one attribute, then *all the identifying attributes* will be underlined. For example, we might wish to record the appointments for a doctor. Each appointment might be identified by the date and the time, so a schema to describe this relation might be:

APPOINTMENT(Date, Time, Patient's-name, Remarks, Diagnosis, Medicine-prescribed, Next-visit)

Activity 3

Using the bracket notation introduced above, describe the schemas for
1 the PERSONNEL relation shown in Figure 9.1
2 the STOCK relation shown in Figure 9.3.
Inventing your own data drawn from suitable domains, draw tables representing relations with the following schemas:
3 a table which represents the wards in a hospital:

HOSPITAL-WARD(Ward-number, Building, Number-of-beds, Number-of-side-wards, Name-of-sister-in-charge, Number-of-nurses)

4 a table representing the cars serviced by a garage:

SERVICE-BOOKING(Date, Car-registration-number, Owner's-name, Owner's-address, Owner's-telephone-number, Mileage, Service-identification, Make, Special-remarks, Service-cost, Labour-cost)

Repeating values

An important feature of a relational database is that presented by the atomic property of the data which says that

at the intersection of any tuple and any attribute there is a *single* value.

For this reason, some of the files and entities which we met earlier could not be represented directly as relations. We could not, for example, have a record such as that shown in Figure 9.4(a) which holds information about the books on loan to a student. The instance here shows that student SALMASIUS currently has three books on loan. At any one time a student may have several books on loan. We would depict this by a schema such as:

LOAN (Student-number, Student-name, (Book-number))

We should instead hold this as *three* tuples each with an entry for a single book borrowed by that student. This is illustrated in Figure 9.4(c). Doing this presents us with further problems—notably with duplication of data. In Chapter 10, we shall see how this is resolved by the process of *data normalization*. The schema for the new relation might be represented by the schema:

LOAN-RECORD (Student-number, Student-name, Book-number)

with a composite key made up of the Student-number and the Book-number.

Implementing a relational database

A file which contains records with no repeating values is called a *flat file* and the records themselves are called *flat records*. This term is used to distinguish a set of flat records from the three-dimensional image shown in Figure 9.4(b).

LOAN

STUDENT	STUDENT NAME	BOOKS BORROWED
89/1234	Salmasius	1234 3746 5767

(a) Repeating values

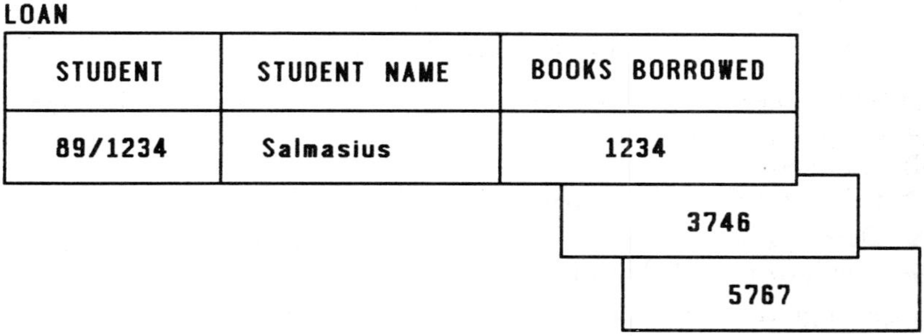

(b) Repeating values - a 3-dimensional image

LOAN

STUDENT	STUDENT NAME	BOOKS BORROWED
89/1234	Salmasius	1234
89/1234	Salmasius	3746
89/1234	Salmasius	5767

(c) Three tuples - as flat records

Figure 9.4 Resolving multiple values into several tuples

Once the data has been reduced to a set of flat records in this manner, it is fairly easy to implement a relation with each tuple becoming a separate physical record. The practical way in which the various rules and constraints are observed—and the reaction of the DBMS if any of the rules are infringed—depends upon the particular DBMS which you are considering.

Processing with relational databases

Before we look at some of the relational DBMSs which are commercially available, we shall look at the formal operations which are provided for the manipulation of such databases. These fundamental operations lie behind the commands and processing which the various data manipulation languages offer.

As we indicated in Chapter 1, the chief processing requirements of a DBMS are that it will allow us to establish relations and to add, change, extract and delete tuples held on the relations. In the context of relations, these operations are:

- Create a new relation
- Add new tuples
- Add new attributes
- Change the value of attributes
- Delete existing tuples
- Display or print the contents of a relation.

Typical data manipulation languages use an operation such as CREATE to establish a new relation, APPEND to add new tuples, REPLACE to change the contents of an attribute, DELETE to remove existing tuples, and DISPLAY to output a specific relation.

All these operations work within the constraints of the security and data integrity imposed on the database. If the user's security does not allow him/her to perform an action on the database, then the request will be rejected. You will see that the formal discussion of relations does not address the problem of security. Real RDBMSs, however, must and do provide features to meet all the requirements which we met in Chapter 6.

Relational algebra

Relations offer far greater processing possibilities than these. In addition to establishing and maintaining the individual tuples, there are also facilities for manipulating entire relations. These operations form what is known as *relational algebra*. Typically, the operations of relational algebra allow us to:

SELECT—extract tuples to form a new relation.
PROJECT—extract attributes to form a new relation.
JOIN—add attributes from one relation to another relation.
PRODUCT—combine all the tuples of one relation will all those of another relation.

UNION—join two relations to form a new relation.
INTERSECT—form a new relation from two relations where the key values are the same.
DIVIDE—extract the tuples from one relation which are identical except for one specific attribute. The required values of that specific attribute are held in another relation.

If you are familiar with the mathematical concept of *sets*, then you will find some of the operations of relational algebra very familiar. The formal language of relational algebra is mathematical in form and differs from that of the commercial RDBMSs. There is also a more formal language—called *relational calculus*—but we shall not discuss that here. For the purposes of explanation, we shall use a stylized form of English to introduce these operations.

Let us illustrate the action of these operations with the aid of the STUDENT relation shown in Figure 9.5.

STUDENT

STUDENT	NAME	ADDRESS	COURSE	RESULT
90/1010	SMITH, P	34 HIGH RD	BIOLOGY	90
90/1020	MARLOWE, C	20 CROMER ST	BIOLOGY	86
90/1030	MURDOCH, I	2 SANDRINGHAM MEWS	MATHEMATICS	90
90/1040	SIDDONS, S	100 HIGH RD	BIOLOGY	50
90/1050	ELIOT, G	1 GAINSBOROUGH RD	PHYSIOLOGY	85
90/1060	BRUNO, G	45 NOLA RD	ART	71

Figure 9.5 A relation—STUDENT

SELECT

The SELECT operation will extract one or more tuples from a relation according to specified conditions to form a new relation. For example, the operation:

BIOLOGISTS = SELECT STUDENT COURSE = BIOLOGY

would select all the tuples from the STUDENT relation which have the value BIOLOGY for the COURSE attribute. These tuples would then be used to produce a new relation called BIOLOGISTS. This is illustrated in Figure 9.6.

BIOLOGISTS

STUDENT	NAME	ADDRESS	COURSE	RESULT
90/1010	SMITH, P	34 HIGH RD	BIOLOGY	90
90/1020	MARLOWE, C	20 CROMER ST	BIOLOGY	86
90/1040	SIDDONS, S	100 HIGH RD	BIOLOGY	50

Figure 9.6 Relational algebra—SELECT

Some further examples of the SELECT operation are:

FIRST-YEAR = SELECT UNDERGRADUATE DATE-JOINED = 1990
RETIRED-MALES = SELECT EMPLOYEE AGE >= 65 AND SEX = MALE
PENSIONER = SELECT EMPLOYEE (AGE > 60 AND SEX = FEMALE) OR (AGE > 65 AND SEX = MALE)

If you are carrying out a complex selection, then it may be simpler to do this in stages. Thus, the second of the above examples could have been produced by the sequence:

RETIRED = SELECT EMPLOYEE AGE >= 65 RETIRED-MALES = SELECT RETIRED SEX = MALE

Activity 4

Using the STUDENT relation and the informal language illustrated above, write down operations which would establish the following relations:

1 A relation called MATHEMATICIANS which includes all the students who are studying mathematics.
2 A relation called PASS which includes all the students who gained a result of 75 or over.
3 A relation called BIOLOGY-PASS which includes all the students who are studying BIOLOGY and who also gained a result of 75 or over.
4 A relation called MEDICAL which includes all the students who are studying BIOLOGY or PHYSIOLOGY or MEDICINE.

In each case, draw the resultant relation.

PROJECT

The PROJECT operation will extract one or more specific attributes from a relation to form a new relation. For example, the operation:

ADDRESS-LIST = PROJECT STUDENT(NAME, ADDRESS)

would select just the NAME and the ADDRESS attributes from all the tuples of the STUDENT relation. These tuples would then be used to produce a new relation called ADDRESS-LIST. This is illustrated in Figure 9.7.

Other examples of the PROJECT operation are:

BIRTHDAY-LIST = PROJECT EMPLOYEE(NAME, DATE-OF-BIRTH, ADDRESS)
SHORT-LIST = PROJECT STUDENT(NAME, COURSE)

ADDRESS-LIST

NAME	ADDRESS
SMITH, P	34 HIGH RD
MARLOWE, C	20 CROMER ST
MURDOCH, I	2 SANDRINGHAM MEWS
SIDDONS, S	100 HIGH RD
ELIOT, G	1 GAINSBOROUGH RD
BRUNO, G	45 NOLA RD

Figure 9.7 Relational algebra—PROJECT

We can also use the PROJECT operation to *re-organize* the attributes of a relation. This is illustrated in Figure 9.8 where we use the operation:

STUDENT-2 = PROJECT STUDENT(NAME, STUDENT, COURSE, RESULT, ADDRESS))

STUDENT-2

NAME	STUDENT	COURSE	RESULT	ADDRESS
BRUNO, G	90/1060	ART	71	45 NOLA RD
ELIOT, G	90/1050	PHYSIOLOGY	85	1 GAINSBOROUGH RD
MARLOWE, C	90/1020	BIOLOGY	86	20 CROMER ST
MURDOCH, I	90/1030	MATHEMATICS	90	2 SANDRINGHAM MEWS
SIDDONS, S	90/1040	BIOLOGY	50	100 HIGH RD
SMITH, P	90/1010	BIOLOGY	90	34 HIGH RD

Figure 9.8 Relational algebra—re-organization with PROJECT

Duplicate tuples

If the PROJECT operation produces duplicate tuples, then—because duplicates are not allowed within the rules governing the relations—only one occurrence is included. This is illustrated in Figure 9.9 where we use the operation:

COURSES = PROJECT STUDENT(COURSE)

to PROJECT just the COURSE attribute of the STUDENT relation. There are several occurrences of BIOLOGY, but only one is included in the resultant relation COURSES.

```
            COURSES = PROJECT STUDENT(COURSE)

                                                  COURSES
 ------------------                               ------------------
 | COURSE         |                               | COURSE         |
 |                |====> duplicate      =====>    |                |
 ------------------      tuples                   ------------------
 | BIOLOGY        |      removed                  | BIOLOGY        |
 | BIOLOGY        |                               | MATHEMATICS    |
 | MATHEMATICS    |                               | PHYSIOLOGY     |
 | BIOLOGY        |                               | ART            |
 | PHYSIOLOGY     |                               |                |
 | ART            |                               ------------------
 |                |
 ------------------
```

Figure 9.9 Duplicate tuples?

Activity 5

Using the HOSPITAL-WARD relation which you developed in Activity 3, write down operations which would establish the following relations:

1 A relation called ACCOMMODATION which includes the Ward-number, the Building and the Number of side wards for all the wards.

2 A relation called BUILDINGS which includes just the Building attribute.

3 A relation called LARGE-WARD which includes the ward number, the building, the name of the sister in charge and the number of beds for all the wards which have more than 20 beds.

In each case, draw the resultant relation.

JOIN

JOIN, or as it is sometimes called the *natural join*, operates on *two* relations and combines those tuples which have a matching field to produce a new relation. You specify which are to be the matching fields.

We can illustrate this by means of the two relations PASS and LECTURER shown in Figure 9.10. We can JOIN these two relations where the tuples have the same values for COURSE (in the PASS relation) and for SUBJECT (in the LECTURER relation), as illustrated in diagram (c).

Cartesian PRODUCT

The action of the JOIN operation may sound rather complicated, but you can think of the process as being carried out in the following manner:

PASS

STUDENT	NAME	COURSE
90/1010	SMITH, P	BIOLOGY
90/1020	MARLOWE, C	BIOLOGY
90/1030	MURDOCH, I	PHYSICS
90/1040	SIDDONS, S	BIOLOGY
90/1050	ELIOT, G	FRENCH
90/1060	BRUNO, G	ART

(a) PASS relation

LECTURER

REF	NAME	SUBJECT
1101	WALSH, A	PHYSICS
2000	BRONTE, E	FRENCH
2003	EVANS, M	GERMAN
3455	COPLEY, E	PHYSICS
6022	MORRIS, W	FRENCH

(b) LECTURER relation

FULL-LIST = JOIN PASS (COURSE) = LECTURER (SUBJECT)

FULL-LIST

STUDENT	NAME	COURSE	REF	NAME	SUBJECT
90/1030	MURDOCH, I	PHYSICS	1101	WALSH, A	PHYSICS
90/1030	MURDOCH, I	PHYSICS	3455	COPLEY, E	PHYSICS
90/1050	ELIOT, G	FRENCH	2000	BRONTE, E	FRENCH
90/1050	ELIOT, G	FRENCH	6022	MORRIS, W	FRENCH

(c) JOINed relation: FULL-LIST

Figure 9.10 Relational algebra—JOIN

1 Combine each tuple of the first relation with each tuple of the second. This produces a large relation known as the *Cartesian product* of the two relations. If there are *n* tuples in the first relation and *m* tuples in the second, then the Cartesian product relation will contain *n* times *m* tuples.
2 Delete those tuples from the Cartesian product in which the specified fields do not match.

With our two relations, PASS and LECTURER, the Cartesian product would be that shown in Figure 9.11. From this would be deleted those tuples for which the COURSE (of the PASS) is not equal to the SUBJECT (of the LECTURER) to produce the FULL-LIST.

The Cartesian product is available as a specific PRODUCT operation on some systems, and is used in operations such as:

CARTESIAN1 = PRODUCT PASS LECTURER

which would produce the relation which we have already mentioned in Figure 9.11.

CARTESIAN1 = PRODUCT STUDENTS LECTURERS

CARTESIAN1

STUDENT	NAME	COURSE	REF	NAME	SUBJECT
90/1010	SMITH, P	BIOLOGY	1101	WALSH, A	PHYSICS
90/1010	SMITH, P	BIOLOGY	2000	BRONTE, E	FRENCH
90/1010	SMITH, P	BIOLOGY	2003	EVANS, M	GERMAN
90/1010	SMITH, P	BIOLOGY	3455	COPLEY, E	PHYSICS
90/1010	SMITH, P	BIOLOGY	6022	MORRIS, W	FRENCH
90/1020	MARLOWE, C	BIOLOGY	1101	WALSH, A	PHYSICS
90/1020	MARLOWE, C	BIOLOGY	2000	BRONTE, E	FRENCH
90/1020	MARLOWE, C	BIOLOGY	2003	EVANS, M	GERMAN
90/1020	MARLOWE, C	BIOLOGY	3455	COPLEY, E	PHYSICS
90/1020	MARLOWE, C	BIOLOGY	6022	MORRIS, W	FRENCH
90/1030	MURDOCH, I	PHYSICS	1101	WALSH, A	PHYSICS
90/1030	MURDOCH, I	PHYSICS	2000	BRONTE, E	FRENCH
90/1030	MURDOCH, I	PHYSICS	2003	EVANS, M	GERMAN
90/1030	MURDOCH, I	PHYSICS	3455	COPLEY, E	PHYSICS
90/1030	MURDOCH, I	PHYSICS	6022	MORRIS, W	FRENCH
90/1040	SIDDONS, S	BIOLOGY	1101	WALSH, A	PHYSICS
90/1040	SIDDONS, S	BIOLOGY	2000	BRONTE, E	FRENCH
90/1040	SIDDONS, S	BIOLOGY	2003	EVANS, M	GERMAN
90/1040	SIDDONS, S	BIOLOGY	3455	COPLEY, E	PHYSICS
90/1040	SIDDONS, S	BIOLOGY	6022	MORRIS, W	FRENCH
90/1050	ELIOT, G	FRENCH	1101	WALSH, A	PHYSICS
90/1050	ELIOT, G	FRENCH	2000	BRONTE, E	FRENCH
90/1050	ELIOT, G	FRENCH	2003	EVANS, M	GERMAN
90/1050	ELIOT, G	FRENCH	3455	COPLEY, E	PHYSICS
90/1050	ELIOT, G	FRENCH	6022	MORRIS, W	FRENCH
90/1060	BRUNO, G	ART	1101	WALSH, A	PHYSICS
90/1060	BRUNO, G	ART	2000	BRONTE, E	FRENCH
90/1060	BRUNO, G	ART	2003	EVANS, M	GERMAN
90/1060	BRUNO, G	ART	3455	COPLEY, E	PHYSICS
90/1060	BRUNO, G	ART	6022	MORRIS, W	FRENCH

Figure 9.11 Relational algebra—PRODUCT

UNION

UNION and *INTERSECT* are used with their usual meaning in the theory of sets. The essential meaning of UNION is *OR*. It operates on two relations and returns those tuples which are present in either or both relations.

GROUP1 = SELECT STUDENT COURSE = BIOLOGY

GROUP1

STUDENT	NAME	ADDRESS	COURSE	RESULT
90/1010	SMITH, P	34 HIGH RD	BIOLOGY	90
90/1020	MARLOWE, C	20 CROMER ST	BIOLOGY	86
90/1040	SIDDONS, S	100 HIGH RD	BIOLOGY	50

GROUP2 = SELECT STUDENT COURSE = PHYSIOLOGY

GROUP2

STUDENT	NAME	ADDRESS	COURSE	RESULT
90/1050	ELIOT, G	1 GAINSBOROUGH RD	PHYSIOLOGY	85

LIFE-SCIENCES = UNION GROUP1 GROUP2

LIFE-SCIENCES

STUDENT	NAME	ADDRESS	COURSE	RESULT
90/1010	SMITH, P	34 HIGH RD	BIOLOGY	90
90/1020	MARLOWE, C	20 CROMER ST	BIOLOGY	86
90/1040	SIDDONS, S	100 HIGH RD	BIOLOGY	50
90/1050	ELIOT, G	1 GAINSBOROUGH RD	PHYSIOLOGY	85

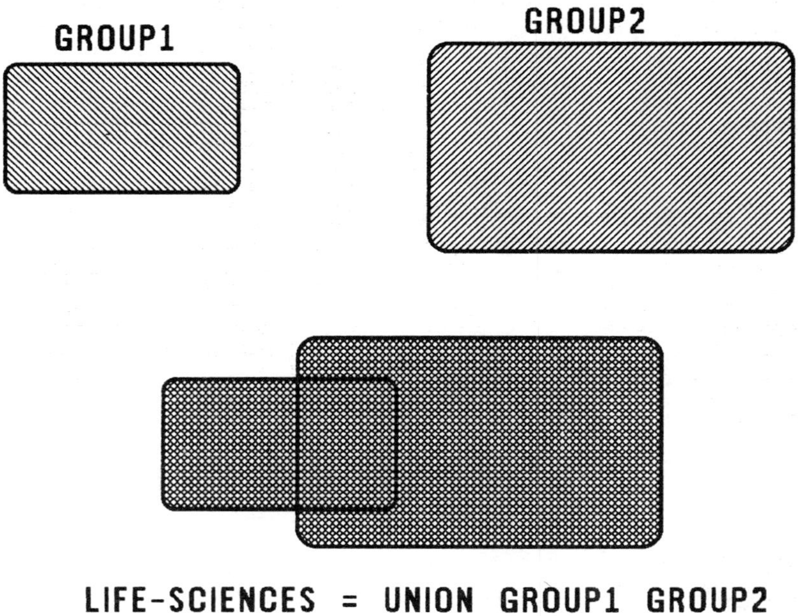

Figure 9.12 Relational algebra—UNION

Starting with the STUDENT relation—shown in Figure 9.5—we might use the UNION operation to produce a list of those students who are studying either BIOLOGY or PHYSIOLOGY. This is illustrated by the sequence of operations:

GROUP1 = SELECT STUDENT COURSE = BIOLOGY
GROUP2 = SELECT STUDENT COURSE = PHYSIOLOGY
LIFE-SCIENCES = UNION GROUP1 GROUP2

in Figure 9.12.

INTERSECT

The essential meaning of INTERSECT is *AND*. It operates on two relations and returns those tuples which are present in *both* relations.

We might use the INTERSECT operation to produce a list of those

GROUP1 = SELECT STUDENT COURSE = BIOLOGY

GROUP1

STUDENT	NAME	ADDRESS	COURSE	RESULT
90/1010	SMITH, P	34 HIGH RD	BIOLOGY	90
90/1020	MARLOWE, C	20 CROMER ST	BIOLOGY	86
90/1040	SIDDONS, S	100 HIGH RD	BIOLOGY	50

GROUP3 = SELECT STUDENT RESULT > 80

GROUP3

STUDENT	NAME	ADDRESS	COURSE	RESULT
90/1010	SMITH, P	34 HIGH RD	BIOLOGY	90
90/1020	MARLOWE, C	20 CROMER ST	BIOLOGY	86
90/1030	MURDOCH, I	2 SANDRINGHAM MEWS	MATHEMATICS	90
90/1050	ELIOT, G	1 GAINSBOROUGH RD	PHYSIOLOGY	85

TOP-BIOLOGISTS = INTERSECT GROUP1 GROUP2

TOP-BIOLOGISTS

STUDENT	NAME	ADDRESS	COURSE	RESULT
90/1010	SMITH, P	34 HIGH RD	BIOLOGY	90
90/1020	MARLOWE, C	20 CROMER ST	BIOLOGY	86

Figure 9.13 Relational algebra—INTERSECT

students who are studying BIOLOGY and who scored more than 80 marks. This is illustrated by the sequence of operations:

GROUP1 = SELECT STUDENT COURSE = BIOLOGY
GROUP3 = SELECT STUDENT RESULT > 80
TOP-BIOLOGISTS = INTERSECT GROUP1 GROUP2

in Figure 9.13.

You will already have realized that the UNION and INTERSECT offer an alternative means of having complicated SELECT clauses.

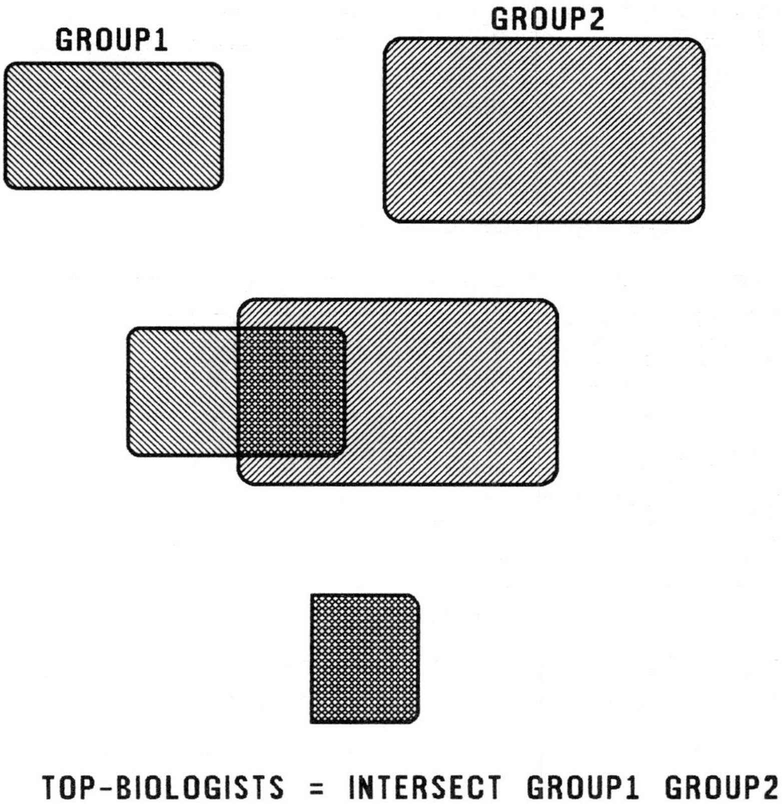

Activity 6

1 Using only the SELECT and PROJECT and JOIN operations, produce the LIFE-SCIENCES relation derived by the UNION operation illustrated in Figure 9.12.
2 Using only the SELECT and PROJECT and JOIN operations, produce the TOP-BIOLOGISTS relation derived by the INTERSECT operation illustrated in Figure 9.13.

DIVIDE

The *DIVIDE* operation will extract the tuples from one relation which are identical except for one specific attribute and in which the required values of that specific attribute are held in the second relation.

To explain this, let us suppose that we have a relation called MEMBERS which shows the students and the clubs and societies of which they are members. Then we have a second relation called CLUBS which shows some of the clubs which are run at the college. The operation:

MAILING = DIVIDE MEMBERS CLUBS

will produce a relation showing those students of the MEMBERS relation who are in *all* of the clubs in the CLUBS relation. We might use this particular example if we want to send letters to everyone who is a member of *both* the Rugby Club and the Football Club, but not to those students who are only members of one or the other, or neither, club.

This is a particularly valuable operation for use when working on tuples which arise from the duplicate values situation which we mentioned earlier.

Activity 7

Using only the SELECT and PROJECT and JOIN operations, produce the MAILING relation derived by the DIVIDE operation illustrated in Figure 9.14.

MEMBERS

NAME	CLUBS
ATTLEE, C	FOOTBALL
BEECHAM, T	RUGBY
BRUNO, G	RUGBY
BRUNO, G	FOOTBALL
BRUNO, G	SQUASH
ELIOT, G	CINEMA
ELIOT, G	RUGBY
SIDDONS, S	RUGBY
SIDDONS, S	FOOTBALL
SMITH, P	CHESS
SMITH, P	FOOTBALL
WATKINS, A	CHESS
WATKINS, A	CINEMA

CLUBS

CLUB
RUGBY
FOOTBALL

MAILING = DIVIDE MEMBERS CLUBS

MAILING

NAME
BRUNO, G
SIDDONS, S

Figure 9.14 Relational algebra—DIVIDE

Activity 8

1 MEMBER and FEE relations
The following relational operations are based upon the MEMBER and the FEE relations which form a part of a computer system for an ex-servicemen's club. The relations are shown in Figure 9.15. In each case, explain the result in your own words and draw the resultant relation.
(a) TEMP1 = SELECT MEMBER TOWN = REDLEY
(b) TEMP2 = SELECT TEMP1 RANK = SERGEANT
(c) TEMP3 = PROJECT MEMBER(RANK, TOWN)
(d) TEMP4 = SELECT MEMBER RANK = SERGEANT
(e) TEMP5 = UNION TEMP1 TEMP4
(f) TEMP6 = JOIN MEMBER (RANK) = FEE (POSITION)

(g) TEMP7 = PROJECT MEMBER(TOWN)
(h) TEMP8 = SELECT MEMBER TOWN = WELFORD
(i) TEMP9 = SELECT MEMBER TOWN = MAJOR
(j) TEMP10 = INTERSECT TEMP8 TEMP9

MEMBER

MEMBER	RANK	TOWN
ADEY	SERGEANT	WELFORD
BARNES	SERGEANT	REDLEY
HAYTER	CAPTAIN	BRETTON
CREAGH	COLONEL	COLBEY
HOROWITZ	MAJOR	WELFORD
KARLIN	MAJOR	REDLEY
HUNTLEY	CAPTAIN	BRETTON
LAGO	COLONEL	COLBEY
SPURLING	MAJOR	WELFORD
MERCHANT	SERGEANT	REDLEY

FEE

AMOUNT	POSITION
30.00	COLONEL
25.00	MAJOR
20.00	CAPTAIN
15.00	SERGEANT
10.00	CORPORAL

Figure 9.15 MEMBER and FEE relations

2 DEPOT and CATALOGUE relations
Look at the relations shown in Figure 9.16. These represent the catalogue of a furniture shop and the depots where the various items are stored.
Write down relational algebraic expressions to meet each of the following requirements. In each case, draw a table representing the resultant relation.
(a) A complete list of all the settees in the catalogue.
(b) A complete list of all settees and chairs.
(c) A list showing the colour of all chairs.
(d) A complete list of all items costing more than 100 pounds.
(e) A complete list of all sideboards which cost more than 150 pounds.
(f) A list showing all the red items which are not chairs.
(g) A list showing the price, type, colour and material of all products held at the Leytonstone depot.

As we go on to look at some real examples of query languages, you will recognize the principles of relational algebra which are embodied—implicitly or explicitly—in such languages.

DEPOT

PRODUCT	DEPOT
CHAIR	WALFORD
DESK	LEYTONSTONE
SETTEE	WALFORD
SIDEBOARD	LEYTON

CATALOGUE

ITEM	TYPE	COLOUR	MATERIAL	PRICE
1200	DESK	GREY	WOODEN	56.00
1234	CHAIR	RED	STEEL	10.00
2000	SETTEE	YELLOW	STEEL	100.00
2200	SETTEE	BROWN	STEEL	10.00
2222	DESK	BLUE	STEEL	56.00
2936	SETTEE	GREY	STEEL	7.00
3000	SIDEBOARD	BLUE	WOODEN	175.00
3579	SIDEBOARD	GREY	SPECIAL	130.00
4000	DESK	BLACK	SPECIAL	56.00
4200	SETTEE	GOLD	WOODEN	10.00
4444	SETTEE	RED	WOODEN	10.00
4545	SETTEE	BLUE	SPECIAL	10.00
5000	SETTEE	ORANGE	WOODEN	10.00
6000	SIDEBOARD	GOLD	STEEL	130.00
6666	SIDEBOARD	ORANGE	STEEL	130.00
7000	DESK	WHITE	WOODEN	56.00
8000	SETTEE	RED	SPECIAL	10.00
8117	SIDEBOARD	GREY	STEEL	130.00
8763	SIDEBOARD	MAROON	WOODEN	160.00
8888	DESK	RED	WOODEN	56.00
9000	SIDEBOARD	YELLOW	WOODEN	130.00

Figure 9.16 DEPOT and CATALOGUE relations

Recap

A relational database is organized as a set of tables of data called relations. Each relation has a name and comprises a number of tuples (rows) and attributes (columns).

The types of value which can appear in each column are taken from the domain for that attribute.

A relation has specific properties: each relation has a name; no two tuples can be the same; the order of the tuples is not important; each attribute must have a unique name; the order of the attributes is significant; at the intersection of any tuple and any attribute there is a single value; the values in any one column are all from the same domain; the primary key must not be null.

The number of columns in a table is a measure of the degree of the relation. The number of tuples in a table is a measure of the cardinality of the relation.

A relation can be described by a schema consisting of the name of the relation, the attributes enclosed in brackets, and the key of the record underlined.

A relational database can be implemented fairly easily by means of a flat file.

A mathematical language called relational algebra is available to manipulate the data. Relational algebra offers a number of fundamental operations to manipulate relations: SELECT—extract tuples to form a new relation; PROJECT—extract attributes to form a new relation; JOIN—add attributes from one relation to another relation; PRODUCT—combine each tuple from one relation with every tuple of another; UNION—join two relations to form a new relation; INTERSECT—form a new relation from two relations where the key values are the same; DIVIDE—extract from one relation those tuples whose values in one attribute match all those of another relation.

The principles of relational algebra which are embodied—implicitly or explicitly—in many of the query languages which we shall meet in the next chapter.

Answers

1 An internal telephone number might simply be the set of all valid telephone numbers consisting of integer numbers in the range 200 to 599.

Some instances might be:

300
200
999

A public telephone number might be the set of all valid public telephone numbers, including the numeric STD dialling code followed by the integer telephone number.

Some instances might be:

01-999 9999
0484-999999
Elmdale 123

2 An alphanumeric code consisting of two alphabetic letters, followed by three pairs of numeric digits followed by an alphabetic code A, B, C or D.
Some instances might be:

AA 11 11 11 A
3 27 45 36 D

3 The set of names of students consisting of an alphabetic surname followed by one or more initials.
Some instances might be:

AAAAAAAAAAAA, AAA
THOMPSON, P
WILSON, JA
LUNKINS, MGC

4 The set of departments within the college consisting of alphanumeric department name.
Some instances might be:

SCIENCES
MATHEMATICS
HUMANITIES

5 The set of subjects studied at the college consisting of alphanumeric subject title.
Some instances might be:

BIOLOGY
MATHEMATICS
HOME ECONOMICS
C AND G 471

10: Relational databases—languages

Objectives

After reading this chapter, you should be able to:

- describe the manner in which some of the commercial DBMS manipulate the relational model of data
- name some of the query languages which are commercially available
- describe the general features of query languages
- use the fundamental features of some of these languages to answer questions which are frequently asked in business.

In the last chapter, we saw how relational databases represent their data and we looked at the formal language of relational algebra which is used as a basis for the manipulation of relations.

In this chapter, we shall look at some of the ways in RDBMSs are implemented in practice and we shall pay particular attention to the languages which are used for this purpose. Obviously we cannot mention or look at every aspect of the languages and the DBMSs described here. But there are many books covering each one in detail if you want to go further.

There are a great many enquiry languages and query languages available for the end-user. Some are associated with a specific DBMS, some are more widely available. Some DBMSs offer several languages.

As you look at the languages illustrated here—and as you come to look at other languages in your work—you will see a great many similarities between them. This is not a consequence of one designer copying from another. It is simply that the languages are attempting to allow the end-user—typically in business and commerce—to express the enquiries and the processing in a manner which seems natural to him or her. Any similarities, therefore, are the result of mimicking the natural language of the English- (or American-) speaking business world.

Access

Access is the query language provided by the Pick Operating System. This operating system and others such as Honeywell Ultimate and McDonnell Douglas Reality which have common roots with Pick, are aimed specifically at *commercial* applications, an area in which the powers of Access are particularly valuable.

There is no formal data description language. The format of the records is specified by a set of *definitions* held on a data dictionary which is associated with each file. A file is created by a statement of the form:

CREATE-FILE STOCK 5 11

indicating how many pages of memory are to be allocated to the data dictionary of the file (5 pages in this instance) and to the data file (11 in this instance).

On the Pick Operating System, we use the word *item* instead of *record*, and each each data item is identified by its *item-id* that is, its key. Each *attribute* (field) is identified by its physical position within the item, as declared by the user.

To see this in practice, let us consider two files: the STOCK file which contains information about items of furniture held by an organization, and the SUPPS file which contains information about the companies which supply those items of furniture. Figure 10.1 shows a typical data item on each file. Diagram (a) illustrates that the STOCK file consists of the item-id (1000 in this instance) followed by seven data attributes. Logically, we shall interpret the attributes as representing the:

1 Description
2 Quantity in stock
3 Location in warehouse

1000	DESK, RED, WOODEN	8	LS/17/81	5600	30	2000	7713

(a) A typical item on the STOCK file

2000	A.B.ATKINS AND CO	HIGH RD	WIDDOP	AL9 9LA	061-999 2375

(b) A typical item on the SUPP file

Figure 10.1 Pick data items—logical

4 Price
5 Minimum stock level
6 Supplier code
7 Date of the last stock movement

of a type of furniture held in the warehouse.

Pick holds its items as a string of characters. The individual attributes are separated by a special character called the *attribute-mark* and another special character called the *segment-mark*, indicates the end of each item. As a consequence of this arrangement, an attribute may be any length and a null (empty) attribute is represented by just its attribute-mark. Figure 10.2 shows how the two items introduced in Figure 10.1 would be held as physical records on the disk. We have shown the attribute-mark as the character ^ and the segment-mark as __ in these illustrations.

```
1000^DESK, RED, WOODEN^8^LS/17/81^5600^30^2000^7713^_
```

(a) A typical item on the STOCK file

```
2000^A.B.ATKINS AND CO^HIGH RD^WIDDOP^AL9 9LA^061-999 2375^_
```

(b) A typical item on the SUPPS file

Figure 10.2 Pick data items—physical

	DESCR	QUANTITY	PRICE	MINIMUM	VALUE	MOVED	SNAME
01	A	A	A	A	A	A	A
02	1	2	4	5	0	7	6
03	DESCRIPTION			MIN			SUPPLIER
04							
05							
06							
07			MD2		MD2	D	
08					A2*4		TSUPPS;V;;1
09	L	R	R	R	R	R	L
10	25	1	6	3	8	9	30

(a) Data dictionary definitions

```
QUANTITY^A^2^^^^^^^R^1^_

DESCR^A^1^DESCRIPTION^^^^^^L^25^_

SNAME^A^6^SUPPLIER^^^^^TSUPPS;V;;1^T^20^_
```

(b) The physical appearance of STOCK dictionary items

Figure 10.3 Data dictionary definitions

The dictionary definitions are held on the dictionary of the file—called DICT STOCK in our case and the definition items are created and maintained by a general-purpose editor. Some typical dictionary definitions are shown in Figure 10.3. It is also possible to have a global dictionary—the master dictionary—which can be used to access data and each of every file. We shall not consider this here.
Figure 10.5 shows examples of the output from some Access enquiries and demonstrates the use of some of these dictionary definitions.

Activity 1

1 What are the contents of attribute 1 of STOCK item 1000 shown in Figure 10.1(a)?
2 What are the contents of attribute 1 of SUPPS item 2000 shown in Figure 10.1(a)?
3 Using the simple format used to describe the seven attributes of the STOCK file, make a list of the attributes which make up the items on the SUPPS file.
4 What are the contents of attribute 3, attribute 8 and attribute 10 of the data dictionary item DESCR shown in Figure 10.3?

Each dictionary item is identified by a unique item-id. This is a name, such as DESCR, PRICE or LOCATION, which will be used as part of the vocabulary of the Access enquiry sentences. As illustrated in Figure 10.3, there are ten attributes in each dictionary definition item and each attribute has a specific significance.

(a) The first attribute is A to identify this dictionary item as an attribute definition.
(b) The second attribute of the definition is a number indicating which attribute of the *data item* is to be identified by this definition. Thus, when we use the name DESCR we shall be referring to attribute 1 of the data items, QUANTITY will identify attribute 2, and so on.
    Each attribute is identified by its physical position within the item: attribute 1 is the first attribute, attribute 2 the second, and so on. Attribute 0 is the item-id (the key).
(c) The third attribute is a title which is to be displayed as a column heading on the output report. This may be blank if the title is to be the same as the definition name. Thus the DESCR attribute will

appear with the title DESCRIPTION, but QUANTITY will have the title QUANTITY.

(d) We do not use attributes 4, 5 and 6 of the definitions in our examples.

(e) The seventh attribute is used to indicate how the data is to be formatted on the output report. If it is blank, then the data will be output unchanged. Our examples use just two of the many possibilities:

- The code MD2 means *mask with 2 places of decimals*, so the PRICE attribute and the VALUE will be displayed in a form such as 25.00 or 125.75 as you see from Figure 10.1, the PRICE attribute is held with a decimal point: this reduces the storage space and simplifies the use of this attribute in arithmetic calculations.
- The code D means that the MOVED attribute is actually a *date*. As you see from Figure 10.1, the MOVED attribute is held as a number—7713 in this instance. This is an *internal date* (it is actually the number of days since 31st December 1968, the date when Pick first established its date routines) and by doing this, we reduce the storage space and make it easier to use the data for sorting purposes. The data value 7713 is the internal form for the date *11 FEB 1989* as shown in the output reports. Because the date is held in this internal format, there are a variety of codes to reformat the date on the output report. Some examples are: D2 would display the date in the form:

  11 FEB 89

  The code D2/ would display it as

  11/02/89

  and the code DWA (alphabetic day of the week) would display the date as

  Saturday

  You may even combine several of these to display the date in a form such as:

  Saturday, 11 February, 1989

  There are a great many such codes for a variety of formatting: change to upper-case or to lower-case; remove a specific character; add currency symbols and commas, and many more. You can even write programs and call them from within your definitions to perform any special, non-standard processing.

One such code also handles certain aspects of data integrity by, for example, preventing the deletion of a item from the CUSTOMER file if there are still outstanding orders on the SALES file for that customer.

(f) The eighth attribute is used to specify the source of the data. If it is blank, then the data will be taken from the position indicated by attribute 2 of this definition. But you may use this part of the definition to pick up data from one or more other places and combine into an output value. Our examples use just two of the many possibilities:

- The code A2*4 which appears in the VALUE definition means that the VALUE is not held on the STOCK file at all, but that it is to be calculated by multiplying data attribute 2(the quantity) by data attribute 4(the price). We could have produced the same result by means of the code

  ```
  A N(PRICE) * N(QUANTITY)
  ```

  instead of A2*4 if we had wished.
- The code:

  ```
  TSUPPS;V;1
  ```

  in the SNAMES definition indicates that the value in attribute 6 of the data items (this is the supplier reference number) is to be used as an item-id to Translate—or pick up—an item from the SUPPS file and the contents of attribute 1 of that item (this is the supplier's name, as you can see in Figure 10.1) are to be shown instead of the original reference number. This avoids having to hold the actual supplier's name (or their address or their discount rates) on the STOCK file. Thus, when we use the name SNAMES in an Access enquiry and process item 1000 on the STOCK file, the following will happen:
  1. The Access language will first consult the definition SNAMES and pick up attribute 6 from STOCK item 1000: this is the value 2000;
  2. This value, 2000, will then be used to read the item with item-id 2000 from the SUPPS file;
  3. Finally attribute 1 will be retrieved from item 2000 of the SUPPS file and then displayed on the Access report as if the actual name had been held on the STOCK file.

  The use of this code is illustrated in Figure 10.3(g).

As with the processing described for attribute 7 of the definition, there are a great many such codes: concatenate two or more data attributes and literal strings; extract just a part of the data, and many more.

It is these codes—for collecting and reformatting the raw data—which make Access virtually unique as a query language. They can change the output appearance of any data attribute in a variety of ways and can combine one or more attributes to produce a new value.

g) The ninth attribute indicates whether the data is to be shown left or right-justified.
h) The tenth attribute indicates the width of the data to be shown on the report.

There may be any number of definitions for the STOCK file. We have only shown a few here. You may also have several definitions for the *same* attribute. So if the people in one ofice know the description as the PRODUCT-SUPPS and those in another ofice call it PART-DETAILS, then you can keep them all happy with their own synonyms.

The data manipulation language of Pick

The data manipulation language takes the form of a number of powerful extensions to Dartmouth Basic. Some versions of the Pick Operating System have additional facilities within the query language to update the data on the files. Generally, however, Access does not perform file updates.

Figure 10.4 shows a Basic program written for the Pick Operating System. This particular program displays part of specific items on the STOCK file, and then accepts a despatch or receipt of goods and updates the stock item accordingly.

This program demonstrates how the STOCK file and its dictionary definitions for the DESCR, QUANTITY and LOCATION can be used as an active feature of the Basic program.

The Access query language

The Access query language is used simply by typing in English sentences. Indeed the McDonnell Douglas Reality operating system uses the name ENGLISH instead of Access.

Some of the features of the language are illustrated by the Access sentences and the resultant output shown in Figure 10.5.

```
*
* PROGRAM TO DISPLAY ITEMS FROM STOCK FILE AND CHANGE THE
* QUANTITY IN STOCK
*
* OPEN THE STOCK FILE
*
    FILE STOCK
*
* MESSAGES AND DISPLAYS
*
    HDR=@(-1):@(15,0):"*** DISPLAY STOCK RECORDS ***":@(0,3)
    PRINT HDR
    MESSAGE0=@(0,20):@(-3)       ; ** = CLEAR BOTTOM LINE
    MESSAGE1=@(0,23):"Enter stock number / END to terminate: '
    MESSAGE2=@(0,23):'Enter quantity / END to abandon: '
    MESSAGE3=@(0,23):Enter +nnn (for receipt) / -nnn for despatch / END'
*
* MAIN LOOP
*
    LOOP
        PRINT MESSAGE1:
        INPUT KEY
        PRINT MESSAGE0:
    UNTIL KEY='END' DO
        READ STOCK FROM KEY THEN
            PRINT HDR
            PRINT '         Part number: ':KEY
            PRINT
            PRINT '         Description: ':STOCK(DESCR)
            PRINT '            Quantity: ':STOCK(QUANTITY)
            PRINT '            Location: ':STOCK(LOCATION)
            LOOP
                PRINT MESSAGE2:
                INPUT CHANGE
            UNTIL CHANGE='END' OR NUM(CHANGE) DO
                PRINT MESSAGE3:
            REPEAT
            IF CHANGE NE 'END THEN
                STOCK(QUANTITY)=STOCK(QUANTITY)+CHANGE
                WRITE STOCK ON KEY
            END
        END ELSE
            PRINT @(0,20):'Record ':KEY:' not found'
        END
    REPEAT
    PRINT 'END OF JOB'
    END
```

Figure 10.4 A Pick Basic program to handle the STOCK file

The Pick database is organized according to many of the principles of RDBMSs—although Pick appeared in the mid-1960s long before much work had been done on the formal specification of relational databases. It does, however, allow any attribute to contain more than one value, thereby conflicting with one of the rules which we met in Chapter 9. The output report in Figure 10.5(c) demonstrates how these are handled by Access in the case of items 1200 and 8763—in which there are several values for the QUANTITY attribute and corresponding values for the LOCATION attribute. There is a facility which will allow items with such repeating data to be displayed in strict relational form.

Example (a) LIST sentence

Display specific fields from the items on the file. The fields appear in the order specified in the Access sentence.

```
     LIST STOCK DESCR QUANTITY MOVED PRICE

STOCK..... DESCRIPTION............. QUANTITY MOVED....  PRICE

1234       CHAIR, RED, STEEL               7 27 AUG 89  10.00
1200       DESK, GREY, WOODEN             16 21 AUG 89  56.00
                                          32 05 SEP 89
1000       DESK, GREEN-BLUE, WOODEN        8 09 SEP 89  56.00
2000       SETTEE, YELLOW, STEEL          18 22 JUL 89 100.00
3000       SIDEBOARD, BLUE, WOODEN        58 10 AUG 89 130.00
8763       SIDEBOARD, MAROON, WOODEN      10 17 AUG 89 130.00
                                           5 01 SEP 89
                                           0 23 AUG 89
```

Example (b) SORT sentence

Sort the lines of the report in ascending order of price.

```
     SORT STOCK BY PRICE DESCR QUANTITY LOCATION PRICE

STOCK..... DESCRIPTION............. QUANTITY LOCATION..  PRICE

1234       CHAIR, RED, STEEL               7 DN/5/88      10.00
1000       DESK, GREEN-BLUE, WOODEN        8 LS/17/81     56.00
1200       DESK, GREY, WOODEN             16 LS/17/1      56.00
                                          32 LS/17/2
2000       SETTEE, YELLOW, STEEL          18 DN/1/69     100.00
3000       SIDEBOARD, BLUE, WOODEN        58 MN/5/56     130.00
8763       SIDEBOARD, MAROON, WOODEN      10 LN/33/4     130.00
                                           5 LN/51/7
                                           0 MN/3/40
```

Example (c) Expand repeating values into a true relation

Using BY-EXP (by-expanded) in the sentence causes all items which are stored in more than one location to generate a separate line - showing the appropriate stock in that location.

```
     SORT STOCK BY-EXP LOCATION DESCR QUANTITY LOCATION
          PRICE

STOCK..... DESCRIPTION............. QUANTITY LOCATION..  PRICE

2000       SETTEE, YELLOW, STEEL          18 DN/1/69     100.00
1234       CHAIR, RED, STEEL               7 DN/5/88      10.00
8763       SIDEBOARD, MAROON, WOODEN      10 LN/33/4     130.00
8763       SIDEBOARD, MAROON, WOODEN       5 LN/51/7     130.00
1200       DESK, GREY, WOODEN             16 LS/17/1      56.00
1200       DESK, GREY, WOODEN             32 LS/17/2      56.00
1000       DESK, GREEN-BLUE, WOODEN        8 LS/17/81     56.00
8763       SIDEBOARD, MAROON, WOODEN       0 MN/3/40     130.00
3000       SIDEBOARD, BLUE, WOODEN        58 MN/5/56     130.00
```

Figure 10.5 Access queries and reports

Example (d) Total the VALUE attribute and print the report

The dictionary definition tells Access that VALUE is to be calculated by multiplying the QUANTITY by the PRICE. Here, we ask Access to display and accumulate the VALUE for each item. The word LPTR sends this report to the line-printer; otherwise, the report would be displayed on the terminal screen.

```
     SORT STOCK BY PRICE DESCR QUANTITY PRICE TOTAL VALUE
          LPTR

STOCK..... DESCRIPTION.............. QUANTITY  PRICE     VALUE

1234       CHAIR, RED, STEEL                7  10.00     70.00
1000       DESK, GREEN-BLUE, WOODEN         8  56.00    448.00
1200       DESK, GREY, WOODEN              16  56.00    896.00
                                           32          1792.00
2000       SETTEE, YELLOW, STEEL           18 100.00   1800.00
3000       SIDEBOARD, BLUE, WOODEN         58 130.00   7540.00
8763       SIDEBOARD, MAROON, WOODEN       10 130.00   1300.00
                                            5           650.00
                                            0             0.00

***                                                   14496.00
```

Example (e) Select according to the PRICE

Select all the items whose price is less than £100, sort the report into descending order of price, and total the value of these items.

```
     SORT STOCK BY-DSND PRICE WITH PRICE < "100.00" DESCR
          QUANTITY PRICE TOTAL VALUE

STOCK..... DESCRIPTION.............. QUANTITY  PRICE     VALUE

1000       DESK, GREEN-BLUE, WOODEN         8  56.00    448.00
1200       DESK, GREY, WOODEN              16  56.00    896.00
                                           32          1792.00
1234       CHAIR, RED, STEEL                7  10.00     70.00

***                                                    3206.00
```

Example (f) Look at the desks only

Select those items which contain the characters DESK anywhere in the DESCR field, and then display just the DESCR field.

```
     LIST STOCK DESCR WITH DESCR = "[DESK]"

STOCK..... DESCRIPTION..............

1200       DESK, GREY, WOODEN
1000       DESK, GREEN-BLUE, WOODEN
```

```
Example (g) Pick up data from the SUPPS file

Here we use the feature which allows us to pick up data -
the supplier name - from the SUPPS file by means of the code
in the definition SNAME.

     LIST STOCK DESCR SUPPLIER SNAME

STOCK..... DESCRIPTION.............. SUPPLIER SUPPLIER.NAME.......

1234       CHAIR, RED, STEEL          2000     A.B.ATKINS AND CO
1200       DESK, GREY, WOODEN         1000     ROGER PETERSEN PLC
                                      3000     3000
                                      2000     A.B.ATKINS AND CO
1000       DESK, GREEN-BLUE, WOODEN   2000     A.B.ATKINS AND CO
2000       SETTEE, YELLOW, STEEL      1000     ROGER PETERSEN PLC
3000       SIDEBOARD, BLUE, WOODEN    2000     A.B.ATKINS AND CO
8763       SIDEBOARD, MAROON, WOODEN  1000     ROGER PETERSEN PLC
```

There are a number of powerful extensions to the Access language. These allow the user to

- Produce labels such as you might use for addressing envelopes.
- Produce spreadsheets. We looked at this in Chapter 6.
- Produce charts and graphs based upon the data on the database. We looked at this in Chapter 6.
- Produce extensive reports based upon data which is organized as a loop structure. We look at this below.

Questions—Access

Answer these questions about the Access language.

1 Is there a data description language?
2 Is there a data manipulation language?
3 Are the data description language, the data manipulation language and the query language identical?

When you are using the query language, ...

4 How do you select specific pieces of data from a file?
5 How do you sort the data into a specific order?
6 How do you produce a total of specific columns of data?

Activity 2

Using the Access language, how would you handle the following situations? Write down the sentences which you would use.

1 To produce a list showing the description, price and quantity of all the red products.
2 To find the total value of the desks.
3 To produce a list of all the products sorted into order of value.

Access with a loop structure

We have already met the loop structure—such as might be used in such applications as a PARTS file with a data structure diagram like that in Figure 10.6. This tells us that some parts on the file are made up of other parts of the same file.

The Access language has a powerful means of handling files which are organized in this manner.

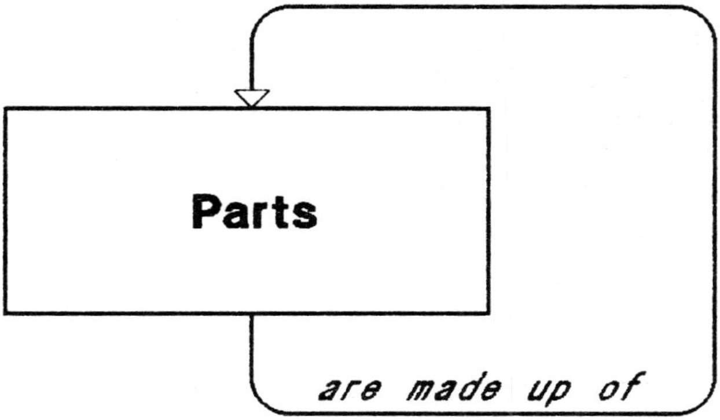

Figure 10.6 A loop structure

As a simple example, let us consider an ofice supply company's catalogue which contains the following records, some of which imply that this part is made up of other parts in the catalogue. For example:

- Record KIT1 is a Teaching kit 1, and comprises 3 student's units, 1 teacher's unit
- Record SU1 is a student's unit, and comprises 1 desk, 1 chair, 1 student literature pack, 1 cassette player

- Record TD1 is a Teacher's desk, and comprises 1 cassette player, 1 desk and some parts are *atomic*, that is, they are not made up of smaller parts:
- Record D1 is a Desk
- Record CH1 is a Chair
- Record CP1 is a Cassette player

We could represent this information by means of the records shown in Figure 10.7. Diagram (a) shows the record structure, and the instances are shown in diagram (b). Note that we must hold the keys of the component parts as repeating values of field 3 of the records.

```
    Key: record number
field 1: description
field 2: quantity in stock, for a primitive component
field 3: keys of subordinate components, if any
field 4: price, for a primitive component

                    (a) The record structure

KIT1^Teaching kit 1^^SU1]SU1]SU1]TU1
KIT2^Teaching kit 2^^SU1]SU1]SU1]SU1]SU1]TU1]TU1
SU1^Student's unit^^D1]CH1]SL1]CP1
TU1^Teacher's unit^^TD1]CH1]TL1]SL1
TD1^Teacher's desk^^CP1]D1
D1^Desk^34^^5600
CH1^Chair^23^^3700
SL1^Student literature pack^56^^1200
TL1^Teacher literature pack^67^^2500
CP1^Cassette player^7^^2600

                       (b) The instances
```

Figure 10.7 Records on a loop file

Having organized our data in this manner, we can then use an Access sentence such as:

LIST WITHIN CATALOGUE 'KIT2' DESCR QTY TOTAL PRICE

using the word WITHIN to produce a report showing the nature, the quantity in stock, and the price of all the stock records which are needed to supply one KIT2. The output from this sentence is shown in Figure 10.8.

```
LEVEL CATALOGUE. DESCR.................... QTY.. PRICE

 1    KIT2        Teaching kit 2
 2    SU1         Student's unit
 3    D1          Desk                         34 56.00
 3    CH1         Chair                        23 37.00
 3    SL1         Student literature pack      56 12.00
 3    CP1         Cassette player               7 26.00
 2    SU1         Student's unit
 3    D1          Desk                         34 56.00
 3    CH1         Chair                        23 37.00
 3    SL1         Student literature pack      56 12.00
 3    CP1         Cassette player               7 26.00
 2    SU1         Student's unit
 3    D1          Desk                         34 56.00
 3    CH1         Chair                        23 37.00
 3    SL1         Student literature pack      56 12.00
 3    CP1         Cassette player               7 26.00
 2    SU1         Student's unit
 3    D1          Desk                         34 56.00
 3    CH1         Chair                        23 37.00
 3    SL1         Student literature pack      56 12.00
 3    CP1         Cassette player               7 26.00
 2    SU1         Student's unit
 3    D1          Desk                         34 56.00
 3    CH1         Chair                        23 37.00
 3    SL1         Student literature pack      56 12.00
 3    CP1         Cassette player               7 26.00
 2    TU1         Teacher's unit
 3    TD1         Teacher's desk
 4    CP1         Cassette player               7 26.00
 4    D1          Desk                         34 56.00
 3    CH1         Chair                        23 37.00
 3    TL1         Teacher literature pack      67 25.00
 3    SL1         Student literature pack      56 12.00
 2    TU1         Teacher's unit
 3    TD1         Teacher's desk
 4    CP1         Cassette player               7 26.00
 4    D1          Desk                         34 56.00
 3    CH1         Chair                        23 37.00
 3    TL1         Teacher literature pack      67 25.00
 3    SL1         Student literature pack      56 12.00

                                                  967.00
```

Figure 10.8   Output from a LIST WITHIN sentence

We could do the same for smaller units or for several units at once, by means of sentences such as:

LIST WITHIN CATALOGUE 'TU1' DESCR QTY TOTAL PRICE
LIST WITHIN CATALOGUE 'TU1' 'SU2' DESCR QTY TOTAL PRICE

dBASE

dBASE—in its various manifestations dBASE II, dBASE III Plus and dBASE IV is a product of the Ashton-Tate Company. Like much DBMS software, dBASE is screen-oriented, interacting with the user in a screen-based dialogue. It is also possible to write applications programs in the dBASE language. The statements used in the programs are essentially the same as the commands which are issued interactively.

To illustrate the features of dBASE we shall handle the relation FURNITURE which is illustrated in Figure 10.9(a). In this discussion, we shall use the dBASE terminology: file, record and field (instead of relation, tuple and attribute).

We must first specify the *structure* for the new file. This is done by means of the

CREATE

command, and we can subsequently change the content and form of the structure by means of the

MODIFY STRUCTURE

command. The structure performs the role of the data dictionary for the file. In creating the structure for the FURNITURE file, we specify for each field in the file the name, type, width and format of the field. This is illustrated in Figure 10.9(b). What do you think the DEC means?

When the file and the structure have been created, data may be added to the file immediately the CREATE operation has finished (at which point dBASE will ask you if you want to input any new data records), or you may add them later by means of the

APPEND

command. In either case, a blank form will be displayed on the screen—based upon the structure of the file—and the user will be allowed to type in the data which is to go into the file.

Records are added—one by one—to the end of a file. They are held in the order in which they are added. dBASE allocates its own record keys and these keys are shown when the file is displayed by means of the

LIST

command. Assuming that we had created the records shown in Figure 10.6(a), then the output from the LIST command would be as shown in

FURNITURE

CODE	TYPE	COLOUR	MATERIAL	PRICE
4600	DESK	GREY	WOODEN	56.00
3000	SIDEBOARD	BLUE	PLASTIC	175.00
5000	SETTEE	ORANGE	WOODEN	10.00
7000	DESK	WHITE	WOODEN	56.00
8000	CHAIR	RED	SPECIAL	10.00
8763	SIDEBOARD	MAROON	WOODEN	160.00
8077	DESK	RED	PLASTIC	56.00
9134	SETTEE	YELLOW	WOODEN	130.00

(a) FURNITURE relation

CREATE FURNITURE

	FIELD NAME	TYPE	WIDTH	DEC
1	ITEM	NUMERIC	4	
2	CODE	CHAR/TEXT	10	
3	COLOUR	CHAR/TEXT	6	
4	MATERIAL	CHAR/TEXT	8	
5	PRICE	NUMERIC	6	2

(b) CREATE command

Figure 10.9 Establishing a dBASE file

Figure 10.10. In order to look at the format and structure of the records, we could use the command:

LIST STRUCTURE

as illustrated in Figure 10.10(b).

There are several statements available if you want to look at specific records:

DISPLAY RECORD 5
to look at a single record.

LIST FOR PRICE > 100
LIST FOR COLOUR = 'RED' OR COLOUR = 'MAROON'
LIST FOR COLOUR = 'RED' AND TYPE = 'DESK'
LIST FOR NOT(MATERIAL = 'ASH' OR MATERIAL = 'MAHOGANY')
to look for records which satisfy certain conditions. Some versions of

LIST

Record £	CODE	TYPE	COLOUR	MATERIAL	PRICE
1	4600	DESK	GREY	WOODEN	56.00
2	3000	SIDEBOARD	BLUE	PLASTIC	175.00
3	5000	SETTEE	ORANGE	WOODEN	10.00
4	7000	DESK	WHITE	WOODEN	56.00
5	8000	CHAIR	RED	SPECIAL	10.00
6	8763	SIDEBOARD	MAROON	WOODEN	160.00
7	8077	DESK	RED	PLASTIC	56.00
8	9134	SETTEE	YELLOW	WOODEN	130.00

(a) LIST file

LIST STRUCTURE

FIELD	FIELD NAME	TYPE	WIDTH	DEC
1	ITEM	NUMERIC	4	
2	CODE	CHAR/TEXT	10	
3	COLOUR	CHAR/TEXT	6	
4	MATERIAL	CHAR/TEXT	8	
5	PRICE	NUMERIC	6	2
Total			35	

(b) LIST STRUCTURE

Figure 10.10 LIST command—dBASE

dBASE may use *.OR.* and *.AND.* and *.NOT.* where we have used OR and AND and NOT.

LIST FOR SUBSTR(TYPE,1,1) 'S'

to list all the records of which the first character of the TYPE is S. dBASE has a large number of functions. The SUBSTR function used here takes a substring of a variable: the parameters are the name of the field, the position of the first character of the substring and the number of characters to be taken.

LIST FOR 'W'\COLOUR

to list all the records which have a W anywhere in the COLOUR field.

LIST CODE, COLOUR, MATERIAL, TYPE OFF

to output specific fields. The word OFF suppresses the record number.

LIST CODE, TRIM(COLOUR)+' '+TYPE

to display the code and the colour and the type concatenated to form a single string. The TRIM function removes trailing spaces from the field.

These and some other examples are illustrated in Figure 10.11 where we show the dBASE command followed by the output produced.

```
DISPLAY RECORD 5

Record £  CODE   TYPE        COLOUR   MATERIAL   PRICE
       5  8000   CHAIR       RED      SPECIAL    10.00

LIST FOR PRICE > 100

Record £  CODE   TYPE        COLOUR   MATERIAL   PRICE
       2  3000   SIDEBOARD   BLUE     PLASTIC   175.00
       6  8763   SIDEBOARD   MAROON   WOODEN    160.00
       8  9134   SETTEE      YELLOW   WOODEN    130.00

LIST FOR COLOUR = 'RED' OR COLOUR = 'MAROON'

Record £  CODE   TYPE        COLOUR   MATERIAL   PRICE
       5  8000   CHAIR       RED      SPECIAL    10.00
       6  8763   SIDEBOARD   MAROON   WOODEN    160.00
       7  8077   DESK        RED      PLASTIC    56.00

LIST FOR COLOUR = 'RED' AND TYPE = 'DESK'

Record £  CODE   TYPE        COLOUR   MATERIAL   PRICE
       7  8077   DESK        RED      PLASTIC    56.00

LIST FOR SUBSTR(TYPE,1,1) = "S"

Record £  CODE   TYPE        COLOUR   MATERIAL   PRICE
       2  3000   SIDEBOARD   BLUE     PLASTIC   175.00
       3  5000   SETTEE      ORANGE   WOODEN     10.00
       6  8763   SIDEBOARD   MAROON   WOODEN    160.00
       8  9134   SETTEE      YELLOW   WOODEN    130.00

LIST FOR 'W'\COLOUR

Record £  CODE   TYPE        COLOUR   MATERIAL   PRICE
       4  7000   DESK        WHITE    WOODEN     56.00
       8  9134   SETTEE      YELLOW   WOODEN    130.00
```

Figure 10.11   LIST and DISPLAY command—dBASE

Our formal relational algebra did not allow for any arithmetic or other processing of the data. This is obviously a commercial requirement and dBASE—like other query languages—has facilities for counting and totalling. These are illustrated in Figure 10.12. In addition to simply totalling a field, dBASE will allow you to store the result in a *variable*—we used SETTOT and DESTOT—and then use these stored values for further calculations.

```
LIST FOR PRICE < 100 AND TYPE = "SETTEE"

Record £  CODE   TYPE         COLOUR   MATERIAL     PRICE
       3  5000   SETTEE       ORANGE   WOODEN       10.00

LIST CODE, COLOUR, MATERIAL, TYPE OFF

CODE   COLOUR    MATERIAL    TYPE
4600   GREY      WOODEN      DESK
3000   BLUE      PLASTIC     SIDEBOARD
5000   ORANGE    WOODEN      SETTEE
7000   WHITE     WOODEN      DESK
8000   RED       SPECIAL     CHAIR
8763   MAROON    WOODEN      SIDEBOARD
8077   RED       PLASTIC     DESK
9134   YELLOW    WOODEN      SETTEE

LIST CODE, TRIM(COLOUR)+' '+TYPE

Record £  CODE   TRIM(COLOUR)+' '+TYPE
       1  4600   GREY DESK
       2  3000   BLUE SIDEBOARD
       3  5000   ORANGE SETTEE
       4  7000   WHITE DESK
       5  8000   RED CHAIR
       6  8763   MAROON SIDEBOARD
       7  8077   RED DESK
       8  9134   YELLOW SETTEE
```

Some dBASE commands such as:

GO TOP
GO BOTTOM
GO 2
SKIP 3
SKIP −1
LOCATE FOR COLOUR = 'RED'

will allow you to browse through the file to locate and look at records. These are illustrated in Figure 10.13.

The contents of the current file record can be changed by a sequence such as:

LOCATE FOR TYPE = 'DESK' AND COLOUR = 'RED'
REPLACE PRICE WITH PRICE + 10.25

or a range of records may be changed by a command such as:

REPLACE ALL TYPE WITH 'S/BOARD'FOR TYPE = 'SIDEBOARD'

```
LIST TYPE, PRICE, PRICE*0.15

Record £  TYPE            PRICE  PRICE*0.15
       1  DESK            56.00        8.40
       2  SIDEBOARD      175.00       26.25
       3  SETTEE          10.00        1.50
       4  DESK            56.00        8.40
       5  CHAIR           10.00        1.50
       6  SIDEBOARD      160.00       24.00
       7  DESK            56.00        8.40
       8  SETTEE         130.00       19.50

COUNT FOR TYPE = "DESK"
             3 RECORDS

SUM PRICE FOR MATERIAL = "PLASTIC"
             2 RECORDS SUMMED
             PRICE
             231.00

SUM PRICE FOR TYPE = "SETTEE" TO SETTOT
             2 RECORDS SUMMED
             PRICE
            140.00

SUM PRICE FOR TYPE = "DESK" TO DESTOT
             3 RECORDS SUMMED
             PRICE
            168.00

STORE DESTOT - SETTOT TO DIFTOT
             18.00

AVERAGE PRICE
             3 RECORDS AVERAGED
             PRICE
             81.63
```

Figure 10.12 Calculations using dBASE

```
GO TOP

DISPLAY 2

Record £  CODE   TYPE        COLOUR   MATERIAL    PRICE
       1  4600   DESK        GREY     WOODEN      56.00
       2  3000   SIDEBOARD   BLUE     PLASTIC    175.00

SKIP 2

DISPLAY 1

Record £  CODE   TYPE        COLOUR   MATERIAL    PRICE
       5  8000   CHAIR       RED      SPECIAL     10.00

GO BOTTOM

SKIP -3

DISPLAY 2

Record £  CODE   TYPE        COLOUR   MATERIAL    PRICE
       5  8000   CHAIR       RED      SPECIAL     10.00
       6  8763   SIDEBOARD   MAROON   WOODEN     160.00

GO 2

DISPLAY 1

Record £  CODE   TYPE        COLOUR   MATERIAL    PRICE
       2  3000   SIDEBOARD   BLUE     PLASTIC    175.00

GO TOP

LOCATE FOR COLOUR = 'RED'

DISPLAY 1

Record £  CODE   TYPE        COLOUR   MATERIAL    PRICE
       5  8000   CHAIR       RED      SPECIAL     10.00
```

Figure 10.13 Browsing through a file

Records can be removed from a file by means of a command of the form:

DELETE RECORD 5

This flags the record(s) for deletion although it does not actually delete them from the file. If you realize that you have made a mistake and you don't really want to delete the records, then the RECALL command

```
DELETE RECORD 5

LIST

Record £   CODE    TYPE           COLOUR     MATERIAL      PRICE
       1   4600    DESK           GREY       WOODEN        56.00
       2   3000    SIDEBOARD      BLUE       WOODEN       175.00
       3   5000    SETTEE         ORANGE     WOODEN        10.00
       4   7000    DESK           WHITE      WOODEN        56.00
       5*  8000    CHAIR          RED        SPECIAL       10.00
       6   8763    SIDEBOARD      MAROON     WOODEN       160.00
       7   8077    DESK           RED        PLASTIC       56.00
       8   9134    SETTEE         YELLOW     WOODEN       130.00

DELETE FOR TYPE = "SIDEBOARD"

LIST

Record £   CODE    TYPE           COLOUR     MATERIAL      PRICE
       1   4600    DESK           GREY       WOODEN        56.00
       2*  3000    SIDEBOARD      BLUE       WOODEN       175.00
       3   5000    SETTEE         ORANGE     WOODEN        10.00
       4   7000    DESK           WHITE      WOODEN        56.00
       5*  8000    CHAIR          RED        SPECIAL       10.00
       6*  8763    SIDEBOARD      MAROON     WOODEN       160.00
       7   8077    DESK           RED        PLASTIC       56.00
       8   9134    SETTEE         YELLOW     WOODEN       130.00

RECALL RECORD 2

LIST

Record £   CODE    TYPE           COLOUR     MATERIAL      PRICE
       1   4600    DESK           GREY       WOODEN        56.00
       2   3000    SIDEBOARD      BLUE       WOODEN       175.00
       3   5000    SETTEE         ORANGE     WOODEN        10.00
       4   7000    DESK           WHITE      WOODEN        56.00
       5*  8000    CHAIR          RED        SPECIAL       10.00
       6*  8763    SIDEBOARD      MAROON     WOODEN       160.00
       7   8077    DESK           RED        PLASTIC       56.00
       8   9134    SETTEE         YELLOW     WOODEN       130.00
PACK

LIST

Record £   CODE    TYPE           COLOUR     MATERIAL      PRICE
       1   4600    DESK           GREY       WOODEN        56.00
       2   3000    SIDEBOARD      BLUE       WOODEN       175.00
       3   5000    SETTEE         ORANGE     WOODEN        10.00
       4   7000    DESK           WHITE      WOODEN        56.00
       5   8077    DESK           RED        PLASTIC       56.00
       6   9134    SETTEE         YELLOW     WOODEN       130.00
```

Figure 10.14 DELETE, RECALL and PACK commands—dBASE

can be used to cancel the deletion flag. When you are certain that you wish to proceed with the deletion, then you will use the PACK command to accomplish this. These commands are illustrated in Figure 10.14.

There may be up to 10 files active at any one time. The command

USE FURNITURE

is used to *open* a new file and to indicate which of several files you wish to process.

Indexing in dBASE

Since dBASE holds the records in the same order that they were added

```
USE FURNITURE
INDEX ON PRICE TO PINDEX
            8 RECORDS INDEXED

USE FURNITURE INDEX PINDEX
LIST

Record £  CODE   TYPE        COLOUR   MATERIAL    PRICE
       3  5000   SETTEE      ORANGE   WOODEN      10.00
       5  8000   CHAIR       RED      SPECIAL     10.00
       1  4600   DESK        GREY     WOODEN      56.00
       4  7000   DESK        WHITE    WOODEN      56.00
       7  8077   DESK        RED      PLASTIC     56.00
       8  9134   SETTEE      YELLOW   WOODEN     130.00
       6  8763   SIDEBOARD   MAROON   WOODEN     160.00
       2  3000   SIDEBOARD   BLUE     WOODEN     175.00

USE FURNITURE
SORT TO PRODUCTS ON TYPE, COLOUR
LIST PRODUCTS

Record £  TYPE        COLOUR
       1  CHAIR       RED
       2  DESK        GREY
       3  DESK        RED
       4  DESK        WHITE
       5  SETTEE      ORANGE
       6  SETTEE      YELLOW
       7  SIDEBOARD   BLUE
       8  SIDEBOARD   MAROON
```

Figure 10.15 INDEX and SORT commands—dBASE

to the file, there must be some means of displaying the records in a specific sequence. This is achieved by means of the

INDEX

command. Figure 10.15 shows the use of this command to display the records sorted into order of price. You may also create a new (sorted) version of your file by means of the SORT verb.

Activity 3

This Activity concerns the BOOK relation of the form shown in Figure 10.16.

BOOK

TITLE	AUTHOR	PRICE	CATEGORY	DATE
MYSTERY OF THE ROCK	WILLIAMS	5.00	FICTION	01/06/89
CATCHING ON	DENISON	7.50	FICTION	02/06/89
THIS IS ASTRONOMY	ABDULKARIM	11.00	SCIENCE	31/01/88
ENGLISH USAGE	CARRINGTON	10.50	LANGUAGE	28/02/88
COBOL 88	LASHLEY	17.95	COMPUTERS	11/05/88

Figure 10.16 BOOK relation

Write down the dBASE command (or commands) which you would use to perform the following:

1 To create the structure for the file. You can handle the date as a character string in the same way as you will handle the title, the author and the category.
2 To list the contents of the file.
3 To list the books in the fiction category.
4 To list the books sorted into order of the author's.
5 To list the computer books bought in 1988.
6 To find the total cost of the fiction books.
7 To find how much more we spend on fiction than we spend on language books.

Security on dBASE

The PROTECT command allows the database administrator to add new users and to maintain their security levels and other parameters, and also to assign security restrictions on specific files, or specific fields of files. This command is itself protected by a password.

Programs in dBASE

dBASE allows you to extend fundamental enquiries, such as those shown above, by creating REPORTs to produce printed output in a formatted manner, and LABELs to produce mailing labels.

But more powerfully, the interactive commands of dBASE are augmented by a set of statements which allow conventional programs (or procedures) to be written in the dBASE language. Programs may be created by the dBASE applications generator, or the dBASE commands may be placed in an ordinary file (with the suffix .PRG if you are using DOS) and then executed by means of the dBASE DO command. Since there is little functional difference between interactive dBASE and dBASE programs, we shall not look at programming in detail, but a few simple examples will show how they offer the full facilities that you would expect of a programming language.

Information may be displayed on the screen by means of statements such as:

```
? 'THERE ARE'
?? REC__COUNT
?? ' RECORDS'

@ 3,1 SAY 'THERE ARE'
@ 3,11 SAY REC__COUNT
@ 3,14 SAY 'RECORDS'
```

The ? and ?? commands are used for producing line by line output (scrolling down the screen): ?? holds the cursor at the end of the output without advancing a line. The first three commands, therefore, have a similar effect to the last three commands except that the @ command offers more powerful screen formatting and—in this example—forces the output to row 3 of the screen.

Data is accepted from the keyboard by statements such as:

```
INPUT "WHAT IS YOUR USER CODE" TO USER__CODE
```

Variables are used as on other programming languages, although, unlike languages such as Cobol or Pascal, dBASE does not require variables to be declared before use. Values are assigned to variables by means of statement such as:

```
STORE 0 TO TOTAL__SALES
STORE SPACE(20) TO CLIENT__NAME
```

A full range of control statements is provided for structured programming. Some of these are illustrated in Figure 10.17.

```
IF USER_CODE = 'X'
    @ 23,0 SAY 'END OF JOB'
    RETURN
ENDIF

DO WHILE OPTION <> 'X'
    DO PROCESS_ROUTINE
ENDDO

DO CASE
    CASE OPTION = 'A'
         DO ADD_RECORD
    CASE OPTION = 'D'
         DO DELETE_RECORD
    CASE OPTION = 'M'
         DO MODIFY_RECORD
ENDDO
```

Figure 10.17 Structured programming—dBASE

Statements such as DO ADD_RECORD are the equivalent of CALL or procedure statements in other languages.

As you might expect, many statements in dBASE are concerned with file access. We have already met SELECT, GO, SKIP and LOCATE. All these statements regard the file as a relational table. A program may use up to ten files at one time (dBASE II only allowed two files).

Questions—dBASE

Answer these questions about the dBASE language.

1 Is there a data description language?
2 Is there a data manipulation language?
3 Are the data description language, the data manipulation language and the query language identical?

When you are using the query language, . . .

4 How do you select specific pieces of data from a file?
5 How could you produce a total of specific columns of data?

Activity 4

Using the dBASE language, how would you handle the following situations? Write down the commands which you would use.

1 To create a new STUDENT file.
2 To indicate that you want to use the name, address, sex, telephone number, date of enrollment, the student registration number, the fee to be paid, whether the fee has been paid yet (assume that this is going to be a Y or N), and the degree for which the student is studying.
3 To add a new student: Miss Mary Shelley of 34 High Street who started to study for a B.Sc on 9th September 1990. Her registration number is 90/36192. She has no telephone and has not yet paid her fee.
4 To produce a list of all students who are studying for the MA degree.
5 To change her record to indicate that Mary Shelley has now paid her fee.
6 To find the total fees still to be paid.
7 To delete the record for student 85/13455.

Using the informal version of dBASE illustrated above, write programs to do the following:

QBE—query by example

Most of the query languages which we consider here—Access, SQL and dBASE—allow the user to type in English-like sentences. QBE is remarkably different from these, in that it allows the user to make his/her enquiries by *filling in a form.*

QBE uses the terms *table*, *row* and *column* for relation, tuple and attribute. To make a simple enquiry about a table called STOCK we would proceed as shown in Figure 10.18:

(a) When we invoke QBE it displays a blank form—this is called a *template.*
(b) We give the name of the table which we want to use.
(c) QBE displays the name of the columns which are available in that table.
(d) We put the code P. to indicate which columns we wish to print.
(e) QBE produces the report.

This method has a number of advantages: the user does not have to remember the names of his columns of data, and there is no stylized English grammar to learn.

The data description language, the data manipulation language and the query language all operate in this same fundamental way. The various activities are indicated by means of codes:

(a) QBE displays the blank template

STOCK						

(b) We request the STOCK table

STOCK	CODE	NAME	QUANTITY	PRICE	MINIMUM	MOVED

(c) QBE fills in the available column names

STOCK	CODE	NAME	QUANTITY	PRICE	MINIMUM	MOVED
	P.	P.		P.		

(d) We indicate which columns are to be printed

CODE	NAME	PRICE
1200	DESK, GREY, WOODEN	56.00
2000	SETTEE, YELLOW, STEEL	100.00
3000	SIDEBOARD, BLUE, WOODEN	130.00
3200	SIDEBOARD, GREY, WOODEN	130.00
4000	DESK, BLACK, SPECIAL	56.00
1000	DESK, RED, WOODEN	56.00

(e) QBE displays the report

Figure 10.18 *A simple QBE enquiry*

P. to print the values in a column,
I. to insert data,
U. to update data,
D. to delete data.

The data description activity applies QBE to a table called TABLES which holds details of all the data on the database. Figure 10.19 shows how this might look when creating our STOCK table.

I.	STOCK I.	CODE	NAME	QUANTITY	PRICE	MINIMUM	MOVED
	TYPE I.	CHAR(4)	CHAR(25)	FIXED	FIXED	FIXED	DATE

Figure 10.19 Creating a new STOCK table

The data manipulation language is concerned with the I. and U. and D. codes. These are illustrated in Figure 10.20. Compare these with the examples used for the other query languages.

In some of these examples we used X and Y. This represents *any* value. Thus:

X * 1.1

means multiply the current price (whatever it is) by 1.1. This increases all the prices by 10%. Similarly,

DESKX

means look for the letters DESK followed by anything. We used the names X and Y just to make them stand out from the rest of the data. In practice, you would use meaningful names for your variables—*PRICE* would have been better than X. Notice that if you use the *same* variable name in different columns of the template, then QBE will look for matching values. You can see this in example Figure 10.21(e) below where we look for rows in which the minimum is the same as the quantity. This facility is also used when you want to *join* two tables.

Some of the features of QBE as a query language are illustrated by the sentences shown in Figure 10.21. Look at the enquiries and you will easily be able to work out what they are doing. Compare these sentences with those of the other query languages.

The SUM operation used in example (c) is one of a number of standard functions offered by QBE. Others include AVG (average), CNT (count), MAX (maximum) and MIN (minimum). These functions operate on all (or selected) values in a column.

STOCK	CODE	NAME	QUANTITY	PRICE	MINIMUM	MOVED
I.	4567	BOOKCASE	25	250.00	10	29/7/90

(a) Add a new row to the STOCK table

STOCK	CODE	NAME	QUANTITY	PRICE	MINIMUM	MOVED
U.				X * 1.1		

(b) Update the prices of all items

STOCK	CODE	NAME	QUANTITY	PRICE	MINIMUM	MOVED
U.		DESKX		Y * 1.1		

(c) Update the prices of all desks

STOCK	CODE	NAME	QUANTITY	PRICE	MINIMUM	MOVED
U.	4567			X * 1.1		

(d) Update the price of product 4567

STOCK	CODE	NAME	QUANTITY	PRICE	MINIMUM	MOVED
	7711			U. 35.50		

(e) Change the price of product 7711

STOCK	CODE	NAME	QUANTITY	PRICE	MINIMUM	MOVED
D.	1234					

(f) Delete the row for product 1234

Figure 10.20 Data manipulation with QBE

You may find some minor differences between your implementation of QBE and that described here: some precede all the *constant* values by the underscore '_' character, so that the formula to increase the prices might be be:

X * _1.1

STOCK	CODE	NAME	QUANTITY	PRICE	MINIMUM	MOVED
		P.	P.	P.		P.

(a) A simple enquiry

STOCK	CODE	NAME	QUANTITY	PRICE	MINIMUM	MOVED
	1290	P.	P.	P.		P.

(b) Looking for item 1290

STOCK	CODE	NAME	QUANTITY	PRICE	MINIMUM	MOVED
		P.	P.	P.SUM.ALL.XXX		

(c) Totalling the prices

STOCK	CODE	NAME	QUANTITY	PRICE	MINIMUM	MOVED
	P.	P.	P.	<100.00		

(d) Selecting according to the price

STOCK	CODE	NAME	QUANTITY	PRICE	MINIMUM	MOVED
	P.	P.	P.XXX		XXX	

(e) Selecting where the quantity is equal to the minimum

Figure 10.21 QBE queries and reports

But whichever version of QBE you use, you and your users will find it much easier to learn and to use than many other query languages which use sentences to make enquiries.

Questions—QBE

Answer these questions about the QBE language.

1 Is there a data description language?

2 Is there a data manipulation language?

3 Are the data description language, the data manipulation language and the query language identical?
When you are using the query language, ...
4 How do you select specific pieces of data from a file?
5 How could you produce a total of specific columns of data?

Activity 5

Using the QBE language, how would you handle the following situations? Write down the templates which you would use.

1 To create a new STUDENT file.
2 To indicate that you want to use the name, address, sex, telephone number, date of enrollment, the student registration number, the fee to be paid, whether the fee has been paid yet (assume that this is going to be a Y or N), and the degree for which the student is studying.
3 To add a new student: Miss Mary Shelley of 34 High Street who started to study for a B.Sc on 9th September 1990. Her registration number is 90/36192. She has no telephone and has not yet paid her fee.
4 To produce a list of all students who are studying for the B.Sc degree.
5 To change her record to indicate that Mary Shelley has now paid her fee.
6 To find the total fees still to be paid.
7 To delete the record for student 85/13455.

SQL

Probably the most well-known query language is SQL—*S*tructured *Q*uery *L*anguage. This was originally designed and implemented by IBM under the name SEQUEL—*S*tructured *E*nglish *QUE*ry *L*anguage, but variations of SQL are now available on many commercial DBMSs, including the DB2 product from IBM. The various implementations of SQL differ slightly from each other, although anyone who has used the language on one system should be able to move easily to some other version.

It is quite similar to the Access language in its form and in the syntax of the sentences. Unlike Access, SQL does have its own data description language.

It is possible to embed SQL commands within a host language such as Cobol, Pascal or PL/1. The SQL commands are distinguished from

```
CREATE TABLE FURNITURE ( CODE CHAR(4) NOT NULL,
                         DESCR CHAR(25),
                         QUANTITY INTEGER,
                         PRICE DECIMAL(5,2),
                         MINIMUM INTEGER,
                         MOVED CHAR(9) )
```

Figure 10.22 Creating an SQL table

the statements of the host language by preceding them with some identifier, such as a special character or keywords such as EXEC SQL.

SQL uses the terms *table*, *row* and *column* for relation, tuple and attribute. To create a table with the name FURNITURE, we use the SQL CREATE TABLE command shown in Figure 10.22. This describes the nature and the format of the columns of our table.

It doesn't matter how you arrange the command when you type it in. We have laid out our examples putting the various parts on separate lines so as to emphasize their meaning.

When you have created a table, SQL uses INSERT, UPDATE and DELETE commands for data manipulation. These are illustrated in Figure 10.23.

```
INSERT INTO FURNITURE
    VALUES ('4567','BOOKCASE','25','250.00','10','29-JUL-89')

          (a) add a new row to the FURNITURE table

INSERT INTO FURNITURE (CODE, DESCR)
    VALUES ('7711','CHAIR, SPECIAL')

               (b) adding a few columns only

UPDATE FURNITURE
    SET PRICE = PRICE * 1.2

            (b) Update the prices for all items

UPDATE FURNITURE
    SET PRICE = PRICE * 1.2
    WHERE CODE = '4567'

           (d) Update the price for product 4567

DELETE FROM FURNITURE
    WHERE CODE = '1234'

           (f) Deleting the row for product 1234
```

Figure 10.23 Data manipulation with SQL

Some of the features of SQL as a query language are illustrated by the sentences shown in Figure 10.24. Look at the enquiries and you will easily be able to work out what they are doing. Compare these sentences with the equivalent Access enquiries shown in Figure 10.5.

```
SELECT DESCR, QUANTITY, MOVED, PRICE
    FROM FURNITURE
```

(a) LIST sentence

```
SELECT DESCR, QUANTITY, LOCATION, PRICE
    FROM FURNITURE
    GROUP BY PRICE
```

(b) SORT sentence

```
SELECT DESCR, QUANTITY, PRICE, SUM(VALUE)
    FROM FURNITURE
    GROUP BY PRICE
```

(c) Totalling the VALUE column

```
SELECT DESCR, QUANTITY, PRICE, SUM(VALUE)
    FROM FURNITURE
    GROUP BY PRICE
    WHERE PRICE < 100
```

(d) Selecting according to the PRICE

Figure 10.24 SQL queries and reports

Questions—SQL

Answer these questions about the SQL language.

1 Is there a data description language?
2 Is there a data manipulation language?
3 Are the data description language, the data manipulation language and the query language identical?

When you are using the query language, ...

4 How do you select specific pieces of data from a file?
5 How could you produce a total of specific columns of data?
6 How could you sort a report by the product code?

Activity 6

Using the SQL language, how would you handle the following situations? Write down the commands and sentences which you would use.

1 To create a new STUDENT file.

2 To indicate that you want to use the name, address, sex, telephone number, date of enrollment, the student registration number, the fee to be paid, whether the fee has been paid yet (assume that this is going to be a single character, Y or N), and the degree for which the student is studying.
Make any assumptions about the size and format of the data in the columns.

3 To add a new student: Miss Mary Shelley of 34 High Street who started to study for a B.Sc on 9th September 1990. Her registration number is 90/36192. She has no telephone and has not yet paid her fee.

4 To produce a list of all students who are studying for the B.Sc degree.

5 To change her record to indicate that Mary Shelley has now paid her fee.

6 To find the total fees still to be paid.

7 To delete the record for student 85/13455.

Views

SQL will allow you to create explicit views for the individual users. A view is a single table—often called a *virtual table* since it has no independent physical existence—which is derived from the data held in other tables. The view can be drawn from a single table—such as the STUDENT table used in the last Activity. Let us imagine that we want a view called BSC_STUDENTS—representing the number, the name, sex and address of all the students who are studying for the B.Sc degree. To illustrate this, we have created the STUDENT table by the command shown in Figure 10.25(a). A view representing just the B.Sc students might be created by the command shown in diagram (b), and used by a command such as that shown in diagram (c).

More powerfully, the view can be drawn from several diøerent tables. You will recognize the JOIN process in this operation. To illustrate this, let us imagine that, in addition to the STUDENT table described in the last Activity, we have a table called DEGREE created with the command and the sample contents shown in diagrams (a) and (b) of Figure 10.26. We now wish to allow a group of users to have access to information held in the view consisting of the student's enrolment number, name and full title of the degree, as represented by the

```
CREATE TABLE STUDENT (STUDENTNAME VARCHAR(15),
                      STUDENTADDRESS VARCHAR(30),
                      STUDENTSEX CHAR(1),
                      STUDENTPHONE CHAR(20),
                      ENROLMENTDATE CHAR(9),
                      STUDENTNUMBER CHAR(8),
                      STUDENTFEE INTEGER(6),
                      PAIDFLAG CHAR(1),
                      STUDENTDEGREE CHAR(6) )
```

(a) Creating the table

```
CREATE VIEW BSC_STUDENTS
    AS SELECT STUDENTNUMBER, STUDENTNAME, STUDENTSEX, STUDENTADDRESS,
    FROM STUDENT
    WHERE STUDENTDEGREE = 'B.Sc'
```

(b) Creating the view

```
SELECT STUDENTNAME, STUDENTADDRESS
    FROM BSC_STUDENTS
    WHERE STUDENTSEX = 'F'
```

(c) Using the view

Figure 10.25 A view drawn from one table

instances in diagram (c). We could create this view and give it the name STUDENT_SUMMARY by means of the command shown in diagram (d). This view can then be used as if it were an ordinary table, as illustrated by the command in diagram (e) and the output in diagram (f).

Having created a view, it is possible to manipulate it exactly as if it were a true table. This is illustrated in Figure 10.26(e). It is also possible to change the values within a view, and in doing so, you will be indirectly changing the actual table(s) from which the view is drawn.

Recap

There are many language available to describe and manipulate relational databases. In this chapter, we looked at some of these individually. Some of the languages are essentially query languages assisted by other tools to allow the programmer to manipulate the database. Other languages are powerful pieces of software representing a combination of data description language, data manipulation and query language.

Most of the query languages offer full facilities for displaying all or some of the data fields of the records, selecting records according to specific criteria, sorting the output into some specific order, totalling numeric fields. The various languages differ in the ease and elegance with which they allow the user to use these facilities.

```
CREATE TABLE DEGREE (DEGREECODE VARCHAR(10),
                     FULLDESCRIPTION VARCHAR(30) )
```

(a) Creating the table

DEGREE

DEGREECODE	FULLDESCRIPTION
BSc	Bachelor of Science
MSc	Master of Science
BA	Bachelor of Arts
MA	Master of Arts
PhD	Doctor of Philosophy

(b) Some instances

STUDENT SUMMARY

STUDENTNUMBER	STUDENTNAME	FULLDESCRIPTION
90/36192	Mary Shelley	Bachelor of Science
90/45112	John Locke	Master of Science

(c) The view

```
CREATE VIEW STUDENT_SUMMARY
    AS SELECT STUDENTNUMBER, STUDENTNAME, FULLDESCRIPTION
    FROM STUDENT, DEGREE
    WHERE STUDENTDEGREE = DEGREECODE
```

(d) Creating the view

```
SELECT STUDENTNAME, FULLDESCRIPTION
    FROM STUDENT_SUMMARY
    WHERE STUDENTNAME = 'Mary Shelley'
```

(e) An SQL enquiry on the view

STUDENT SUMMARY

STUDENTNUMBER	STUDENTNAME	FULLDESCRIPTION
90/36192	Mary Shelley	Bachelor of Science

(f) The output

Figure 10.26 A view drawn from several tables

The data manipulation languages allow the user to add new records, change existing records and delete existing records.

Access is the query language provided by the Pick Operating System. There is no formal data description language, but the format of the data records is specified by a set of definitions held on a dictionary which is associated with each file.

The data manipulation language takes the form of a number of powerful extensions to Basic.

As a query language, Access is virtually unique in that it can change the output appearance of any data field in a variety of ways and can combine one or more fields to produce a new value.

We looked at the contents of the data dictionary and saw how this controls the format of the output reports.

dBASE is a combination of data description language, data definition language and query language. It is screen-oriented, interacting with the user in a screen-based dialogue. It is also possible to write applications programs in the dBASE language. The statements used in the programs are essentially the same as the commands which are issued interactively.

Some dBASE commands will allow you to browse through the file to locate and look at records. The contents of the data records can be changed interactively.

QBE is different from the other languages considered, in that it allows the users to make their enquiries by filling in a form.

QBE uses the terms table, row and column for relation, tuple and attribute.

When invoked, QBE displays a blank called a template, the user enters the name of the table which is to be used and QBE displays the name of the columns in that table.

The users then enter codes according to whether they wish to print the values in a column, to insert data, to update data, or to delete data.

SQL is probably the most well-known query language. It is a combination of data description language, data manipulation language and query language. It is possible to embed SQL commands within a host language such as Cobol, Pascal or PL/1.

SQL uses the terms table, row and column for relation, tuple and attribute.

SQL will allow you to create explicit views for the individual users. A view is a single table—often called a virtual table since it has no independent physical existence—which is derived from the data held in other tables.

Answers

Access

1 No, the editor is used to create dictionary definition records on the DICT for each file.
2 Yes, it is an extended form of Basic.
3 No
4 Use the WITH modifier in a sentence.
5 Use the BY modifier in a sentence.
6 Use the TOTAL modifier in a sentence.

dBASE

1 Yes, it is an extension of the query language.
2 Yes, it is an extension of the query language.
3 Yes
4 Use FOR with a selection condition.
5 Use the SUM command.

QBE—query by example

1 Yes, it is an extension of the query language.
2 Yes, it is an extension of the query language.
3 Yes
4 Specify the selection condition in the appropriate column.
5 Write P.SUM.ALL.*XXX* in the appropriate column.

SQL

1 Yes, it is the CREATE TABLE command which is an extension of the query language.
2 Yes, it is an extension of the query language with commands such as INSERT, UPDATE and DELETE. SQL commands may also be embedded in a host language such as Cobol, Pascal or PL/1.
3 Yes
4 Use the WHERE modifier in the sentence.
5 Use the SUM function in the sentence.
6 Use GROUP BY in the sentence.

11: Database design

Objectives

After reading this chapter, you should be able to:

- define the terms *key*, *functional dependency* and *repeating group*
- recognize the terms *synonym* and *homonym*
- use the terms *schema* and *sub-schema*, and *local data model* and global data model
- use a notation for recording sub-schemas
- identify functional dependency between attributes
- use a notation and diagrams to represent functional dependencies
- describe the process of *data normalization*
- perform the steps of data normalization as far as third normal form
- describe the terms *composite key* and *foreign key*
- describe the way in which the local data models are combined to derive the schema for the database.

File design

During the preparatory stages of the development of a computer system, the analyst will carry out a full investigation of the needs of each individual user and each group of users within the organization. Based upon the results of the systems investigation and the systems analysis activities, the analyst is able to decide which data to hold in the database: the data must be able to produce all the reports and to support all the enquiries which are needed by the users. The analyst will then combine these to build a database which meets the requirements of all the users. This led us to the concept of *entities*, objects about which we need to hold information.

We have seen that an entity may be quite different from a file; the information about a STUDENT entity may be held on several different physical files. So how do we make the transition from entities to files? How do we decide which pieces of data are to be held in the records on our files? How do we design the schemas for our files? These are some of the questions which we shall answer in this chapter.

We shall base our work upon *relational schemas*, but the general concept and principles apply equally well to the hierarchical and network models which we have considered.

A formal definition of a key

We have used the word *key* on many occasions, and in Chapter 2 we developed an intuitive idea of what we mean by a key. We must now produce a formal definition so that we can use this in our data analysis. We shall define the key of a relation as follows:

> A key is the smallest subset of attributes from the relation such that the key is unique for each tuple.

Let us illustrate this by looking at the table which holds information about the tours offered by a coach hire company. We have shown a section of the table in Figure 11.1.

Date	Destination	Fare	Seats	Bookings
18/7	Stonehenge	50.00	30	15
18/7	London	30.00	30	2
18/7	Lake District	75.00	25	25
19/7	Stonehenge	50.00	30	17
19/7	Rye and the coast	30.00	30	30
19/7	London	30.00	30	7
20/7	Lake District	75.00	25	22
20/7	London	30.00	30	9

Figure 11.1 Tables of tours

The owner of the company has decided to hold this information on a computer database as a part of a seat reservation system. We need to identify the key. The attributes of the relation are:

- The date on which the tour operates,
- The destination of the tour,
- The fare for each passenger,
- The number of seats,
- The number of bookings.

Clearly, none of these attributes *alone* can be used to identify each line uniquely:

- Date: there are several tours on any one date (so we can't use the Date as the key).
- Destination: there are several tours to Stonehenge, for example (so we can't use the Destination).
- Fare: there are several tours which cost £30.00 for example (so we can't use the Fare).
- Number of seats: there are several tours limited to 30 seats (so we can't use the Seats as the key).
- Number of bookings: the number of reserved seats cannot be a key since it will change whenever another seat is booked.

Let us see what happens when we try the attributes in pairs.

- Date and destination: this is possible since each combination of these attributes is unique.
- Date and fare: this is not unique (this combination for Rye and for London on 19/7 would be the same).
- Date and seats: this is not unique (this combination for Rye and for London on 19/7 would be the same).
- Destination and fare: this is not unique (this combination for Stonehenge on 18/7 and 19/7 would be the same).
- Destination and seats: this is not unique for the same reasons as *destination and fare*.
- Fare and seats: this is not unique (this combination for Rye and for London would be the same).

We have, therefore, satisfied the conditions for a key to this relation and we need look no further: the *date* and the *destination* give us a key. There is no *smaller* key (neither the date nor the destination alone would suffice) and any other combination of attributes must be a *larger* subset. This means that in order to identify any specific tour, we need to know the date and the destination of the tour. If you wanted to reserve a seat on a particular tour, you would have to tell the booking clerk both the date and the destination of the tour, these two pieces of information are sufficient to identify any particular tour: if you gave only the destination or only the date, the clerk would not have enough information to know which tour you wanted; if you gave more than this information—the price, for example—then this would be unnecessary, redundant information.

Questions

1 Describe a situation or some circumstances in which the combination of date and destination would not uniquely identify each tour.
2 What would happen if there were *two* tours to London on the same date, one starting at 9:00 am and another at 2:30 pm? How would the above discussion change and what would the new key be?
3 Carry out an inspection similar to the one in the text, so as to derive a possible key for the table shown in Figure 11.2. This represents a list of organized parties who wish to visit a food factory.

Date of visit	Name of person making booking	Organisation	Time of arrival
20/1/92	Mrs Hudson	Keyes School	9:00
20/1/92	Mr Barrymore	Keyes School	11:00
20/1/92	B.A.Ross	P.W. College	2:30
21/1/92	Chairman	Golf Club	2:30
22/4/92	Chairman	R.P. Institute	10:30
20/6/92	Mrs Hudson	Keyes School	11:00

Figure 11.2 Visits to the food factory

Relational sub-schemas

We shall record the proposed sub-schema for a relation like this:

TOUR (Date, Destination, Fare, Seats, Bookings)

and when we have decided upon a suitable key, we shall underline the attribute (or attributes) which make up the key, like this:

TOUR (<u>Date</u>, <u>Destination</u>, Fare, Seats, Bookings)

This gives us a concise and precise means of recording the contents of the relations.

It may be that the structure of our relations will change as we proceed with the design of the files, so it is important to keep these sub-schemas up-to-date and to ensure that they reflect the current state of our investigations.

In practice, when you are developing sub-schemas such as this, you will not be doing it for just *one* relation; you will be developing *several* sub-schemas at the same time. Each sub-schema will describe the view of one user. In the case of the coach hire company, in addition to the timetable which we have been looking at, there may be another sub-schema to describe the information about the passengers (their names, addresses and telephone numbers), another to describe information about the fares paid (the name of the passenger, the amount paid, the date paid, any amount outstanding), and possibly others besides. Each sub-schema will represent one *local data model.* For this reason, it is good practice to choose meaningful and explicit names for the attributes. This will help you to avoid confusion when we come to consolidate and combine the several local data models into a single *global data model.* This is particularly true of attributes such as Date, Price, Cost, Value, Description and Name. In most commercial applications, there are many situations in which Date and Price are used, and it is easy to make a mistake and confuse them. The Name on a STUDENT relation would not be the same as the Name on a LECTURER relation; it would be much better to use Student-name (or even Student-surname) and Lecturer-name.

When you are performing your investigation, you will find situations where:

1 Different names are used to described the same piece of information; a sales assistant might use the word PRICE to describe the amount to be paid for the goods, whereas a clerk in the office might use the word COST for the same thing, both words describing the same piece of data. When different names are used to describe the same piece of data, these names are called *synonyms.*

2 The same name is used to describe different pieces of information. A sales assistant might use the word PRICE to mean the amount which the customer has to pay *after* VAT has been added, whereas a clerk in the office might use the word PRICE to mean the amount to be paid *before* VAT has been added. When the same name is used to describe different pieces of data, these names are called *homonyms.*

Choosing explicit and meaningful names avoids such situations. It also has a further advantage because it makes you think about what data you will be holding in the relation. In fact, the TOUR relation might be better written:

TOUR (Departure-date, Destination, Adult-fare, Maximum-number-of-seats, Current-number-of-bookings)

and you see how this forces the systems analyst to ask further questions about the fare: what about other sorts of fare—Children's, Old-age pensioners'—how are they to be charged? By asking such questions and incorporating the answers into the design for the data and the system, the analyst is able to ensure that the design covers all eventualities, even those which were not obvious to him/her earlier.

In this discussion, however, I have shortened my names so as to make them easier to type and to remember.

Activity 1

We have seen that *Name* might mean *Student-name*, *Student-surname*, or *Lecturer-name*. Give some possible meanings of the following attributes as you might meet them within a system designed for a Department Store:

1 Date
2 Description
3 Price
4 Value
5 Cost
6 Name

Choose more explicit names which would indicate clearly the true nature of the data.

Repeating groups

When we were looking at the formal aspects of relations in Chapter 9, we said that *at the intersection of any tuple and any attribute there is a single value*. However, when you are investigating your real-world data, you may find that certain pieces of data are *repeated*. That is, within any one entry (tuple) of the table (relation), a certain attribute may have several values. For example, we may have decided to hold the *names* of the people who are going on each tour of the food factory. So that a single entry might look like that in Figure 11.3(a). We would record this sub-schema using bracket notation, like this:

> FACTORY-TOUR (Date, Person-booking, (Visitor-name), Organization, Time)

enclosing the *Visitor-name* in *brackets* to show that this attribute may be repeated several times. When this situations occurs, the data is said to be a *repeating group*.

Later, we shall look at the ways in which we can remove these repeating groups so that the relation retains the properties which we looked at in Chapter 9. We have mentioned that a relation which has

Date of visit	Name of person making booking	Name of visitor	Organisation	Time of arrival
20/1/92	Mrs Hudson	A.Christie G.Green T.Mann H.Newbolt	Keyes School	9:00

(a) FACTORY-TOUR relation

Borr' No.	Book No.	Book Title	Date Borrowed	Date due Back	Name	Dept.	Date Joined
19288	8465 4232 2300	HEAT I HEAT HEAT II	10/11/92 10/11/92 10/11/92	24/11/92 24/11/92 24/11/92	JONES	PHYSICS	10/10/92

(b) LIBRARY-MEMBER relation

Student Number	Exam Code	Paper Number	Marks	Result	Degree	Class
92/1922	BA001	BA001/1	79	PASS	B.A.	2
		BA001/2	60			
	BA002	BA002/4	65	FAIL		
		BA002/5	43			
		BA002/7	40			
	BA003	BA003/1	90	PASS		
	BA003	BA003/9	98			

(c) DEGREE relation

Figure 11.3 Repeating groups

no repeating groups is known as a *flat file*. By resolving our relation into one or more flat files, we shall be able to avoid many of the difficulties which such repeating groups present.

Some sub-schemas can be quite complicated with several attributes within a repeating group. We might, for example, have produced a relation like this:

LIBRARY-MEMBER(<u>Borrower-number</u>, (Book-number, book-title, Date-borrowed, Date-due-back), Name, Department, Date-joined-library)

Here there are several sets of

(Book-number, book-title, Date-borrowed, Date-due-back)

for any one Borrower-number. Such a sub-schema may have instances like those in Figure 11.3(b). You may even encounter *repeating groups within repeating groups*:

DEGREE(Student-number, (Examination-code, (Paper-number, Marks), Result), Degree, Class)

where there are several sets of

(Examination-code, (Paper-number, Marks), Result)

for each Student-number, Degree and Class, and there are several sets of

(Paper-number, Marks)

for each Examination-code and Result. Such a sub-schema may have instances like those in Figure 11.3(c).

Activity 2

Use the bracket notation to write down the relation sub-schemas for each of the following tables:

1 The Video Tape Catalogue relation shown in Figure 11.4.

VIDEO NUMBER	TITLE	RECENT TITLE	HIRE RATE			MINS
			WEEK	DAY	WK-END	
700	THE INCAS	*	4.00	1.50	1.75	120
056	WILLY WONKA		3.00	1.00	1.50	60
078	SOUND OF ROME		3.00	1.00	1.50	145
340	THE THING II		3.00	1.00	1.50	120
600	WATER MARGIN	*	4.00	1.50	1.75	60
734	SENTRIES	*	4.00	1.50	1.75	220
098	WONDERS		3.00	1.00	1.50	140
534	THE GANGES	*	4.00	1.50	1.75	140

Figure 11.4 A video tape catalogue

2 The table shown in Figure 11.5 which represents the transport log book kept by the manager of a road haulage company. The table shows the dates and route for a number of journeys, the registration number of the lorry which made the journey, the identity number of the containers which the lorry carried, and the charge rate for carrying the container.

3 The patient's record card shown in Figure 11.6.

Rte	From	To	Reg	Cont	Chrge Rate	Date
102	Lincoln	Leeds	G 123 ABC	FT36 AG44 AH19 PL32	D A E B	13/09/92
003	Manchester	Lincoln	F PQR 321	AL77 AG08 AM10	D C C	13/09/92
103	Lincoln	York	F PQR 321	AG03 AG07 AM10	C A C	14/09/92
302	York	Norwich	DEF 123 A	AG09 FT10	E F	14/09/92
003	Manchester	Lincoln	F PQR 321	AH19 AG03 PL32 AL77 FT36	E C B D D	15/09/92

Figure 11.5 TRANSPORT-LOG relation

National Insurance Number: ZZ 88 77 66 C

Name: Henderson, Mary Elizabeth, Miss

Date of birth: 16 June 1953

Address: 12 Main Street, Redbexton, Sussex

Telephone: 01-999 4500

Last Visit: 7 July 1990

Contact: Mrs Alice Henderson, 01-999 4500, Mother
Miss Mary Johnson, 01-999 3456, Friend

Visits:

Date	Symptoms	Diagnosis	Medications
01/01/87	Cold		Paracetamol
03/03/87	Headache	Migraine?	Paracetamol
07/07/88	Sunburn		Calamine lotion
12/07/88	Headache		Migraway
07/07/90	Vaccinations	Travelling	Smallpox vaccine

Hospital Visits:

Date of Admission	Hospital	Reason	Date Discharged	Doctor
01/10/86	Fowler	Minor Burn	02/10/86	Dr Jobson Dr Oddson
01/11/86	Fowler	Remove sutures	01/11/86	Dr Bodson

Figure 11.6 PATIENT relation

Functional dependency

We have seen that if we know its key, we can find any tuple in the relation. In other words, the key determines the tuple. There are, however, other pieces of data in the relation which are associated one with another, such that, if we know the value of one piece of data, we can find the value of the other.

If a passenger is interested in going to, say, Stonehenge, then he can look at the table and see that the fare is £50.00. We say that the *fare* is functionally dependent upon the *destination*: knowing the destination determines the fare that the passenger must pay. A more formal way of saying this is:

> If we know the value of the *destination* attribute, then we can find the corresponding value for the *fare* attribute. The *fare* attribute is therefore functionally dependent upon the *destination* attribute.

and this leads us to a definition:

> An attribute A is functionally dependent upon another attribute B, if attribute A can be uniquely identified when the value of attribute B is known.

Let us look at the table of tours shown in Figure 11.7. This has changed slightly from the one which we met earlier; our user has now decided that she wants to show the income from the bookings on each tour.

Date	Destination	Fare	Seats	Bookings	Income
18/7	Stonehenge	50.00	30	15	1125.00
18/7	London	30.00	30	2	60.00
18/7	Lake District	75.00	25	25	1875.00
19/7	Stonehenge	50.00	30	17	850.00
19/7	Rye and the coast	30.00	30	30	900.00
19/7	London	30.00	30	7	210.00
20/7	Lake District	75.00	25	22	1650.00
20/7	London	30.00	30	9	270.00

Figure 11.7 Tables of tours

Looking at the table, we will find situations in which:

- One attribute is functionally dependent upon several combined attributes: the combination of the date and the destination enable us to find the number of bookings and also the income; the income is functionally dependent upon the combination of the fare and the number of bookings.

- Several attributes are functionally dependent upon one attribute: the fare is functionally dependent upon the destination; the number of seats is functionally dependent upon the destination.

We can write these facts using the following notation:

- destination → fare
- destination → seats
- fare, bookings → income
- date, destination → bookings

the arrow telling us that:

- The *fare* is functionally dependent upon the *destination* (that is, if we know the *destination* then we can find the *fare*).
- The number of *seats* is functionally dependent upon the *destination* (if we know the *destination* then we can find the number of *seats*).
- The *income* is functionally dependent upon the *fare* and the number of *bookings* (if we know the *fare* and the number of *bookings* then we can find the *income*).
- The number of *bookings* is functionally dependent upon the *date* and the *destination* (if we know the *date* and the *destination* then we can find the number of *bookings*).

These same functional dependencies can be shown diagrammatically as in Figure 11.8.

Some analysts use other diagramming techniques such as that shown

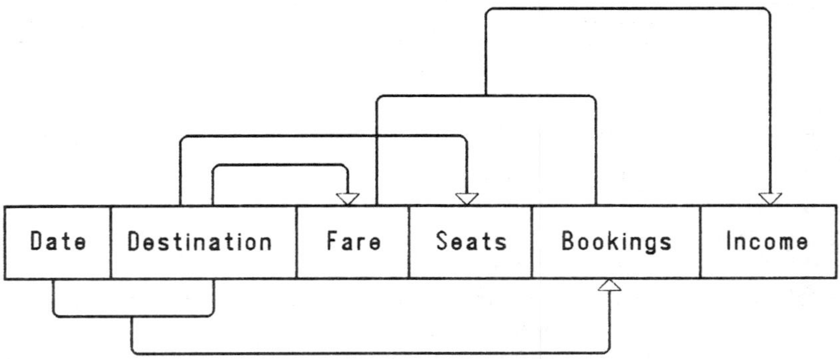

Figure 11.8 Functional dependencies—1

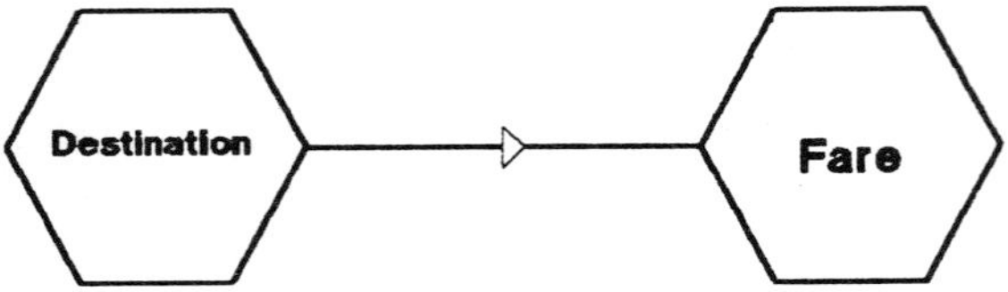

(a) Destination → Fare

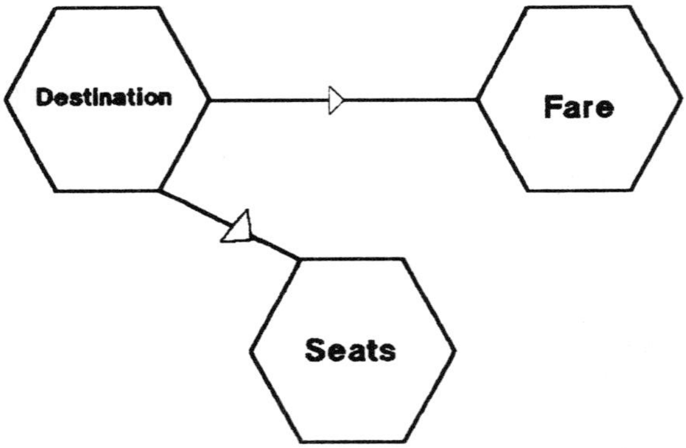

(b) Destination → Fare, Seats

Figure 11.9 Functional dependencies—2

in Figure 11.9. Diagram (a) tells us that the fare is functionally dependent upon the *destination*. The individual attributes are represented by hexagons, and the functional dependency is shown by a line with an arrow-head pointing towards the dependent attribute. The number of seats is also functionally dependent upon the destination. We can extend the diagram to show this, as llustrated in Figure 11.9(b).

Figure 11.10 shows how this technique depicts the situation where an attribute is functionally dependent upon several attributes. For example, if we know the date and the destination, we can find the number of bookings. This is represented in Diagram (a). We can com-

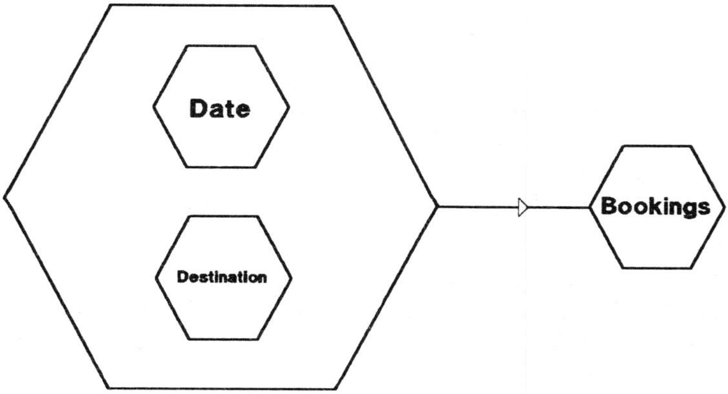

(a) Date, Destination → Bookings

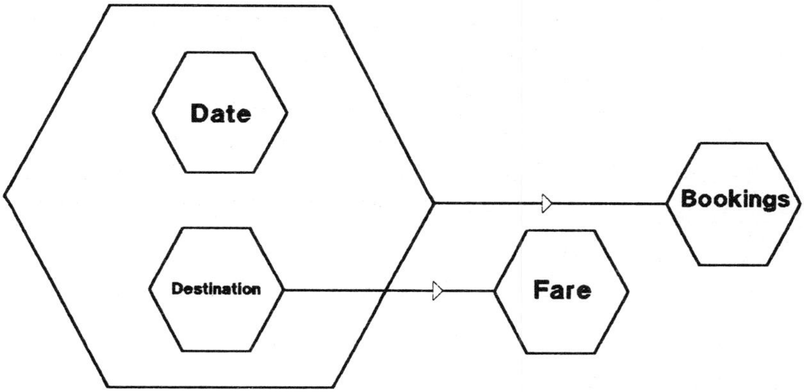

(b) Date → Fare
Date, Destination → Bookings

Figure 11.10 Functional dependencies—3

bine these diagrams to represent several such facts by a diagram like that shown in Figure 11.10(b).

When an identifying key consists of two or more pieces of data, this is called a *composite key*. So the combination of Fare and Bookings is a composite key enabling us to find the Income.

Functional dependency diagrams, such as these, can be a valuable tool when you are trying to clarify your thoughts about the inter-relationship and the dependency of the various attributes in an entity. We shall use the concept of functional dependency later when we discuss data normalization.

Activity 3

In this section, we have seen three ways of recording the functional dependency between the attributes of a relation. Use each of these three methods in turn to show the functional dependencies within the following four relations.

1 The video tape catalogue relation shown in Figure 11.11.

VIDEO NUMBER	TITLE	RECENT TITLE	HIRE RATE WEEK	HIRE RATE DAY	HIRE RATE WK-END	MINS
700	SUNDAY II	*	4.00	1.50	1.75	120
056	WHISPERERS		3.00	1.00	1.50	60
078	SALAD IN ROME		3.00	1.00	1.50	145
340	THE THING		3.00	1.00	1.50	120
600	WATER MARGIN	*	4.00	1.50	1.75	60
734	RAMBO XCIX	*	4.00	1.50	1.75	220
098	CARRY OUT		3.00	1.00	1.50	140
534	YES, SIR	*	4.00	1.50	1.75	140

Figure 11.11   A video tape catalogue

2 The local football league table shown in Figure 11.12.

Team	Position	Won	Lost	Drawn	Points	Played
Whites	1	3	2	4	8	9
Greens	2	2	3	3	7	8
Blues	3	2	3	4	7	9
Reds	4	1	2	5	4	8

Figure 11.12   Football league table

3 The relation represented by the sub-schema:

STUDENT (<u>Name</u>, Address, (Subject, Exam-result), Enrolment-date, Registration-number, Sex, Date-of-birth, Age)

4 The relation represented by the sub-schema:

ROOM-ALLOCATION (<u>Building</u>, <u>Room-number</u>, <u>Study-period</u>, Tutor, (Student), (Equipment-available), Subject)

What is the difference between this sub-schema and:

ROOM-ALLOCATION (<u>Building</u>, <u>Room-number</u>, <u>Study-period</u>, Tutor, (Student, Equipment-available), Subject)

and which is most likely to be correct? Notice the brackets around Student and Equipment-available. Explain the differences in your own words and give instances of each.

Data normalization

In order to transform our data designs from relations to files, we shall look at the data which they represent and perform a process known as *data normalization*. This will produce a set of suitable relations which we can use to hold the data.

The formal techniques for performing data normalization were developed by Ted Codd for use with relational databases, nevertheless, they form a suitable basis for the design of data which is to be used in other situations.

Essentially, data normalization involves arranging the data in such a way that it meets the database requirements that the data should be accessible to all who need it and that each piece of data be held in one place only.

We shall start by looking at each relation or a small group of relations in turn. When these have been normalized to produce a set of *local data models*, we combine and consolidate the various sub-schemas to arrive at a *global data model*—the *schema*. It is this final global data model which will form the basis for the database.

The starting point for the normalization process is the reports and documents which are produced by the proposed computer system. The whole purpose of the database is to satisfy the reporting needs of the system. In order to know what data to put into the database and what data to hold on the files, we must know what data is required from it. We therefore collect together all the layouts for the screens, reports and enquiries which will be concerned with the database.

If we are re-organizing an existing system, then we should gather all the current reports and screen layouts and—after checking that they are still to form a part of the system and amending them to meet the users' requirements—we shall use these as our starting point. If we are designing a completely new system, then we should gather all the designs for the proposed reports and screen layouts and use these as our starting point.

It is convenient to think of each document as requiring its own local data model. Three standard steps are followed in the process to normalize a relation so as to produce a local data model. We can summarize these:

1 *First normal form*
The first step is *to remove any repeating groups from the relation*. When this step has been taken, the data is said to be in the *first normal form*.

2 *Second normal form*
The second step is to ensure that, if the relation has a composite key then *any data attribute in the relation should be functionally dependent upon the whole key and not just a part of the key.* A data attribute which is functionally dependent upon just a *part* of a composite key should be removed to form a new relation. When this step has been taken, the data is said to be in the *second normal form.*

3 *Third normal form*
The third step is to ensure that you *remove any attributes which are functionally dependent upon other attributes and put these in a separate relation.* When this step has been taken, the data is said to be in the *third normal form.*

There is some academic discussion about fourth, fifth and even higher normal forms, but these are outside the scope of the present text. Indeed third normal form is perfectly adequate for almost any commercial database management system.

We shall illustrate the process of data normalization by working through two examples. One example is based upon the LIBRARY-MEMBER entity which we met earlier, the second is based upon an invoice such as you might receive when you order goods from a mail-order supplier.

Question

4 Using that data shown in Figure 11.13, draw up a sub-schema for the Invoice entity. Indicate a suitable key or composite key for the entity. We shall use the solution to this Question in the work which follows.

First normal form

Before we start the process of normalization, we must write down the *name* and the sub-schema for the relation which we are going to normalize, and indicate a suitable key. We shall use the bracket notation to do this.

Let us look at our first example, the LIBRARY-MEMBER relation which now has the sub-schema:

LIBRARY-MEMBER(Borrower-number, (Book-number, Book-title, Author, Category, Date-borrowed, Date-due-back), Student-number, Name, Address, Department, Telephone-number, Date-joined-library)

Acme Sports Goods Ltd

34 High Street, Braddersfax, West Yorkshire BF9 9BF 0274-999274

I N V O I C E

Order Number 111111

Order Date 02/02/92

Delivery Date 02/05/92

Customer 33333

ORWELL FOOTBALL CLUB
34 HIGH STREET, YORK

Ref	Description	Qty	Unit Price	Cost
4/4444	TRAINERS	5	66.00	330.00
7/7777	TRACK SUIT	8	99.00	792.00
			Total	1122.00
			Vat	168.30
Credit limit: 10000.00			Amount Due	1290.30

Figure 11.13 A sales invoice

Assignment 1

Using the LIBRARY-MEMBER sub-schema shown here, draw up a relation showing instances for about 10 borrowers each of whom may have up to three books.

- Invent your own values for the names, titles and other attributes.
- Highlight the keys for each entry in the relation.

The first step is *to remove any repeating groups*. The attribute(s) which we remove will form a new relation and the key for this new relation will be made up of the key for the original relation plus an attribute which will produce a unique key for each tuple of the new relation. In this example, we would remove the repeating group:

(Book-number, Book-title, Author, Category, Date-borrowed, Date-due-back)

to produce the two relations:

LIBRARY-MEMBER2(Borrower-number, Student-number, Name, Address, Department, Telephone-number, Date-joined-library)
BOOK-LOAN(Borrower-number, Book-number, Book-title, Author, Category, Date-borrowed, Date-due-back)

Where LIBRARY-MEMBER2 is the original relation with the repeating group removed (we have called it LIBRARY-MEMBER2 to avoid confusing it with the original LIBRARY-MEMBER), and BOOK-LOAN is a new relation made up of the original key and the attributes from the repeating group.

The choice of key for the new BOOK-LOAN relation depends on how we wish to use the data. We have chosen a *composite key* made up of Borrower-number (from the original relation) and Book-number (from the repeating group). This means that the composite key is considered to be unique and implies that:

- We are assuming that one borrower will only borrow each book once. This is obviously true (only one person can borrow a book at any one moment).
- We do not want to distinguish between the several occasions on which a borrower borrows the same book. That is, if a student ever borrows the same book again, we are no longer interested in the previous occasions on which he borrowed that book.

If the users and the analyst are not happy with these implications, then it may be necessary to modify the design and use an alternative composite key:

BOOK-LOAN2(Borrower-number, Book-number, Book-title, Author, Category, Date-borrowed, Date-due-back) Telephone-number, Date-joined-library)

which only assumes that a given borrower will only borrow a given book *once* on a given date. Now let us repeat the process for the INVOICE relation.

INVOICE(Invoice-number, Invoice-date, Delivery-date, Customer-number, Customer-name, Customer-address, (Reference-code, Description, Quantity, Unit-price, Line-cost), Total-cost, Vat-due, Credit-limit, Total-amount-due)

The only repeating group is the order line:

(Reference-code, Description, Quantity, Unit-price, Line-cost)

Removing this, we derive:

INVOICE2(Invoice-number, Invoice-date, Delivery-date, Customer-number, Customer-name, Customer-address, Total-cost, Vat-due, Credit-limit, Total-amount-due)
ORDER-LINE(Invoice-number, Reference-code, Description, Quantity, Unit-price, Line-cost)

As before, by having a composite key made up of the Invoice-number and the Reference-code, we are assuming that that this key will be unique and that any particular product will only be shown once on each invoice. If there were two lines both for TRAINERS, for example, then this key would not be unique and we should have to think of some other key. One possibility might be to use the item-number or the order-line-number; item-number 1 for the first order-line, item-number 2 for the second, and so on. We must check this with our users to ensure that our keys are satisfactory.

Assignment 2

1 Using the instances which you produced for the LIBRARY-MEMBER relation, draw up the corresponding instances of the LIBRARY-MEMBER2 and BOOK-LOAN relations. Highlight the keys for each entry in the relations.
2 Using the data in the original invoice shown in Figure 11.13, draw up the corresponding instances of the INVOICE2 and ORDER-LINE relations. Highlight the keys for each entry in the relations.

If the original relation contained more than one repeating group, then you would remove each in turn to produce a new relation.

If you had repeating groups *within* repeating groups, then you would first remove the outer repeating groups, and then from these you would remove the inner repeating groups. We can illustrate this with a relation such as:

DEGREE(Student-number, (Examination-code, (Paper-number, Marks), Result), Degree, Class)

would yield first:

DEGREE2(Student-number, Degree, Class)

EXAMINATION(Student-number, Examination-code, (Paper-number, Marks , Result)

and finally:

DEGREE2(Student-number, Degree, Class)

EXAMINATION2(Student-number, Examination-code, Result)

PAPER(Student-number, Examination-code, Paper-number, Marks)

This first step in normalization results in one or more flat files, and the data is said to be in the *first normal form.*

Activity 4

1 Using the instances shown in Figure 11.3, draw up the corresponding tables for the DEGREE2, EXAMINATION2 and PAPER relations whose sub-schema is shown above. Highlight the keys for each entry in the relations.
2 Using your previous results, derive the first normal form of the TRANSPORT-LOG relation.
3 Using your previous results, derive the first normal form of the PATIENT relation.

Second normal form

The second step uses the idea of functional dependency which we introduced earlier, and is to ensure that, if a relation has a composite key then *any attribute in the relation should be functionally dependent upon the whole key and not just a part of the key.*

The LIBRARY-MEMBER2 relation does not have a composite key, so we can ignore it at this stage. However, the other relation,

BOOK-LOAN(<u>Borrower-number</u>, <u>Book-number</u>, Book-title, Author, Category, Date-borrowed, Date-due-back)

does have a composite key. We must therefore look at each attribute and check whether it depends upon the *whole* key or just a *part* of the key. Doing this, we find that:

- Book-title is functionally dependent upon Book-number. This means that, in order to find the Book-title, we need to know only the Book-number. The Book-title is functionally dependent upon just the Book-number part of the key.
- Author is functionally dependent upon just the Book-number part of the key.
- Category is functionally dependent upon just the Book-number part of the key.
- Date-borrowed is functionally dependent upon Borrower-number *and* Book-number. This means that, in order to find the Date-borrowed, we need to know both the Borrower-number and the Book-number; other borrowers who have borrowed (or will borrow) the same book will be due back on different dates, and other books borrowed by the same borrower may also be due back on different dates. Only the combination of Borrower-number and Book-number will enable us to find the correct Date-due-back.
- Date-due-back is functionally dependent upon Borrower-number *and* Book-number.

Using the notation we introduced earlier, we write:

Book-number → Book-title
Book-number → Author
Book-number → Category
Borrower-number, Book-number → Date-borrowed
Borrower-number, Book-number → Date-due-back

Having identified the functional dependencies, we remove those attributes which are functionally dependent upon just a part of the key and use these to establish new relations. We would then produce the new relations:

BOOK-LOAN2(<u>Borrower-number</u>, <u>Book-number</u>, Date-borrowed, Date-due-back)

BOOK(<u>Book-number</u>, Book-title, Author, Category)

You will see that the attributes of the new relation are such that the data attributes (Book-title, Author and Category in this example), are those which are functionally dependent upon the key (Book-number) of the new relation.

Repeating the process for the INVOICE relation, we see that of the INVOICE2 and ORDER-LINE relations, only the ORDER-LINE has a composite key and is to be considered for processing at this stage. We look at each attribute and check whether it depends upon the whole key or just a part of the key. Doing this, we find that:

- Description is functionally dependent upon Reference-code,
- Quantity is functionally dependent upon Invoice-number and Reference-code,
- Unit-price is functionally dependent upon Reference-code,
- Line-cost is functionally dependent upon Invoice-number and Reference-code.

Using the notation we introduced earlier, we write:

Reference-code → Description
Invoice-number, Reference-code → Quantity
Reference-code → Unit-price
Invoice-number, Reference-code → Line-cost

This enables us to derive the relations:

INVOICE2(Invoice-number, Invoice-date, Delivery-date, Customer-number, Customer-name, Customer-address, Total-cost, Vat-due, Credit-limit, Total-amount-due)

ORDER-LINE2(Invoice-number, Reference-code, Quantity, Line-cost)

PRODUCT(Reference-code, Description, Unit-price)

The reason for reducing the data to second normal form is that it avoids duplication of data. If we held the product Description on every order line, then we should have to change every order line if the description of the product were to be changed.

Assignment 4

1 Using the instances which you produced for the LIBRARY-MEMBER2 and BOOK-LOAN relations, draw up the corresponding instances of the BOOK-LOAN2 and BOOK relations. Highlight the keys for each entry in the relations.
2 Using the instances which you produced for the INVOICE and ORDER-LINE relations, draw up the corresponding instances of the ORDER-LINE2 and PRODUCT relations. Highlight the keys for each entry in the relations.

When this step has been taken, the data is said to be in the *second normal form.*

Activity 5

1 Using your previous results, derive the second normal form of the TRANSPORT-LOG relation.
2 Using your previous results, derive the second normal form of the PATIENT relation.

Third normal form

The third step again uses the idea of functional dependency to ensure that you *remove any attributes which are dependent upon other attributes and put these in a separate relation.*

The current versions of our relations are:

LIBRARY-MEMBER2(<u>Borrower-number</u>, Student-number, Name, Address, Department, Telephone-number, Date-joined-library)

BOOK-LOAN2(<u>Borrower-number</u>, <u>Book-number</u>, Date-borrowed, Date-due-back)

BOOK(<u>Book-number</u>, Book-title, Author, Category)

We now look at each in turn.

1 In the LIBRARY-MEMBER2 relation, we see that:

Student-number → Name
Student-number → Address
Student-number → Department
Student-number → Telephone-number

and we use this fact to remove the dependent attributes and use them to create a new relation (let us call this STUDENT) and use the attribute upon which they depend as the key to the relation. This produces:

LIBRARY-MEMBER3(<u>Borrower-number</u>, Student-number, Date-joined-library)
STUDENT(<u>Student-number</u>, Name, Address, Department, Telephone-number)

An attribute such as Student-number which is a data attribute in the LIBRARY-MEMBER3 relation and the key attribute of the STUDENT relation is known as a *foreign key* in the context of the LIBRARY-MEMBER3 relation.

You might feel that holding a foreign key within a data record conflicts with our attitude to duplicated data within the database. However, a foreign key is simply a way of linking from one record to another—to show their relationship—and since the key is unlikely to change, there is no danger to the integrity of the database. We shall see later how some DBMSs allow us to avoid holding foreign keys by holding the necessary linkage between related relations as a part of their own control data for each record. Do you recall the chains of records we met when we were looking at Network DBMSs?

2 In the BOOK-LOAN2, you may feel that the Date-borrowed is functionally dependent upon the Date-due-back, suspecting that a book is always on loan for three weeks. On checking with the users, we learn that this is generally so, but some students ask for a special extension and the loan may be anything from three weeks to six months in some cases. So this dependency does not exist.

3 In the BOOK relation, we have seen that all the attributes are dependent only upon the key. You may feel that there is some (intuitive) link between Book-title and Category, and between Author and Category, but this is not generally so: a book entitled THE STARS OVER TEXAS may be about astronomy, geography, politics or it may be a romance, so there is no link between Book-title and Category, and many authors of fiction write their travel guides and autobiographies, so there is no link between Author and Category.

Summarizing, we see that only the LIBRARY-MEMBER2 relation has changed at this stage and we are left with:

LIBRARY-MEMBER3(<u>Borrower-number</u>, Student-number, Date-joined-library)
BOOK-LOAN2(<u>Borrower-number</u>, <u>Book-number</u>, Date-borrowed, Date-due-back)
STUDENT(<u>Student-number</u>, Name, Address, Department, Telephone-number)
BOOK(<u>Book-number</u>, Book-title, Author, Category)

We now look at each in turn.

1 In the INVOICE2 relation, we see that:

Customer-number → Customer-name
Customer-number → Customer-address
Customer-number → Credit-limit

You may also feel that there is some connection between the Total-cost and the Vat-due and the Total-amount-due. The Vat-due is generally 15% of the Total-cost, but it may be that the VAT rate on some goods will change in the future, so we cannot rely on this functional dependency. However, the Total-amount-due is always the sum of the other two, so we need not hold this at all.

Combining these facts and decisions, we derive the relations:

INVOICE3(Invoice-number, Invoice-date, Delivery-date, Customer-number, Total-cost, Vat-due)
CUSTOMER(Customer-number, Customer-name, Customer-address, Credit-limit)

The Customer-number is a foreign key since it is used as a data attribute in the INVOICE3 relation and as a key in the CUSTOMER relation.

2 In the ORDER-LINE2 relation, there is a similar decision to be made about whether or not to hold the Line-cost. We could always derive the Line-cost by multiplying the Quantity by the Unit-price held on the PRODUCT file. This is possible, but we are only concerned with functional dependency between the attributes of one relation, and it is not possible to derive the line cost from the attributes of the ORDER-LINE relation alone.

There are no changes to be made to the PRODUCT relation, so only the INVOICE2 relation has changed at this stage and we are left with:

INVOICE3(Invoice-number, Invoice-date, Delivery-date, Customer-number, Total-cost, Vat-due)
CUSTOMER(Customer-number, Customer-name, Customer-address, Credit-limit)
ORDER-LINE2(Invoice-number, Reference-code, Quantity, Line-cost)
PRODUCT(Reference-code, Description, Unit-price)

The reason for reducing the data to third normal form is that it avoids duplication of data. If we held the Customer-address on every invoice, then we should have to change every invoice if the customer ever changed his/her address.

Assignment 4

1 Using the instances which you produced for the LIBRARY-MEMBER2, BOOK-LOAN2 and BOOK relations, draw up the corresponding instances of the LIBRARY-MEMBER3 and STUDENT relations. Highlight the keys for each entry in the relations.
2 Using the instances which you produced for the INVOICE2 relation, draw up the corresponding instances of the INVOICE3 and CUSTOMER relations. Highlight the keys for each entry in the relations.

When this step has been taken, the data is said to be in the *third normal form.*

Activity 6

1 Using your previous results, derive the third normal form of the TRANSPORT-LOG relation.
2 Using your previous results, derive the third normal form of the PATIENT relation.

Consolidating the entities

We have now derived the third normal form for our data. However, normalization is not concerned with just one entity or one relation in isolation. When we look at one document as we have just done with the Invoice, or when we consider one report, we derive only a single *local* data model. We must look at all areas of the organization and merge the separate local data models to produce the *global* data model for the entire organization or at least that part of the organization which will be associated with our proposed computer system.

For example, the relations:

INVOICE3(Invoice-number, Invoice-date, Delivery-date, Customer-number, Total-cost, Vat-due)
CUSTOMER(Customer-number, Customer-name, Customer-address, Credit-limit)
ORDER-LINE2(Invoice-number, Reference-code, Quantity, Line-cost)
PRODUCT(Reference-code, Description, Unit-price)

which we produced during our analysis of the data on the Invoice represent just one user-view, one local data model. Elsewhere in the company, a user in the publicity department may be concerned only with the code-number, description and price of a product. A sub-schema developed from such investigation might be:

PUBLICITY-PRODUCT (Code-number, Description, Price)

Our work with the person who is responsible for reordering goods for delivery to the warehouse might have produced a relation:

REORDER-PRODUCT (Product-code, Description, Quantity-in-stock, Reorder-quantity, Date-of-last-order, Date-of-last-delivery, Supplier-reference)

Whilst another user in the warehouse may be concerned with the dimensions of the packing cases containing each item, its code-number, its location in the warehouse, how many there are in stock, and the date on which deliveries of the item were last received from the supplier:

WAREHOUSE-PRODUCT (Reference-Number, Length-of-box, Width-of-box, Height-of-box, Location, Quantity- in-stock, Date-last-received)

You will notice how we have used explicit and meaningful names for each of the entities and their attributes. This will help avoid confusion during the investigation. To be consistent, we should call our original PRODUCT entity by the name INVOICE-PRODUCT.

So we have three user-views of the data generating three individual—local—data models.

Assignment 5

Using the data in the instances which you produced earlier for the entities of the Invoicing system, produce some instances for the PUBLICITY-PRODUCT, the REORDER-PRODUCT, and the WAREHOUSE-PRODUCT entities. You will have to use your imagination with some of the data values. Make notes about any assumptions which you are making about the meaning and form of the data. In practice, the analyst will have to check with the users to see that any assumptions are correct before continuing with the design.

If we compare the sub-schemas for these different user-views, we see that four of the relations *have the same key*:

INVOICE-PRODUCT (<u>Reference-code</u>, Description, Unit-price)
PUBLICITY-PRODUCT (<u>Code-number</u>, Description, Price)
REORDER-PRODUCT (<u>Product-code</u>, Description, Quantity-in-stock, Reorder-quantity, Date-of-last-order, Date-of-last-delivery, Supplier-reference)
WAREHOUSE-PRODUCT (<u>Reference-Number</u>, Length-of-box, Width-of-box, Height-of-box, Location, Quantity-in-stock, Date-last-received)

The name for the key is different for each relation, how do we know it's the same key? The systems analyst will make notes about the meaning of each attribute and there will be examples of each. Normally, the analyst will try to use the same name for the attribute, but this is not always possible, as we have seen in this situation. Incidentally, a data dictionary can be very useful in sorting out complications such as this.

When several relations have *exactly the same key*, it is possible to consolidate them into a single relation. We do this by making a list of the attributes so as to ensure that each attribute required for each relation is present in the list. Our list is shown in Figure 11.14.

Attribute	INVOICE PRODUCT	PUBLICITY PRODUCT	REORDER PRODUCT	WAREHOUSE PRODUCT
Product-number	*	*	*	*
Description	*	*	*	
Unit-price	*	*		
Quantity-in-stock			*	*
Reorder-quantity			*	
Date-of-last-order			*	
Date-of-last-delivery			*	*
Supplier-reference			*	
Length-of-box				*
Width-of-box				*
Height-of-box				*
Location				*

Figure 11.14 Consolidating the entities

If there is space in your table, it is a good plan to show the names by which each attribute is known within each separate relation. This information will be useful if you are constructing a data dictionary so that each individual user can use their own names for the attributes.

Combining the contents of each relation in this way, we arrive at a final schema for the global data model of the PRODUCT relation:

PRODUCT (Product-number, Description, Unit-price, Quantity-in-stock, Reorder-quantity, Date-of-last-order, Date-of-last-delivery, Supplier-reference, Length-of-box, Width-of-box, Height-of-box, Location)

This will satisfy all our users.

The files

This schema is now the responsibility of the database designer and the database administrator. They will decide exactly how the physical data is to be organized to support the schema which the analyst has derived. For example, it may be decided that the schema:

PRODUCT (Product-number, Description, Unit-price, Quantity-in-stock, Reorder-quantity, Date-of-last-order, Date-of-last-delivery, Supplier-reference, Length-of-box, Width-of-box, Height-of-box, Location)

is to be held physically as:

PRODUCT (Product-number, Description, Unit-price)
PRODUCT-QUANTITY (Product-number, Quantity-in-stock, Reorder-quantity, Location)
PRODUCT-ORDERING (Product-number, Date-of-last-order, Date-of-last-delivery, Supplier-reference)
PRODUCT-SIZE (Product-number, Length-of-box, Width-of-box, Height-of-box)

This may seem a backward step: the analyst goes to a lot of trouble consolidating the sub-schemas, only to find that the DBA disperses them again. There are a number of reason for doing this:

- Certain groups of data are frequently used at the same time. If we can write, store and read this data together, we can process these data fields more eficiently.
- Dispersion makes each record smaller and when you only want to know the Product Description, for example, you don't have to read and write a huge record including the dimensions of the box, for example, which you might not need at that time.
- Since the records are smaller, it is possible to speed up the physical access by packing more records into a single bucket of the file.
- There may be other physical constraints imposed by the DBMS. Allowing the analyst to work without thinking about these and without having to know too much about the way in which the DBMS goes about its work simplifies the tasks of systems development and data design.

The ways in which *relationships* are represented are also the responsibility of the DBA. In our investigation, we saw a number of relationships. For example, the library system used these relations:

LIBRARY-MEMBER3(Borrower-number, Student-number, Date-joined-library)
BOOK-LOAN2(Borrower-number, Book-number, Date-borrowed, Date-due-back)
STUDENT(Student-number, Name, Address, Department, Telephone-number)
BOOK(Book-number, Book-title, Author, Category)

Directly, or indirectly, there are relationships implied by the fact that the data in one relation is the key to another relation—foreign keys—or by having keys or part of keys in common. For example:

- LIBRARY-MEMBER3 is related to STUDENT by way of the foreign key student-number.
- BOOK-LOAN2 is related to BOOK by way of the Book-number in the composite key.
- LIBRARY-MEMBER3 is related to BOOK-LOAN2 by way of the Borrower-number.

and so on.

On some DBMSs, it may not be necessary to hold foreign keys within the data of the record. The DBMS may hold the necessary information in its own linkage fields. Again, the DBA need be the only person who is aware of these facts. The users—and even the analysts and programmers—can perform their work quite ignorant of exactly how the physical data is arranged.

Recap

When you as a systems analyst are carrying out your investigations, you will obtain, produce and design a number of documents, screen layouts and reports which will form a part of the proposed computer system. From these you will develop a series of local data models, the sub-schemas: there will be one sub-schema for each document, and it will contain all the data which is necessary to support that document.

In this Chapter we have looked at the steps which you will follow in taking the data from the document through to the final global data model for the database.

We defined the key of a relation as the smallest subset of attributes from the relation such that the key is unique for each tuple, and then we went on to look at the ways in which we can decide upon a suitable key for a relation.

We introduced a bracket notation for relating the contents of our sub-schemas, giving meaningful names to the attributes and underlining the attribute (or attributes) which we shall use as the key.

We looked again at repeating groups and at the way in which these are represented in our sub-schema notation. A relation which has no repeating groups is sometimes known as a flat file, and by resolving our relation into one or more flat files, we shall be able to avoid many of the difficulties which repeating groups present.

If we have two attributes A and B, and if attribute A can be uniquely identified when the value of attribute B is known, then we say that attribute A is functionally dependent upon atribute B.

We saw that a single attribute may be functionally dependent upon a combination of several attributes, and several attributes may be functionally dependent upon one attribute. We introduced a number of diagrammatic ways of representing functional dependence.

The technique of data normalization enables us to make the transition from raw data to the final design for our database. The general aim of normalization is to produce a set of entities which will support the users' needs and which will conform to the requirements of the database.

We start by looking at each entity in turn to produce a local data model, and then combine and consolidate the various local data models to arrive at a global data model. It is this final global data model which will form the basis for the database.

Three standard steps are taken to normalize an entity to produce a local data model:

1 The first step is to remove any repeating groups.
2 The second step is to ensure that, if the relation has a composite key then any single attribute in the relation should be dependent upon the whole key and not just a part of the key.
3 The third step is to ensure that you remove any attributes which are dependent upon other attributes and put these in a separate relation.

When these steps have been taken, the data is said to be in the third normal form.

We illustrated the process by looking at a number of different examples.

Having normalized the data for each user-view in order to produce a set of sub-schemas, we now merge these to produce the global data model, the schema. This requires us to produce a comprehensive schema which represents each individual sub-schema.

As far as the data design tasks are concerned, the analyst's work is over. The database administrator now takes over and converts the global data model—the logical model of the data—into the true physical model which tells the DBA exactly where and how each piece of data is held. This final transition will be made with the DBMS in mind.

Answers

1 If it were possible for there to be more than one tour to a given destination on one day.
2 We should arrive at a composite key made up of the *time*, the *date* and the *destination*.
3 Based upon the information given, the date and the time will uniquely identify the visit for a particular party.
4 We shall use the following sub-schema in our discussion of normalization.

INVOICE(Invoice-number, Invoice-date, Delivery-date, Customer-number, Customer-name, Customer-address, (Reference-code, Description, Quantity, Unit-price, Line-cost), Total-cost, Vat-due, Credit-limit, Total-amount-due)

Note that we have changed the names of some of the fields to make their meaning clearer.

12: Fourth generation languages and databases

Objectives

After reading this chapter, you should be able to:

- Identify and describe some of the differences between *third generation languages* and *fourth generation languages.*
- Describe the general nature of *procedural* and *non-procedural* languages.
- Describe the features of a typical 4GL.
- Describe some of the ways in which a 4GL changes the nature of the programming task.
- Describe the nature of *prototyping.*

For a great many years, people wrote computer programs in machine code (often called *first generation languages*) before they moved on to Assembly languages (*second generation languages*). Later, it became more efficient to use Cobol, Algol, Fortran and more recently Pascal and Basic (*third generation languages*). But in the last few years, a great many commercial programming departments have started to move from these languages towards *fourth generation languages*—4GLs.

Procedural or non-procedural?

There is one chief difference between the earlier languages and a 4GL: all the earlier languages represent *procedural* ways of solving a particular computer problem, whereas fourth generation languages are *non-procedural* solutions.

To explain this, let us imagine that you have been invited to dinner at a friend's new house. You ask her for details of how to get there. There are two ways in which she can give you directions:

- She can give you a list of instructions: turn off the M4 on to the A33; head towards the centre of town; turn right at the hotel; follow the

road round to the right; she lives at the second house on the left past the school. These are *procedural* instructions for finding her house.
- She can draw you a map. This is a *non-procedural* instruction for finding the house.

This is a very close analogy to programming languages. In a first, second or third generation programming language, you write a *procedural* series of instructions, and the computer obeys these instructions in turn. When you are using a 4GL, you will produce a series of *non-procedural* pictures:

- Report formats showing the name of each piece of data and whereabouts on the printed page each piece of data and text is to appear.
- Screen layouts —showing the name of each piece of data and whereabouts on the printed page each piece of data and text is to be displayed, and whereabouts on the screen each piece of data is to be input.

Most 4GLs have some sort of *screen painter* to allow you— the analyst or the programmer—to design the report formats and screen layouts. This is done by typing in the text and names of the pieces of data which are to appear on the screen and then moving them around, changing them, deleting them until you have produced a satisfactory layout.

More importantly, the 4GL will allow you to use the same screen in many different programs. For example, you might like to use exactly the same screen layout in a program which adds new student records, and in another which displays specific student records, and even in a third which lets you change the contents of a student's record.

A 4GL usually performs two main tasks: the first—the program specification and development phase—allows the programmer to paint the screen and report formats, and describe any processing which is to be performed; the second—the execution phase—interprets the programmer's specifications and performs the necessary processing.

You must not confuse a fourth generation language with tools such as *program generators* and *code generators*. These generators take your program description—this is usually a sort of shorthand version of Cobol or Basic—and translate this into a complete Cobol or a Basic program. In contrast, most 4GLs take your specifications and use these as parameters to tailor their own generalized input and output routines to your precise requirements.

Data dictionary

The 4GL will use some form of *data dictionary* to enable the programmer to use names such as STUDENT.NAME, STUDENT.ADDRESS for the data which is to be processed, and to indicate the physical location—which file, which field—where that piece of data is to be found. Whenever a program needs to handle data which is held (or is to be held) on the database, the programmer simply uses these datanames and the 4GL will consult the data dictionary and obtain the correct information.

It is no longer necessary for the programmer to give explicit instructions to:

- Read data from the database
- Check whether or not the record exists
- Update the data within the record
- Write the record back to the database.

Just as—by looking at your friend's map—you know that if the road bears right then you must bear right, so a 4GL knows that if you want to display the STUDENT.NAME for a record which already exists on the file, then it must first read that piece of data from the database. If you have changed the contents of, say, the STUDENT.SCORE, or if you have input a new value, then the 4GL knows that you must want to update this field on the database and it will write the record for you—you don't have to give a specific write instruction.

Special processing within a 4GL

Although it can handle most of the ordinary, routine pieces of processing, there will inevitably be some particular processing which the 4GL cannot know about. Although it can make reasonable assumptions about when you want to read and write your data records, it cannot tell exactly what calculations you want to perform on the data. For such situations, the 4GL allows you to describe your own particular processing and calculations. So you might describe a process to mark the students' exams by a sequence like this:

```
STUDENT.TOTAL = STUDENT.TOTAL + STUDENT.SCORE
IF STUDENT.SCORE > 95 THEN STUDENT.GRADE = 'PASS'
```

The 4GL will handle all the input/output necessary to get the current values of STUDENT.TOTAL, STUDENT.GRADE from the database and to accept STUDENT.SCORE from your layout for the screen input. It will then pass control to your special calculation routine and when you have performed the calculations, it will put the amended values of STUDENT.TOTAL and STUDENT.SCORE back into the database.

Note that the special processing descriptions are written in a form of third generation (procedural) language.

There are a number of places within the overall process at which most 4GLs will allow you to pass control to your own particular routines. For example, you may want to:

- Perform some particular process before a data field is accepted from the screen;
- Perform some reformatting of the data after it has been input;
- Carry out some processing on the record key before the 4GL gets your data from the database;
- Take some special action if a record cannot be found;
- Perform some additional processing if a record is to be deleted;
- Carry out some special processing before a record is updated on the database;
- Carry out further processing after a record has been written back to the database;
- Take some special action if an error or an exception- condition is detected.

All that you—as the programmer—need do is write the processing descriptions to handle these situations, and the 4GL will execute them as and when they are required. Now let us look at a 4GL in action.

Looking at a fourth generation language

As an illustration of a fourth generation language, we shall look at PRO IV. This 4GL is available on many computers, from mainframes to PC personal computers, and is completely portable between hardware.

Our example, presents a function which will allow us to add records to a file called STUDENT. A *function* is the PRO IV equivalent of a program.

The information which is required to define the function is shown in Figure 12.1 through to Figure 12.6. For clarity and because we have chosen not to use them in this particular function, we have removed some parts of the screen display—such as those relating to the security aspects of the system. However, the information shown is all that is required to produce the working function.

Let us look at each part of the PRO IV function in turn.

1 Figure 12.1 shows the FIELD DEFINITION. This is the data dictionary for the STUDENT file and will be used by all the functions which process the STUDENT file. The data dictionary itself is maintained by the DBA and made available to each function which mentions the STUDENT file in the SCREEN CHARACTERISTICS illustrated in Figure 12.5.

In this function, we do not use all the fields of the STUDENT RECORD.

```
File Name : STUDENT

Fld  Type  Variable Name    Len

---  ----  ---------------- ---

001   K    ST.ENROLMENT       4
002   A    ST.NAME           25
003   A    ST.PHONE          20
004   A    ST.ADDRESS        30
005   N    ST.COURSE          8
006   A    ST.HISTORY        30
007   N    ST.SCHOOL         10
008   N    ST.DOB             6
009   N    ST.ADMIT.DATE      6
```

Figure 12.1 File Definition

2 Figure 12.2 shows the FUNCTION DEFINITION. This is largely devoted to documentation and represents a verbal description of the action of the function.

The programmer has indicated that this function is of type S. This means that it is a *S*creen function. A Screen carries out a dialogue between the function and the user. Other possibilities are a Menu function (to offer the user a means of selecting the work he/she wants to do), or a Report function (to generate printed reports with no user intervention), or an Update function (to process a large number of records on the files without any user intervention).

The *link* information instructs the function to return to another function called STUDENT.MENU when this function ends or if there is any error which is not handled by the programmer.

```
Function Name: STUDENT.ADD      Title: STUDENT FILE MAINTENANCE

         Type: SCREEN                  Analyst: MBULL
                                    Entry Date: 29/07/92
    Exit Link: STUDENT.MENU           Reset On: 29/07/92    17:27:15
   Error Link: STUDENT.MENU                 By: MBULL

Ln£  -----------------------  D e s c r i p t i o n  -------------

001  This function adds new records to the STUDENT records file.
002  The function will ask for the STUDENT NUMBER of the new
003  student.  It will then ask for the NAME, ADDRESS, TELEPHONE
004  NUMBER, COURSE, DATE OF BIRTH, and the ADMISSION DATE (the
005  default value is today's date).
006
007  The STUDENT ENROLMENT NUMBER will be assembled from the year
008  followed by the STUDENT NUMBER = 92 / nnnn
009
010  The new record will then be written away and the function
011  will repeat.
012
013  To stop the process, the user should type .  When a new
014  student number is requested or / at any other time
```

Figure 12.2 Function Definition

The dates and times are maintained automatically by PRO IV.

3 Figure 12.3 shows the SCREEN FORMAT. This is painted by the programmer and specifies the text which is to be displayed on this screen. This is the basis for the scren layout.

```
                         Screen Format ID: 1

            1         2         3         4         5         6         7
   1234567890123456789012345678901234567890123456789012345678901234567890
   ----------------------------------------------------------------------
01:
02:29/07/92        ** STUDENT MAINTENANCE ** ADD A NEW RECORD **
03:
04:
05:                STUDENT NUMBER :
06:
07:    STUDENT ENROLMENT NUMBER :
08:
09:                          NAME :
10:
11:                       ADDRESS :
12:
13:              TELEPHONE NUMBER :
14:
15:                        COURSE :
16:
17:                 DATE OF BIRTH :
18:
19:                ADMISSION DATE :
20:
21:
22:
23:
   ----------------------------------------------------------------------
   1234567890123456789012345678901234567890123456789012345678901234567890
            1         2         3         4         5         6         7
```

Figure 12.3 Screen Format

4 Figure 12.4 shows the SCREEN FIELD DEFINITION. This is a section describing the data which is to be input and to be displayed.

```
Function Name: STUDENT.ADD     Title: STUDENT FILE MAINTENANCE

-------------------------------------------------------------

                                      Fill                 M D Lgc
Fld  Variable Name Row  Col Len Code  Display Code I O  ID

---  ------------- ---  --- --- ----  ------------ - - ---

001  £NUMBER         5   32   4  LFZ                Y     2
     ENTER NUMBER FOR NEW STUDENT

001  ST.ENROLMENT    7   32   7                       Y

003  ST.NAME         9   32  25                     Y
     ENTER THE STUDENT'S NAME

004  ST.ADDRESS     11   32  30                     Y
     ENTER THE STUDENT'S ADDRESS

005  ST.PHONE       13   32  20                     Y
     ENTER THE STUDENT'S TELEPHONE NUMBER

006  ST.COURSE      15   32   4                     Y
     ENTER THE COURSE TO BE FOLLOWED

007  ST.DOB         17   32  11       DATE          Y     3
     ENTER THE STUDENT'S DATE OF BIRTH

008  ST.ADMIT       19   32  11       DATE          Y

009  $$MSG          23    1  60                       Y

010  $RESP          23   45   1                     Y
```

Figure 12.4   Screen Field Definition

Each field is given a name. This may be the name of a data field from the database, or it may—as in the case of £NUMBER, $$MSG and $RESP—be a work variable used by the program and not held on the database. The variables beginning with £ are used to hold numbers, those beginning with $ are used to hold short alphanumeric strings, and those beginning with $$ are used to hold long alphanumeric strings.

You can probably guess the significance of the headings fld (field), variable, row, col (column) and Len (length). The Fill Code indicates how the user's input data is to be handled: LFZ means that the number must be left-filled with zero. So an input value of 99, for example, would be changed to 0099 by the PRO IV processor. Similarly, the Display Code indicates how the value is to appear when it is displayed: DATE means that this is a date field and will be displayed in the correct form. You may also specify a code such as 4.2 to indicate that a numeric value be displayed in a form such as 9999.99 or 4.0 to display an integer number in a form such as 9999 with no decimal places.

Of particular interest are the three headings MI (this means Mandatory Input—that is, the user *must input* a value here). DO (this means that this field is only to be displayed), and Lgc ID (this stands for Logic Identifier, and refers to the processing routine which is to be carried out immediately after this field has been input or displayed). So these definitions tell the PRO IV processor that

a) the user must input a numeric value which PRO IV is to place in the variable called £NUMBER. When this has been done,
b) PRO IV will process the programmer's routine number 2(as indicated in the Lgc ID column). We shall look at this routine later, but it's action is to take the year number 92 and join this to the student number (held in £NUMBER) to produce the student's enrolment number. So a student number 0023 would be used to build the enrolment number 92/0023 and this would be placed (by routine 2) into the variable ST.ENROLMENT.
c) PRO IV will then display the value of ST.ENROLMENT.

When the function is executed, the fields are accessed in the order indicated on the Screen Field Definition, starting with the first field and then inputting or displaying as specified, and processing any Logic ID indicated. This is a procedural description of the data handling which is required.

In this example, all the fields in the Screen Field Definition will be processed one by one, until we reach the bottom and the variable $$MSG will be displayed and the user asked to enter a value into $RESP. $$MSG is a message asking the user if the data is correct, and $RESP will hold the user's reply. This will be / if the user wants to cancel the record (as we shall mention in a moment, the / is the PRO IV convention for cancelling the current action), it will be null if the user just hits the RETURN key.

When all the fields have been processed, then PRO IV will take the fields which represent data to he held on the database—ST.ENROLMENT, ST.NAME, ST.ADDRESS and so on—and use these to build a new student record and add this to the STUDENT file.

PRO IV has a number of conventions for use when inputting data:

the / instructs the PRO IV processor to abandon whatever is happening and go to the top of the screen and start again; a / at the first data input of a screen means abandon this function and go to the function named in the Exit Link of the Function Definition; a . means accept the information which has been entered so far on this screen and then stop the processing of this function.

5 Figure 12.5 shows the SCREEN CHARACTERISTICS. The first two lines show the identity number of the screen. This screen ties in with the Screen Format and the Screen Field Definition which we specified earlier. Our example shows a fairly simple screen, but there may be any number of screens in a function and they may have windows and other effects.

We then specify some details about this screen: we ask that the screen be cleared before the screen image is displayed (we may have wanted to superimpose this on another image); we say that this screen is only going to be used once for each new student record; when the screen is displayed we ask that our procesing routine (Lgc ID) number 1 be carried out (this sets up the message in $$MSG, as we shall see below); the first input field in number 1(of the Screen Field Definition) and the final field is number 10—after that PRO IV can update out files.

The Screen Characteristics also describe the database files which we shall be using. We are only using the STUDENT file and the key to the record (Rd Fld) is field number 2 of the Screen Field Definition (the ST.ENROLMENT field).

The A tells PRO IV that we are adding records to the file. We could Change records, Delete records, or just Look at them, according to the codes which we put here.

Notice that PRO IV uses this part of the specification to let us carry out our own processing routines at various stategic points in the file-handling: before we read from the file, after we have read a record and found an error, after we have read a record without any errors, and before we write to the file. To use these, we would simply enter the number of our processing routine under the appropriate heading.

6 Finally we come to the LOGIC DEFINITION shown in Figure 12.6. This is the part of the function specification where we write our own pieces of coding to perform special processing. These bits of code are known as logic IDs in PRO IV. We have used just three: Logic ID 1 is called in when we enter the screen (as requested on the Screen Characteristics); Logic ID 2 is called in after the user has input the

```
Function Name: STUDENT.ADD          Title: STUDENT FILE MAINTENANCE

------------------------------Screen Info-------------------------

Logical Screen: 1
     Format ID: 1

Clear CRT: Y              Start Fld:     1
 One Time: N              End Field:    10

Logic ID: 1

-----------------------------File Information--------------------

 File                      Rd  Err  Modes   Before  After-Read   Before
Access    File Name        Fld Rtn A C D L   Read   Error No-err  Write
------ ----------------- --- --- ------- ------ ----- ------ ------

  01   STUDENT             1      A                                2
```

Figure 12.5 Screen Characteristics

student's number (as requested on the Screen Field Definition); Logic ID 3 is called in after the user has input the student's date of birth (as requested on the Screen Field Definition) and loads today's date (indicated by the code @DATE) into the field ST.ADMIT.DATE which will be displayed on the screen and added to the student's record.

There are a number of standard mathematical and other functions available for use within your Logic IDs.

```
Function Name: STUDENT.ADD          Title: STUDENT FILE MAINTENANCE

Lgc
ID  Ln£ Step ---------------------S t a t e m e n t-------------

001 001 *    Set up prompt for CONTINUE? Message
    002      $$MSG = "Press <RETURN> to add record or / to ignore"

002 001 *    Build student enrolment number in BEFORE-WRITE logic
    002      ST.ENROLMENT = "92/" + £NUMBER

003 001 *    Assign the current system date to ST.ADMIT.DATE
    002      ST.ADMIT.DATE = @DATE
```

Figure 12.6 Logic Definitions

So there you have it: six pages of information. That is all you need to write a program to add new records to a file. Six screens of information created by the programmer sitting at the terminal. To a large extent, the routine programming tasks—file description, input and output formatting—are reduced to simple form-filling exercises. The only complicated part is design and creating of the Logic IDs, the pieces of special processing.

How long would it take you to write a similar program in Cobol or in Basic? It took me eight minutes to write this function in PRO IV, just one of the many fourth generation programming languages which are available today.

Activity

1 Describe some of the ways in which the 4GL described above interacts with the database.

2 You are required to write a fourth generation language program in the style of the PRO IV function discussed informally in the text.

The purpose of the program is to allow the user to enter a student enrolment number, and then display the following details about that student: name, telephone number, address, course course, date of birth and admission date.

It will also calculate and display the age of the student today and the age when the student was admitted to the college. The ages will be expressed in a form such as 18.75 years.

Perform the following:

a) Design a screen layout which will contain all the required input and output information.

b) Draw up the Function Definition.

c) Draw up the Screen Format information based upon your design from part (a).

d) Draw up the Screen Field Definition.

Remember to include the Logic ID references which will allow you to calculate the student's age before displaying it.

e) Draw up the Screen Characteristics. Note that we are only Looking at the STUDENT file.

f) Draw up the Logic Definition which will calculate the age of the student today and when he/she was admitted. A special YEARDAY function has been written which will allow you to convert a date into the number of days since the beginning of the century. Your Logic IDs can call this function and put the equivalent number of days into a work variable by means of a statement such as:

```
£BIRTHDAYS = YEARDAY(ST.DOB)
£ENROLDAYS = YEARDAY(ST.ADMIT.DATE)
```

Do not concern yourself with the precise syntax of the language used. It is sufficient if you make the intention of your coding clear.

Efficiency of 4GLs

When you have designed a screen layout, you can use this same layout in many different programs. This makes it easy to standardize the screens which the user sees. You can also use the same processing description within many different programs. All this speeds up the process of writing a program. All that the programmer has to do is bolt together a collection of pre-written sections, add any special processing and formats for this particular program—and the job is done. Because all the other parts are tested and working, only the special processing routines need be tested.

This increase the productivity of the programming department. With the aid of a 4GL, a programmer might produce a working and tested program in five days; using Cobol, the same programmer might take five weeks to produce the same program. It is this increase in productivity that has resulted in in the popularity of fourth generation languages in the commercial programming world.

Such routine development of computer systems does not mean that the work of the systems analyst and the programmer will become routine, tedious or boring. Instead, 4GLs remove the tiresome and repetitive coding of standard routines—open the file, read the record, write the record, work out the column positions for the screen display—and allow the programmer to concentrate on the complicated logical and detailed processing routines. This has always been the best, the most challenging, the most interesting part of programming.

And when that fearful day arrives on which a program has to be maintained or modified, the task of making the program modifications is simply an extension of the original development activity.

Many 4GLs offer self-documenting facilities. This also makes them more attractive to all who are involved with programming and programming productivity.

Prototyping

The speed and ease with which a program can be written and more importantly the ease with which it can later be changed and modified, has introduced a new concept known as *prototyping*. This technique allows the systems analyst to talk briefly to the users so as to get a *general outline* picture of their requirements, and then the programmer can quickly produce a sample program—the *prototype*. This prototype can be demonstrated to the users and then gradually refined and modified to their precise requirements. This is illustrated in Figure 12.7.

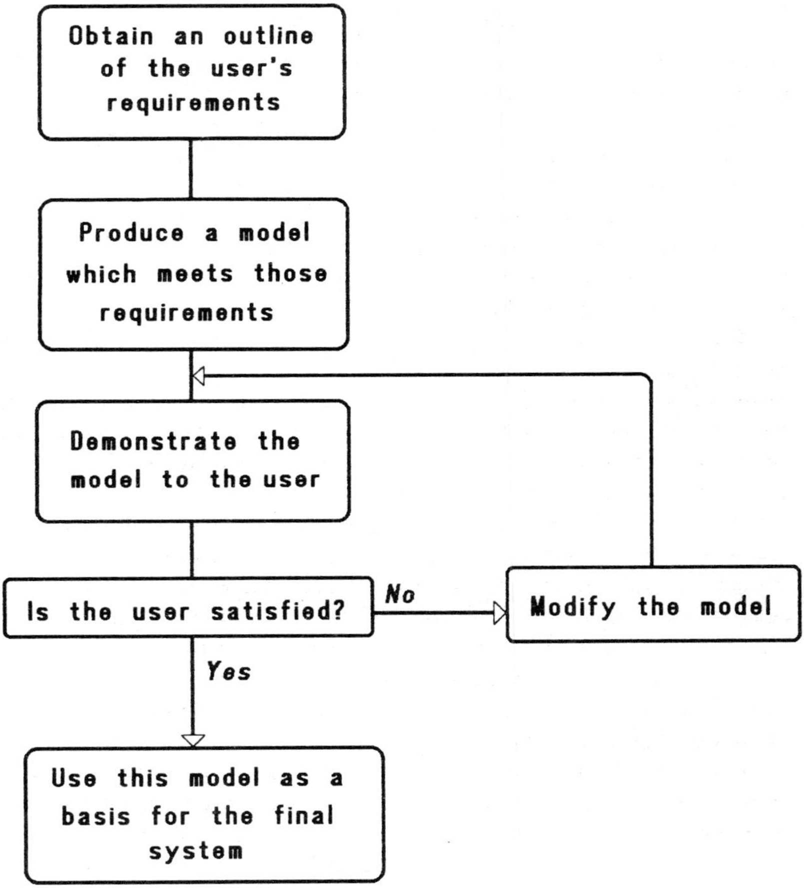

Figure 12.7 Prototyping

In some cases, the final program represents a *process model* which can be used as the basis for the specification and design of some other language such as Cobol or Basic. This is done because some 4GLs are not very efficient when they are executing. However, many 4GLs are so efficient that the prototype can be used directly as the finished working version of the users' program.

Prototyping has a number of advantages:

1 The system is tailored precisely to the users' requirements *as their requirements develop*, by allowing the users to recognize, build

up, and specify their own requirements after they have seen what can be done. It is a fact of life for the systems analyst and the programmer that *users rarely know exactly what they do want, but they always know what they don't want.* The prototype gives them something on which they can base their requirements.
2 The users are actively involved in design and development.
3 There is great scope for misunderstanding between the systems analyst and the users. With prototyping, there is less room for confusion between what the users want and what the users say they want, and between this and what the systems analyst thinks they want.
4 There is a gradual learning and understanding on the users' part because they grow up with the system and therefore there are reduced user-training requirements.
5 There is a shorter development lead time. A prototype system can be produced within a few hours to give the users a flavour of what the final system will look like.
6 At this preliminary stage, the user may make a decision to accept—or reject—the feasibility of the proposed system. This encourages the users and leads to an early commitment and involvement on their part.

The major disadvantage is that it does demand considerable time and commitment on the part of the users. If the users are unable to accept these greater demands on their time, then the development cycle more closely follows that of the traditional methods, with the systems analyst accepting greater responsibility as the users' representative.

Some 4GLs are so easy to use that the end-user—the clerk, the manager, the accountant—can quickly learn the language and produce their own prototypes and even their own programs. Although the data processing department will usually find some reason for objecting to this, it does cut out the middle man and allows the person who has the problem to be the person who is best suited to recognize and to work out the solution. In these days of shortages of suitable analysis and programming staff, this can be no bad thing.

Recap

Many commercial programming departments have started to move from languages such as Assemblers, Cobol, Algol, Fortran, Pascal and Basic, towards fourth generation languages—4GLs.

Fourth generation languages and databases

The early languages represent procedural ways of solving a computer problem in which the programmer writes a series of instructions, and the computer obeys these in turn. Fourth generation languages are non-procedural and enable the problem to be described by means of a series of formats and layouts.

When the program is executed, the fourth generation language processor interprets these specifications and performs the necessary processing.

4GLs use some form of data dictionary to define the data fields on the database. The data dictionary names and describes the data which is to be processed and indicates the physical location of the data. The programmer uses these datanames in the programs and the 4GL consults the data dictionary to obtain the correct information.

It is no longer necessary for the programmer to give explicit instructions to read data from the database, update the data within the record, or write the record back to the database. If you use the name of a data field, the 4GL will automatically fetch it from the database and—if you are changing the data—it will return it to the database at the end.

By declaring whether you are adding, changing, deleting or just looking at a file, the 4GL will take the appropriate action for each record.

The 4GL allows you to describe your own calculations and these are incorporated at the specified point in the file handling process.

By reducing the amount of work to be done during coding (and thereby removing much of the scope for making mistakes), the use of 4GLs can speed up the development of a computer system and improve the productivity of the programming department.

The technique of prototyping allows the systems analyst to use just an outline picture of the users' requirements in order to produce a sample program—the prototype—which can be demonstrated to the users and gradually refined and modified to their precise requirements.

The final program may be used as the basis for the specification and design of a program written in a more familiar language such as Cobol or Basic. However, many 4GLs are so efficient that the prototype can be used directly as the finished working version of the program.

We looked at a 4GL called PRO IV which is available on many computers, from mainframes to PC personal computers, and is completely portable between hardware.

Index